CITIES
IN
STRESS

Volume 30, URBAN AFFAIRS ANNUAL REVIEWS

CITIES IN STRESS

A New Look at the Urban Crisis

Edited by
M. GOTTDIENER

Volume 30, URBAN AFFAIRS ANNUAL REVIEWS

SAGE PUBLICATIONS
The Publishers of Professional Social Science
Beverly Hills   Newbury Park   London   New Delhi

For information address:

SAGE Publications, Inc.
275 South Beverly Drive
Beverly Hills, California 90212

SAGE Publications Inc.
2111 West Hillcrest Drive
Newbury Park
California 91320

SAGE Publications Ltd.
28 Banner Street
London EC1Y 8QE
England

SAGE PUBLICATIONS India Pvt. Ltd.
M-32 Market
Greater Kailash I
New Delhi 110 048 India

Printed in the United States of America

Library of Congress Cataloging-in-Publication Data

Main entry under title:
Cities in stress.

(Urban affairs annual reviews; v. 30)
Includes bibliographies.
 1. Cities and towns—United States—Addresses, essays,
lectures. 2. Urban Policy—United States—Addresses,
essays, lectures. I. Gottdiener, Mark. II. Series.
HT108.U7 Vol. 30 [HT123] 307.7′6 s 85-22223
ISBN 0-8039-2575-1   [307.7′6]
ISBN 0-8039-2576-X (pbk.)

FIRST PRINTING

Contents

Introduction

M. GOTTDIENER

□ "URBAN CRISIS" is a general term for separate phases of the metropolitan restructuring that has occurred over the past two decades. Associated with dramatic and highly publicized events, the urban crisis began with the ghetto riots of the 1960s, which became an index of racial problems and the failure of American society to integrate black people into its mainstream. A decade later cities were menaced by the specter of default. In this "fiscal crisis" funding sources for deficit spending dried up under conditions that cities had taken for granted. Consequently, municipalities were faced with instituting painful austerity measures and/or restructuring public finance, or bankruptcy.

Although the threat of crisis concerned only a few cities, it ferreted out a more generic condition of "fiscal strain" that characterized a larger group of urban regimes that seemed to be reeling under the impact of uncoordinated urban growth. Following each of these crises, the one social and political, the other economic and fiscal, urban areas were plunged into a phase of restructuring involving other levels of government and organized public policy that attempted to ameliorate their effects and alleviate their causes. In sum, the much publicized "crises" were linked to an almost equally scrutinized series of initiatives, involving both the public and the private sector, that addressed urban problems including service delivery, welfare, unemployment, infrastructure repair, economic decline, and the restructuring of revenue sources.

7

Crisis events, inquiries into their underlying causes, and the societal response to them have all become foci for what continues to be a burgeoning subfield of urban academic literature. At present, analyses of the urban malaise are dominated by the most recent phase, namely, fiscal concerns and the "fiscal crisis of the state" (O'Connor, 1973). From the very onset of this literature (see, e.g., Alcaly and Mermelstein, 1977; Shefter, 1977), however, it has been clear that the social problems of the 1960s and the fiscal concerns of the 1970s were linked. In short, the urban crisis literature constitutes a global inquiry into the complex social, economic, and political changes that have affected cities since at least the 1960s. Furthermore, because it focuses in a concrete manner on the complex articulation between the state, the economy, and the shifting manifestations of class, race, gender, and lifestyle status captured by demographic description, the urban crisis has emerged as a principal means of understanding the nature of contemporary society and its patterns of restructuring.

Virtually all of the literature on the urban crisis, until the 1980s, was concerned with its causes and immediate effects. This hardly seems surprising for a new field that was precipitated by concrete events and the need to understand them in order to direct public policy. It is easy to reject these early inquiries for their political biases or lack of sophistication; however, past work should be viewed as necessary first attempts that provided more recent research with a strong foundation. Even the media spectacle of crisis, however overrated, drew the excited attention of researchers to the more sober inquiry into the nature of urban change and restructuring.

In retrospect, it appears that the urban crisis was attacked from at least three separate and fundamental lines of thought. First, traditional Marxists linked the appearance of public sector breakdowns to the political economy of capitalism. Initially conceived as an extension of economic crisis theory to the field of political relations, this approach specified a tendency to public sector indebtedness propelled by private sector demands and the logic of monopoly capitalist development that required increasing levels of state spending. It was hypothesized that progressively advancing debt would overshoot the capacity of revenue sources to make up the difference and float government budgets. Eventually, the general crisis of capital accumulation, brought about by the long-term tendency of the rate of profit to fall, would give birth to a twin—a general crisis of public finance—because capital in crisis would no longer be able to sustain ever-increasing state budgets.

This crisis theory formulated first by O'Connor (1973), has been criticized by Marxists themselves because of its casting in terms appropriate to the national level of the state and as a general, univariant condition of society (Friedland et al., 1978). Analysts have found it difficult to apply this theory to the local level where other aspects of state structure and considerable variability between urban regimes greatly modify the conditions under which cyclical transformations in the economy express themselves in the field of political relations. Even early attempts at explaining the fiscal crisis of cities rejected O'Connor's theory in favor of other approaches (Alcaly and Mermelstein, 1977; see, also, Pickvance, 1980).

Recently, O'Connor (1981) has suggested that, despite such limitations, fiscal crisis theory advanced orthodox Marxism specifically by its introduction of separate streams of capital canalized by state auspices. These streams include, first of all, "social investment capital" or government spending on projects that direct resources back to the private sector—a feature lauded by "free enterprise" advocates as promoting a good "business climate." The two remaining streams involve, respectively, "social consumption capital," which is utilized in the reproduction of labor power by providing workers with resources normally purchased by wages, such as subsidized housing, transportation, and medical care; and, "social expenses capital" or state expenditures to keep the peace and promote system legitimation. This threefold distinction has been used repeatedly by Marxian-style commentators on the fiscal crisis, tending to substantiate O'Connor's claim regarding the lasting significance of his perspective.

It should be remembered that O'Connor's theory requires all three streams acting in concert to effect his particular fiscal crisis of the state. Recently, the inexorability of this orchestration has been called into question on both theoretical and empirical grounds. In the first case, the capital stream approach has been refuted by other Marxian political economists, especially those in Europe, who have critiqued successfully the theory of collective consumption (see Theret, 1983; Mingione, 1981; Gottdiener, 1985). Although acknowledging the role of state spending in the process of capital accumulation, it is questionable whether separate streams of capital can be identified that are conditioned by the crisis base of capitalism and that reproduce labor power or manage legitimation problems specifically through the state itself. Without a clear foundation for the existence of separate streams in the political economy of capitalism, such as "expenses capital," work that also follows the role of the state in supporting capital accumulation—incorporating alternate perspectives on crisis—such as those of Habermas (1975) and the work of neo-Fordists, also retain their appeal.

In the second, more empirical case, recent events within cities testify to the failure of social and fiscal crises to materialize. Cities have privatized many of their services, cut back on municipal employment, controlled the masses of poor and unemployed, and, in general, managed fiscal strain rather than surrender to it. The nature of this successful management is examined in the chapters of this book.

A second line of thought on the urban crisis is tied somewhat to the first but focuses directly on social conflict rather than on systemic disorganization. It emerged out of the early period of urban crisis experience to address the city-based social movements that appeared in the 1960s both in the United States (Piven and Cloward, 1979; Katznelson, 1981) and in Europe (Touraine, 1981; Lefebvre, 1969). According to this approach, modernity had spawned fundamental cleavages that could no longer be absorbed by traditional political institutions or forms of expression, and, consequently, that exploded in collective acts against the system. Dramatic incidents based upon this activism rejected conventional political discourse in favor of an oppositional logic that called the society itself into question (Habermas, 1975; Eyerman, 1984). In the United States this impluse was exemplified best by the ghetto riots of the 1960s that placed race on the agenda of mainstream politics and, for a period, moved racial issues to the head of a long list of historically pertinent urban problems.

After some time the social movement for equality became obscured by the fiscal problems of the cities because the effort to bring social justice to America was abandoned at the national level and turned over to the whims and limited resources of local government. Although academic analysis was able to keep separate the distinction between social and fiscal crisis, in practice the identification of the movement for social change and the identification of fiscal difficulties, both in the same city, helped hasten a decline of activism that remains with us today.

Because the overarching national mobilization for social equality and justice evaporated with the failure of left-liberal national politics, militancy and activism at the local level became out of place in cities struggling with capital abandonment and fiscal decline. At present mythologists of capitalism's crisis have kept alive an interest in the concept of "urban social movement" despite clear evidence that its existence has waned and that its theoretical significance, itself, is highly overrated (see Pickvance, 1985; Ceccarelli, 1982). Instead, it is apparent that the real political failure has been at the intermediate and national levels of politics rather than at the populist level of the grass roots. The political environment once nurturing local insurgency has largely disappeared. Several factors are now at work that have enabled crisis restructuring and austerity to proceed with remarkable quiescence and social control rather than effective organized protest. Several of the chapters in this book, such as those by Jeff Henig, Dennis Judd, and C. G. Pickvance, will address this issue.

Finally, and most commonly, the urban crisis became the object of a loosely structured discourse on city decline that was tied to capitalist crisis theories only in weak ways. Urban ecologists, for example, ignored the events of crisis entirely by subsuming the new realities of much-changed cities under the old category of "urban problems" (see Berry and Kasarda, 1977; Hawley, 1981). The failure to examine the nature of the urban crisis on its own terms prevented mainstream urban sociologists from developing the very concepts needed to understand the trajectory of decline and restructuring taking place in cities today. Thus Clark and Ferguson's (1983: 33) otherwise important study of fiscal strain is handicapped by the unfortunate importation from ecology of the concepts "adaption" and "equilibrium" to characterize the local political process in an analysis that confuses structuralism with general systems theory.

Most concerned urbanists addressed the city malaise, but did so in a descriptive manner. General characterizations of decline and restructuring based on census data, correlational studies on the geographical movement of capital, and case studies of central city change were all combined to construct ways of talking about cities under siege and in transformation (Sternlieb and Hughes, 1977; Tabb and Sawers, 1978; Smith, 1984). Both mainstream and Marxist analysts shared in common a pool of concepts and labels that made it easy to talk about sociospatial changes, such as the frostbelt/sunbelt distinction, even if deep-level theoretical ideas went unaddressed and languished for lack of attention. This discourse has been notable over the last few years in identifying proximate causes of crisis, such as job loss; however, these were often taken to be fundamental determinants and combined with concepts from Marxian crisis theory and nonspecified signifiers of structural analysis in a discourse on urban decline and restructuring. More often than not, among Marxists, this crisis discourse displayed a confusion about underlying theoretical ideas, especially those associated with the European theory of structuralism (see, for example, Fainstein and

Fainstein, 1982). Thus the relation between economic transformations and sociospatial restructuring was explained away rather than understood by invoking the signifier "capitalist" as some black box mechanism of explanation.

After a fashion, discourse won out over analysis. The theoretical issues produced by the failure of both fiscal crisis theory and the theory of urban social movements have not been addressed. Instead, we have been left with a neatly wrapped package explaining the urban crisis as a phenomenon of capitalist society despite its relative absence elsewhere in that global camp. More accurately, we have been left with two neat packages—one carried by Marxists and the other by conservatives. In the former case, as already indicated, the crisis is explained by the discourse of "political economy"—conscienceless capital flight, private expropriation of profit, and even the magical creation of "new" faces for capitalism, such as a mutated high technology mode.

Among conservatives, in contrast, the urban crisis is viewed as essentially a political product brought on by the failure of liberal welfare statism. Poor choices made by the political regimes of the frostbelt in catering to the demands of its constituencies are considered most to blame for city ills. Instead of pursuing policies that provided capital with a "proper business climate," the fiscally distressed places fell victim, it is alleged, to their generosity by supporting redistributive programs that were doomed to fail. Further, conservatives assert that social welfare policies begot a social welfare politics with every group organizing itself as a separate interest capable of making recognizable demands on city budgets. In short, for conservatives, the urban crisis reflects the price paid for liberalism and social welfarism and is a creation of the city itself, whereas for Marxists, the urban crisis is preeminently a product of external forces produced by a malevolent capitalism in the throes of its own serious crisis of profit taking.

Currently, the urban malaise is old news. Just as we have no coherent urban policy at the national level that can guide sociospatial change, we no longer have a coherent inquiry into the condition of urban decline and restructuring. Instead we possess politicized domains of discourse—one belonging to the left and the other to the right. As each camp points an accusing finger at the other regarding what went wrong within American cities, residents continue to pay the costs of uncoordinated growth and the persisting decline in the quality of life.

Yet, because so much theoretical importance has been placed on the dramatic outbreak of crisis, understanding why the dire predictions of analysts have not materialized enables us to assess contemporary perspectives on the urban condition in a concrete way. In particular, understanding how the urban crisis has been managed throws new light on some of the most central subjects of contemporary social thought addressing the relation between the state and society including the following: the nature of the reproduction of social relations; the articulation between the local state and the economy; the role of state managers in urban change; the management of the class struggle; social control of racial problems; the problematical provision of housing, employment, and public services within the city; the restructuring of American capital and urban space according to the world system; and, finally, the relation between public policy and social process. For some time, prior to the 1980s, these issues were rarely addressed by mainstream urban analyses; indeed, a few of the above subjects could not even have been thought of at all using a conventional perspective. At present they form the core topics around which a new, more relevant field of urban studies is currently coalescing.

The chapters that follow place the enigma of crisis restructuring and relative social quiescence in comparative perspective. The contributors explore a variety of themes that have emerged in fiscal strain research over the last few years. John Matzer, Jr., Dennis Judd, and Irene and Herbert Rubin call attention to the changing nature of urban politics under the impact of fiscal crisis. At present city regimes are characterized by a growing professional expertise caused by the need to manage budgetary stress; by privatization and cutbacks affecting the quality of community life; by an excessive and unwarranted orientation toward economic development as a means of combating future fiscal problems; and by a conflict between the pristine, rational administration of budgets and bureaucrats, on the one hand, and the in-fighting of have-nots and new minority voices, on the other hand, in order to combat the uneven development of fiscally managed growth. New styles of leadership, new political coalitions, and, in short, a "new" urban politics have emerged in cities under stress that set the tone for a style of city governance that will probably be with us for some time.

A second group of chapters addresses the record of urban sociospatial change and exposes as limited the common discourse of crisis restructuring mentioned above. First, Todd Swanstrom's study of Cleveland, the only major city to default, details the political and voluntaristic nature of default that refutes its alleged structural determinants. Extreme fiscal crisis in Cleveland was caused by a parochial conflict between greedy banks and local government, despite the particulars of frostbelt decline. Second, Stein et al., in a national sample of 500 cities, show that the commonly accepted indicator of stress, measures based on total spending, leads to spurious conclusions about crisis and restructuring. They use a better indicator, municipal employment, that produces a clearer picture of strain and response than that drawn by the mainstream approach to fiscal crisis management.

Finally, chapters by Alberta Sbragia, C. G. Pickvance, and Jeff Henig attack the reductionist understanding of both Marxian political economy and mainstream political science. The link between capitalism and city events is not simple but complex. It represents neither a direct translation of economic crises to political concerns nor a direct reflection of changes in the mode of production to instantly concordant new city forms. These chapters redefine the contents of political economy toward a more fruitful direction of inquiry. The implications of these discoveries are explored in a final section on urban theory by me that evaluates the preceding chapters from the context of what has been said elsewhere about urban crisis and change.

In sum, this book reports and assesses recent work on the urban crisis and challenges the conventional wisdoms from both the left and the right regarding its nature, dynamics, and significance. Rather than accepting some easily available answers in the search for understanding that have contributed over the years to a decline in interest in urban questions, the following chapters search for new answers, issues, and modes of understanding in an effort to revitalize an important subject.

REFERENCES

ALCALY, R. and D. MERMELSTEIN [eds.] (1977) The Fiscal Crisis of American Cities. New York: Vintage.

BERRY, B. and J. KASARDA (1977) Contemporary Urban Ecology. New York: Macmillan.

CECCARELLI, P. (1982) "Politics, parties and urban movements: Western Europe," in S. Fainstein and N. Fainstein (eds.) Urban Policy Under Capitalism. Beverly Hills, CA: Sage.

CLARK, T. and L. FERGUSON (1983) City Money. New York: Columbia University Press.

EYERMAN, R. (1984) "Social movements and social theory." Sociology (February): 73-82.

FAINSTEIN, S. and N. FAINSTEIN [eds.] (1982) Urban Policy Under Capitalism. Beverly Hills, CA: Sage.

FRIEDLAND, R. et al. (1978) "Political conflict, urban structure and the fiscal crisis," in W. Tabb and L. Sawers (eds.) Marxism and the Metropolis. New York: Oxford University Press.

GOTTDIENER, M. (1985) The Social Production of Urban Space. Austin: University of Texas Press.

HABERMAS, J. (1975) Legitimation Crisis. Boston: Beacon.

KATZNELSON, I. (1981) City Trenches: Urban Politics and the Patterning of Class in the U.S. New York: Pantheon.

LEFEBVRE, H. (1969) The Explosion. New York: Vintage.

MINGIONE, E. (1981) Social Control and the City. New York: St. Martins.

O'CONNOR, J. (1981) "The fiscal crisis of the state revisited." Kapitalistate 9: 41-61.

——(1973) The Fiscal Crisis of the State. New York: St. Martins.

PICKVANCE, C. (1985) "The rise and fall of urban movements and the role of comparative analysis." Environment and Planning D: Society and Space 3: 31-53.

——(1980) "Theories of the state and theories of urban crisis." Current Perspectives in Social Theory 1: 31-54.

PIVEN, F. and R. CLOWARD (1979) Poor People's Movements. New York: Vintage.

SHEFTER, M. (1977) "New York's fiscal crisis: the politics of inflation and retrenchment." Public Interest 48 (Summer): 98-127.

SMITH, M. (1984) Cities in Transformation. Beverly Hills, CA: Sage.

STERNLIEB, G. and R. HUGHES [eds.] (1975) Post-Industrial America. New Brunswick, NJ: Rutgers University Press.

TABB, W. and L. SAWERS [eds.] (1978) Marxism and the Metropolis. New York: Oxford University Press.

THERET, B. (1983) "Collective means of consumption, capital accumulation and the urban question." International Journal of Urban and Regional Research, 6, 3: 345-371.

TOURAINE, A. (1981) The Voice and the Eye. New York: Cambridge University Press.

Part I

Historical Perspectives

☐ THIS INTRODUCTORY SECTION contains two chapters that provide a historical perspective on the chapters that follow. Eric Monkkonen, an urban historian, places the crisis of the 1970s within a historical context. He demonstrates that for three dimensions of crisis—fiscal, welfare, and crime—the cities of the past were more beseiged by problems than they are today. These results are based on statistical analyses of time series data that merely identify rates of change that are "significantly" different from background rates. This analysis can be misleading without qualitative interpretation. Monkkonen is sensitive to this issue because he acknowledges the compositional effects of the contemporary crisis, especially its differential effects on the poor and on minorities. Although more can be said about the qualitative significance of this phenomenon than Monkkonen volunteers (see Judd, Ganz, and Pickvance, below), his chapter complements others in the book that examine the differential impact of crisis and the social failure to renew the attack on society's intractable problems produced by uneven development.

Beyond this observation, however, Monkkonen's chapter is important because of its assessment of extant perspectives that have tried to link social and fiscal crises with theories of economic and political organization. According to Monkkonen, what we expect from cities depends largely on how we view them. In the past, local governments have always served first the interests of growth. Over the years progressively more social functions have been ascribed to them. Their limits, therefore, must be assessed against the changing aspects of social expectations—an emergent "discourse" about the purpose of city government. Thus in recent years the city has been burdened with the problem of controlling crime—a problem that for Monkkonen it can never solve. In short, the way we view what city governments are supposed to be doing not only drives local politics but also influences greatly social theories of public policy.

For Alex Ganz, an urban economist, the past decade represents an unprecedented and dramatic recovery for most city economies. Talk of city "decline" may be ill advised after reading Ganz's chapter. Urban cores have been effectively restructured from manufacturing to service, administrative, and banking centers. Occurring together with economic development has been a restructuring of central city fiscal expenditures and revenue sources. Two-thirds of Ganz's sample of the thirty largest cities have cut effectively their municipal payrolls. Service expenditures and slashes in delivery have also been made. In short, our largest cities have followed dutifully the demands of the business and banking community that surfaced in the late 1970s as a private sector precondition for bailing out local finances by cutting expenditures on services, reducing payrolls, and promoting growth.

Yet Ganz observes that this successful management of economic decline does not mean that the urban crisis has gone away. In fact, he argues that the very same structural features of social unrest present prior to the ghetto riots of the 1960s are still very much with us. Most city employment goes to suburban commuters, racial segregation and deprivation are as high as ever, and unemployment and poverty or working poverty remain characteristic of most inner-city dwellers. Thus a tale of two cities emerges that testifies to the flexible and responsive nature of growth, on the one hand, and to the intractable problems of capitalist development that have adversely affected the urban underclass, on the other. Ganz suggests that enlightened city administrations must move quickly to close the gap between the two cities and provide the means by which growth may benefit the larger population. This suggestion brings us back to dilemmas facing the country two decades ago and to demands to increase spending on redistributive social programs at a time when fiscal policy is controlled tightly by private sector constraints. This dilemma involving the "two faces" of city politics is explored by other contributions to this volume (see Henig, Judd, and

Gottdiener). In sum, Ganz's chapter raises the following question: Will the failure of the society in the past to alleviate urban uneven development be repeated in the new round of calls for social justice? It is but a small step from this question to another: Can the urban riots of the 1960s occur again?

1

The Sense of Crisis:
A Historian's Point of View

ERIC H. MONKKONEN

☐   FOR THE PAST two decades historians of the American city have researched the prior occurrences of contemporary urban problems, ranging from poverty to disease to social control to politics to corruption. Although their conclusions vary, a constant theme has emerged, usually stated in terms relative to current events. Crime seems to have been worse in the past; political corruption greater; class and ethnic conflict more ugly; neighborhood instability greater; policymaking more inconsistent. Because historians have so often taken their particular substantive concerns from present-day problems does not mean, however, that they have then taken their evidence to address present problems. For often having found that "it" was "worse" in the "good old days," they have also found that "it" was so different that careful historical analysis has precluded their direct comment on the present scene. As a consequence of their hard-gained and often counterintuitive knowledge, most urban historians make no claims about their special standing as experts on today's urban world. This is a pity, for the historian's view serves as an important way to get leverage on current policy problems. The leverage may not show the way to go, but it does show where others have been and in so doing gives a healthy dose of often subduing medicine.

AUTHOR'S NOTE: *An earlier version of this essay benefited considerably from thoughtful readings by James Q. Wilson and Mark Gottdiener, for which I am most grateful. A grant from the Academic Senate of the University of California helped support the research reported here.*

One of the arguments of this essay is that previous crises dwarf the current urban fiscal crisis to the extent that calling current problems "crises" is analytically incorrect. This does not mean that the current fiscal problems of local government do not exist. Obviously they do. But it does mean that these problems have been faced before in much greater magnitude. And it suggests that they are not unique to our era. Moreover, it tells us that we should face our current fiscal problems with knowledge of what our predecessors did and with the knowledge that such problems are unlikely to be quickly resolved. We should continue to try very hard to resolve urban problems and should not be discouraged by setbacks and small successes, for time may be on our side though it may not be even the next generation that benefits from our attempts. This is a difficult proposition to accept and may make for poor policy argumentation, but one hopes that short-range vision does not make up the only source of our self-understanding. It is in fact the very shortsightedness of our self-understanding that allows us to lose those gains that were so hard for people to achieve 75 years ago.

Perhaps every discouraged urban dweller, visiting the most decrepit downtown areas, should be reminded that the era in which our great-grandparents were born saw homeless children selling newspapers on the street, sleeping in boxes, while the major form of charity in the cities came from small private agencies or from daily handouts by the police. The service apparatus of the modern city was only just being formed, and cities could still experience such public health disasters as the Memphis yellow fever epidemic of 1878-1879, which killed 5000, mainly poor Irish immigrants. The building of the modern service-oriented local government has been difficult and slow. It will in all likelihood continue to be so. And to define all current problems as crises diminishes the gains that have been made in such a way as to call into question the modest machinery we have created.

In any kind of reasonable historical time span, the urban crisis that began in the mid-seventies is to a large extent an imaginary event. Its scope and existence have depended on very limited historical knowledge, research, or analysis, especially in the case of urban fiscal history. With only a handful of exceptions, the literature on the crisis has been the province of nonhistorians and the nonhistorical—both social scientists and journalists (Shefter, 1977; Hoffman, 1983). And as most urban historians have not been attending to the city other than as a container of social history, few have become interested in researching urban political or economic crises. In fact, as the fiscal crisis of the seventies became a larger urban crisis, most urban historians were still debating urban issues only in the sense that the subjects of the research attention were urban dwellers. Social and geographical mobility, bosses and reformers, everything but government, its finance and policy, had become the stuff of the "new urban history" (Thernstrom, 1971). Urban history has in fact been mainly social history and almost never city history.

This, no doubt, is one of the reasons so few of those labeled as urban historians have seen fit to comment on a subject that has become its own scholarly subindustry in other social sciences. Yet historians have important, even crucial, contributions to make to the understanding of the current fiscal crisis. Although the historian can share the amazement of others when examining the enormous growth in government expenditures since the Depression, the fiscal and social straits of cities in the seventies seem trivial when compared to the local crises during the Depression of the 1930s, or that of the 1890s, or that of the 1870s. Like old-timers recounting ever-worse blizzards, urban historians want to say, "Why, you shoulda seen the soup lines in '93," or, "Take a look at city reports from the Depression 'cause they won't last long—the city couldn't buy anything but newsprint for their published reports." This essay first takes the old-timer's position by looking backward at previous fiscal crises. This backward look throws a chill of cold water on most speculations surrounding the fiscal problems of post-World War II cities, for it supports a claim that essentially things have never been so good for the U.S. city.

In addition to providing an empirical historical context, the historian can make other important contributions to understanding the urban crisis, for many of the theoretical problems implicit in the study of the crisis also inform the historical study of urban institutions. The problems implicit in these various approaches stand out more boldly when placed in the historical perspective, for it becomes clear that the reading of history has all too often been used to bolster and justify theoretical positions rather than to develop critical insights.

This essay deliberately eschews the positions of functionalists and social control theorists, particularly as applied to the plight of the urban poor and to urban crime. Caught between the Scylla of functionalism and the Charybdis of quasi-Marxism, few who write the histories of urban social service organizations or of fiscal behavior have sailed undamaged into an examination of recent city crises. Both camps have had their exciting days in the sun. And they continue to encompass the predominant modes of analysis. But both have suffered seriously from their theoretical blinders. Functionalists too often make the city a marvelous machine functioning more smoothly than its observers may at first have comprehended (Merton, 1949; Hofstadter, 1955; Kolko, 1973). Social control theorists, on the other hand, see deep crises, basic contradictions, and repression at every turn of event (Piven and Cloward, 1971; Katznelson, 1981).

With the exception perhaps of Foucault (1979), we have not a dialogue but two monologues, the arguments of each side constructed prior to and virtually unaffected by any empirical research. The functionalists have the city cast as a passive responder, dealing with problems on an ad hoc basis. The social control theorists also see the city as a maintainer of the status quo, but so doing in an inherently unstable and crisis-prone economic context. As forms of historical analysis, both positions have proven useful, at least in a heuristic sense. Both have guided researchers toward asking provocative questions, and both have allowed the researchers to construct parsimonious and often intellectually engaging accounts. Yet neither has grappled with the central empirical and theoretical flaws implicit in its approach, and consequently neither has given us an adequate descriptive or explanatory account of the perceived urban crisis that began to be discussed in the 1970s.

Historians are often charged with being atheoretical. They probably are not guilty of such charges, but given the state of theory on urban crises and social control, their theory shyness certainly would be well justified. Had they been even less theoretical, they might have responded to Cleveland's default in 1979 and the New York City crisis and near default of 1973 more aggressively, trying to put these events in some deeper perspective. Instead, they too fell into the functionalist or social control camps, both of which could happily watch the drama of those years unfold with an "I told you so" smirk.

Two historians did respond to New York City's crisis, indirectly, by writing about the impending crises in New York State (McClelland and Magdovich, 1981). The authors suggest that they had begun with the intention of producing a full-fledged econometric and historical analysis but in the end had to satisfy themselves with organizational charts and an orderly list of data about the state's stupendously complex finances and indebtedness. Their book testifies convincingly to the difficult research problems that face anyone trying to alter the high proportion of bombast to data analysis in the fiscal crisis literature. Untangling urban finance might drive the most avid researcher to the brink apparently reached by Magdovich and McClelland, who ended up finding in the person of Nelson Rockefeller the causal mechanism that so eluded them in their search for decent data.

Although it seldom has been recognized, the historical and nonhistorical crisis literature share a great deal, for actually a great deal of historical research can speak to the analysis of the urban crisis of the seventies and eighties (McDonald and Ward, 1984; Anderson, 1977). In addition, the social control and functionalist perspectives are in themselves essentially historical analyses, and the contemporary application of these perspectives depends for many of its assumptions on historical research (McDonald, 1985; Muraskin, 1976). Fortunately, one must not necessarily be saddled with either of these two perspectives to build a historically sensitive analysis of the urban crisis, if indeed there is a crisis. By judicious selection and careful confrontation with the historical record, it may even be possible to use the historical past as a navigational guide to sail between Scylla and Charybdis.

The following three sections of this essay describe the urban histories of debt, welfare, and crime; each has been constructed to address current issues that swirl around the problem of urban crisis.

DEBT: PRINCIPLES AND INTERESTS

The fiscal history of U.S. cities has yet to be explored in the detail it demands and deserves. Yet certain features are sufficiently established to alter or emphasize some of the truisms about the urban fiscal crisis that seems to have begun in the early seventies. The four main points to be made here are the following: (1) The post-World War II era is unusually stable and free from defaults; (2) only the massive defaults of the 1930s demonstrate a nonrandom deviation from the historical series of defaults; (3) most defaults have been "caused" in their deeper as well as more immediate sense by conscious political decisions; and (4) the most important change since the Depression is in the disassociation of residential property owners from the specifics of local finance. The consequence of the latter is that urban finance is now an arrangement worked out between financiers and multiple layers of government, with the formerly important third party, city dwellers, no longer included as directly interested participants. Recent experience in various state-level tax limitation movements emphasizes this point: Taxpayers have complaints, many very specific and some purely self-interested, and want changes in government (Sears and Citrin, 1982). They can make effective voting coalitions only with "meat axe" proposals, the most famous being California's Proposition 13, which affected local government most dramatically yet registered more discontent with the federal government (Citrin and Levy, 1981: 13).

Defaults supply one dramatic index of fiscal crisis. When all annual defaults between the mid-nineteenth century and the end of the Depression are analyzed through a Box-Jenkins impact analysis, only the Depression is shown to have any marked impact on the series. Although the years of earlier depressions have a visible increase in the number of city defaults, only the Depression of the 1930s, when some 3,000 local governments went into default, as opposed to the 100 or 200 of earlier depressions, was a clearly external cause of local government defaults (Monkkonen, 1984). The internal accounts of several spectacular nineteenth- and early twentieth-century defaults show how these indeed came during times of severe financial crisis but were nevertheless politically contested decisions made as alternatives to continued debt repayment.

Again, the Depression and the Bank Holiday were the exceptions, for then local governments simply could not pay. It may be the case that even then some local governments took advantage of the widespread crisis in order to postpone debt repayment until a more convenient time. No single default was of the magnitude that New York's might have been in the 1970s, although had New York defaulted its geographical solitude would not have matched the thousands of widespread Depression defaults.

The table in the Appendix shows the impact of the Depression and shape of the postwar local revenue structure. Several points should be emphasized. First, one major aspect of the general default crisis of the 1930s was the very high proportion of expenses going to pay interest on debt. Second, the proportion of revenue accounted for by property tax plunged to new lows after the Depression and stayed there permanently. In the context of historically high working-class homeownership and thus concern and control over the city debt and budget, the decrease in property tax contributions indexes a general distancing of homeowners from the local fiscal process. Out of the Depression came an unheralded transition in the relationship of homeowners to local government.

Declining property tax contributions to city revenue amplified the impact of the increase in federal monies going to city governments. In the late 1920s and early 1930s, property taxes contributed a majority of state and local government receipts—around 60%. During the latter part of the Depression this figure had dropped to a stable 45%. With the onset of World War II, a steady decrease in the proportion began, not bottoming out until 1980 at just under 18% (Appendix). In fifty years the historic relationship of taxpayers to local government had been dramatically reversed. Had property tax contributions stayed high, the power of federal aid would have been considerably diluted. The impact of federal aid to cities has come as a consequence of the removal of voters from close ties of self-interest to fiscal policy rather than because of the federal impulse alone.

Finally, the proportions of city expenditures going to meet interest payments are usually taken as an indicator of the general health of a city's fiscal affairs. Again, the general picture for the 1970s is not nearly so grim as it was in the Depression. For instance, in the 1970s, 5% of all local government expenditures went to debt interest, contrasting with 8% in the mid-1930s (Appendix). It is only in the most recent data for the 1980s that interest payments might be taken as a seriously imbalanced aspect of post-Depression urban finance.

WELFARE: ARE THE POOR NECESSARY?

The historiographical battle that has raged within the ranks of social welfare historians reproduces the general intellectual dialogue between social control theorists and functionalists. Piven and Cloward's (1971) *Regulating the Poor* and Trattner's *From Poor Law to Welfare State* (1974) and *Social Welfare or Social Control? Some Historical Reflections on Regulating the Poor* (1983) epitomize the poles of the debate. Piven and Cloward accurately ferret out the control elements in social welfare, whereas Trattner just as accurately documents the reform responses to the social problems of poverty and destitution. The essential disagreement represented by the two analyses is not over accurate evaluations of reform motives, but over the deeper causal springs of modern social welfare systems.

Control theorists take their cue from Richard Hofstadter's (1955) devastating analysis of Progressive refomers that claimed that they were not progressive at all but rather yearned for the power their class positions had formerly given them. His critique of the seemingly pure Progressives opened a flood of revisionist criticism of progressivism. The social welfare systems Progressives had so carefully constructed represented little more than limited ways to assuage the social damage caused by the iniquities of capitalism. Even more, the administration of welfare was and still is a crude form of social engineering, designed to change the behavior of the victims of capitalist development, indoctrinating the poor with self-blame for their poverty, confusing class consciousness, and deflecting class-conscious criticism and action (Rogers, 1982; Banner, 1973; Hall, 1974/1975).

For the functionalists, in contrast, the systematic nature of welfare is not significant. Instead, it is seen in a humanitarian and pragmatic sense. The functionalist historical analysis portrays benevolent, motivated, and concerned individuals working to create social change. The narrative that emerges from this position is essentially progressive in that it portrays the story of progress, of change from less humanitarian to more caring kinds of social organizations. The implied causal model is "natural" in that one event follows predictably from another, just as spring follows winter. Trattner (1974: 44-45), for instance, states as a fact the model underlying the functionalist perspective: Immigration, industrialization, and urbanization increased poverty and the costs of poor relief; this in turn "increased concern about poverty" and "attempts to eliminate it."

In the social control perspective, then, the deep capitalist structure is the protagonist, the poor its victims. In the functionalist story, indifference and callousness make up the enemy's ranks, reformers are the protagonists, and the creation of care and control institutions represents their triumphs.

Social control theory is more intellectually appealing than the functionalist model of social change in that it accounts for the two most apparent contradictions. First, welfare reformers were simultaneously working for the poor and yet harshly critical of them, often expressing racist or other forms of contempt for the very people whom they worked to assist. Second, in spite of the century of work in intense reform efforts, poverty continued to be a major social problem, suggesting that its elimination might not be possible in capitalist society. Social control theory resolves these two contradictions, asserting that the purpose of welfare is to preserve the economic status quo.

The functionalist account, although unable to resolve deep contradictions, also has its appeal. First, its work is much more empirical—the researchers in this mode simply know more. Second, their implicit analytic appeal to humanitarian values strikes a chord in most readers, who feel that helping the poor is a good thing and that the motives of a lifelong welfare reformer were probably less greedy than those of, say, the robber barons. It is hard to see Florence Nightingale as accomplishing the same kind of tasks as John D. Rockefeller. Moreover, most modern readers can relate more to the hope for incremental change that functionalist analysis contains than they can to the either/or, revolution or exploitation model implied in social control theory. In a sense, the functionalist perspective, though lacking any intellectual pizzazz, would seem to offer a better guide to mundane reality.

This long digression on these two conflicting and fashionable models of the relationship of cities to poor people is important because each informs a separate analytic perspective on the larger urban crisis. Piven and Cloward (1977) saw New York's crisis of the 1970s in the social control perspective, interpretng it as a near failure of the control mechanisms. The welfare system had failed in its main task of social control; the poor had begun to make political demands; and the crisis was a political subterfuge to rein in the potentially revolutionary forces. The functionalists (Schultz et al., 1977) on the contrary saw the problem as a simple balance sheet difficulty: too many poor relative to the resources. Neither position actually says much of any great significance, one claiming that the poor had become too powerful, the other that the city had become too poor.

Even the briefest comparison of the crisis of the mid-1970s with the urban response to poverty during the Depression suggests the fatuity of both the functionalist and social control analyses. During the Depression, the fourth largest city in the country, Detroit, probably felt the most swift and severe impact. It quickly went into default as it simultaneously attempted to aid the unemployed, about one-third of its working population. During this Depression there were no federal programs for the poor, and poverty across the United States became more widespread and desperate than ever before (or, one hopes, since). The significance of the urban impact of the Depression was its suddenness and directness. There were no multiple, mediating agencies of complex responsibilities and with varied sources of funding to cushion or diffuse the impact. One cannot help but be struck by the finality of the bank closures and subsequent Bank Holiday in 1931. Cities expended their cash on hand and then had no more monetary resources, period.

In contrast to the thousands of Depression-caused crises in local governments, the crisis of the 1970s had a widely diffused impact because four actively involved governmental layers (city, county, state, and federal) and many more separately funded government agencies dealt directly with the urban poor. The cushion of multiple sources of funds allowed administrators to ease short-run crises, to make transitions slowly, and in this way to make changes somewhat less dramatically visible.

The growth of the welfare state since the 1920s has, through such programs as AFDC and Social Security, mediated individual-level poverty and diffused social responsibility. Although the theoretically alert examination of federal city relations has yet to be done, one can say that the welfare state has eased considerably the city's responsibility for the poor. This alone has probably made a greater impact on the city than any of the more sensational federal urban programs of the 1960s. Without Social Security and AFDC, one can imagine that the belt tightening of fiscally troubled cities in the 1970s might have taken a different turn and that the poor would have suffered severely.

CRIME: PROTOREVOLUTIONARIES OR LUMPEN?

Even those who wish to hold a functionalist or social control analysis of urban poverty must find the causal nexus of poverty and the larger urban crisis murky. That is, are the urban poor to be understood as victims, political agents pressuring for more expenditures, or irrelevant to the urban crisis? Yet as unclear as these causal positions may be, that for crime is even more ambivalent. First, of course, there is the problematic relationship of crime to poverty: Whatever this relationship may be, it compounds the relationship of poverty to crisis. That is, if poverty causes any kind of criminal behavior, then crime has an even more complex causal structure than does poverty.

As with the social control and functionalist confusion over the analysis of welfare, several ideological positions further confuse the understanding of crime and crime control. There is one argument that sees the criminal offenders as prepolitical rebels and the organizations intended to control them as counterrevolutionary. Harring (1983), for instance, claims that the police were created by late nineteenth-century capitalists in order to contain the revolutionary violence of the working class. A more subtle argument concerns the various reform aspects of crime control organizations, claiming that such ameliorative agencies as juvenile institutions are really a form of class control (Platt, 1969).

Functionalists, on the other hand, assume that crime, like poverty, is a natural concomitant of urban scale, and argue that it and the organizations controlling it bear a lawlike, nonpolitical relationship to one another (Johnson, 1979). Big cities beget big crime, which in turn begets big crime control organizations.

Yet whether one sees crime as natural or revolutionary, it is clearly costly in myriad ways and is perhaps the major contributor to the social ills so visible in central cities in the second half of the twentieth century. As U.S. cities lurched through the troubled seventies, the fear of crime occupied citizen perceptions as a central urban problem, even more worrisome than taxes. After 1974, for instance, fear of crime ranked second behind concern over inflation in public opinion polls (Flanagan and McLeod, 1983: 222). And the most feared crimes are indeed urban. As Cook (1983: 1) has pointed out, "Robbery is the quintessential urban crime." Virtually one-fifth (18%) of all robberies in the United States in 1980 occurred in New York City alone. Cities with over 250,000 population contained 19% of the total U.S. population but had 60% of all robberies and 46% of all homicides. And in New York City, over half of all white homicide victims were killed during the course of a robbery.

During the 1960s and 1970s, the demographic anomaly that accounted in part for the era's fiscal peculiarity also accounted for at least a part of its increase in urban crime and poverty. It is well known that most criminal offenders are young, between the teenage years and the thirties. For instance, in 1980, 78% of all arrests were of persons between 13 and 34, although only 38% of the population was in this age group. More to the point, 16- to 24-year-olds, who were 17% of the population, accounted for 46% of all arrests (Flanagan and McLeod, 1983: 398). To the extent that arrestees reflect actual offenders, 16- to 24-year-olds account for about three times as much crime as other age groups.

Prisoners, on the other hand, tend to be somewhat older than those arrested for criminal offenses. This is partly because a youthful offender's recidivism and record of prior offenses builds up to finally earn him or her a longer prison sentence (Langan and Greenfield, 1983). Thus the older members of the age group now committing most crimes were unusual simply in their great number in the 1970s and, for this reason alone, were largely responsible for the great surge in criminal behavior in the cities. They now account for the prison crisis—too many prisoners (over 600,000 counting those in local jails) and too few beds—for similar demographic reasons (Blumstein et al., 1982).

Thus, for reasons entirely independent of the postwar urban situation, the baby boom's criminal legacy exacerbated city problems and seemed to be another signal of serious urban ills. It is no wonder that observers in the mid-seventies could see the only effects of the baby boom in the rise in homicide and violent crime rates and tied their analyses of these to a similar increase in urban fiscal strain, wrongly concluding that a virtual urban Armageddon had begun. Alcaly and Mermelstein's (1977) book dramatically captured this impression, particularly in its paperback version's cover of flames, symbolizing the era's somewhat hysterical analytic conclusions.

Often in crises, otherwise ahistorical social analysts turn to history for precedents, policy suggestions, and a bit of security. The President's

Commission on Civil Disorders had included a strong dose of historical analysis to calm itself and comprehend the riots of the 1960s. Strangely, no such similar turn to the past occurred in the 1970s. For the most part, crime observers looked at the frightening rise in criminal offenses and attempted to think of the future without examining the past.

Had analysts of this period bothered to try to establish a longer perspective rather than so curiously limiting themselves to the highly idiosyncratic postwar era, they would have found a far more significant set of long-term crime indicators. Although imperfect and therefore speculative, these indicators all point toward a century-long decrease or at least stasis in criminal behavior. They make starkly apparent the fact that the crime bulge of the late 1960s and 1970s was indeed an anomaly, one that temporarily countered a very long trend toward less crime in Western society. "Violence," as H. Rap Brown was so often quoted, may have been "as American as apple pie," but this tradition, like so many, was one in abeyance (Gatrell, 1980; Gurr, 1981; Lane, 1979; Monkkonen, 1981).

Short of another baby boom, we can probably expect criminal behavior to resume its long, slow, downward trend. We do not know why this is the trend. It may in fact be a stochastic drift. We do not know if it will reverse. We do not know what is a realistic expectation or goal to set even if we did know how to control crime trends. The best argument for an urban crime control policy must be simply that it is appropriate for humanitarian as well as local economic reasons to continue to try to eliminate crime.

In recent times a disproportionate amount of violent criminal offenders are black (Schuster, 1981; Silberman, 1978: 161). The immediate and long-run causes of this remain the subject of an important set of debates (McNeely and Pope, 1981), but several specific consequences relate directly to the urban crisis. First, in the course of the twentieth century the black population of the United States has dramatically relocated itself, changing from the most rural group to the most urban one, from 23% urban in 1900 to 73% urban in 1960 (Farley, 1968: 255). Located in central cities, blacks contribute a disproportionate amount of the city's high crime rate. Because of the relative poverty of blacks, white racial antagonism, and non-race-specific fear of crime, central-city concentration of blacks has helped in creating a place more dangerous than the suburb or than places with a small number of blacks. Many urban locational decision makers—both residential and business—take this into account, adding to their long list yet one more reason to avoid the central city (Wilson, 1983b: 79-82). When added to the greater crime

control burden already assumed by the central city, the fiscal consequences are incalculable and probably high.

Second, partly because more violent offenders are black, black people are more at risk than whites to become victims of violent criminal
offenses. In a personal sense, the black community has to bear the social
and psychological costs of living in a dangerous environment. Because
of its concentration in racially segregated sections of the city, the black
community lives with the fact of violent crime. Recent estimates show
that black males have an incredible 1 in 21 lifetime chance of being
murdered—a probability six times greater than that for whites (Irwin,
1985). Additionally, recent work has shown that not only do blacks
make up a disproportionate number of victims but that they are less
likely to have their original criminal complaints taken seriously by the
police (Smith et al., 1984). Thus blacks are denied a major urban service,
that of timely and responsive policing. Cities suffer, black people suffer,
and the whole society suffers.

It is appropriate here to introduce, if briefly, the historical innovation
represented in the modern police system. As we know them, salaried,
uniformed, systematically organized, and acting under the executive
branch of government, city police are no more than 140 years old. The
United States has lagged behind all other Western nations in adopting
uniformed, salaried police. Moreover, its police are uniquely urban and
local. Not until the last two decades of the nineteenth century were all
American cities policed. Britain, in contrast, had regular police patrolling in both rural and urban places by the mid-nineteenth century. The
introduction of the uniformed police was expected to accomplish several goals, including crime control. But no one anticipated the new
expectations for public order and freedom from crime that resulted,
partly from the simple physical presence of identifiable agents of local
government and partly from the shift of prosecution costs from the
victim to government (Monkkonen, 1981; Steinberg, 1984). The expectation that society can control crime and violence, that it is an obligation
of government to do so, has resulted in the past decade in ever-
increasing demands for victims' rights.

This has, in turn, created a new crisis, one of three dimensions: in
service (that is, crime control), in racial justice, and in the diseconomy of
urban dangerousness. If nothing else, local urban government has legit-
imized itself not as a governing body but as a provider of services. These
services maintain either the physical or social infrastructures that in turn
provide the stage for social and economic action. The failure to provide
any of these now customary services undermines local government's

legitimacy. Citizens now feel that they can demand freedom from crime. Therefore the presence of crime and disorder threatens the very basis of local government. This expectation represents a fundamental shift in the role of local government, a shift toward greater responsibility. The shift has been completed in the post-World War II era, bringing with it a serious problem: Government does not really know how to control crime. Ironically then, U.S. city governments have earned a major function in social engineering that they may not be capable of providing. Social problems have become urban problems and urban problems are the unique provenance of local government.

The crisis in racial justice follows from that in service. Those who have few choices in their residential areas and must live in central cities are at risk to be victims of crimes. Recent immigrants, minority groups, the elderly, and the poor cannot escape to safer suburbs or different cities. Through no fault of their own they cannot lead safe and predictable lives. The very dangers that make cities unattractive as residential centers multiply inward toward particular populations. The indirect costs of crime then become differentially borne by blacks, Hispanics, and poor whites, and the direct costs of crime control amplify the city's fiscal stress and provide both a monetary and a social reason to escape. Although a disproportionate number of black people are violent offenders, other blacks suffer disproportionately. This unfair distribution of violent crime will not disappear as the overall level of crime subsides, even though its visibility lessens.

CONCLUSION

The basic trajectory of U.S. urban history is short, dating from the second or third decade of the nineteenth century. During the first century of its short history, small but real crises were common occurrences. The Depression of the 1930s was of a far different magnitude, more widespread and longer lasting; but this was not so much a difference of kind as it was of scale, for at the level of the individual city, fiscal disasters had been unusual but not entirely unpredictable. One might compare such crises to California's earthquakes—for the most part small, common, and widespread.

For crucial analytic reasons, the period following World War II should concern us more in that it was the truly atypical time for U.S. cities, if 150 years is long enough to justify such an observation. The post-World War II era saw unprecedented demographic and economic growth. This growth was unprecedented in its smoothness and in the fact that for the most part it could exploit existing organizational structures without the buccaneering entrepreneurialism of the nineteenth century. The mid-1970s shocked U.S. cities with a hint of their traditional instability and proneness to crisis.

The historical myopia of urban observers saw no further back in time than about 1956 and the Federal Highway Act. Thus the unusual period of postwar growth and stability made the relatively minor crises of the 1970s loom prophetically and disproportionately large to a pampered and wealthy generation.

The concern of the social control theorists with the organization and power of city governments reflects, ironically enough, their essentially reformist position. Presumably, if the various welfare and control organizations supported every democratic goal the critics espoused, their criticism would be answered. Only the untestable proposition that a capitalist society cannot provide a fair distribution of wealth and justice makes social control theory radical. And if city organizations responded quickly to every social or economic problem that appeared on the horizon, the functionalists would also be satisfied. Both positions are embedded in the historical assumptions and concepts that serve to make our cities modern. Neither is radical for neither steps beyond the boundaries of the modern, service-providing city. The social control position is in fact profoundly innocent of understanding the historical origins of the modern U.S. city, for to be shocked at the city's servile position relative to finance institutions or its deliberate efforts to make its inhabitants more economically productive is to be unaware of the essence of the modern city. The essential model of the modern American city, developed in the mid-nineteenth century, is nonregulatory and growth (both demographic and economic) promoting.

To "discover" that cities work aggressively in these directions is to be either incredibly naive or historically ignorant. Our conception of the ideal modern city is one new to the world. Its form was hammered out by experimentation and experience in the nineteenth century. It is not traditional. It has abandoned the tight control over social and economic affairs of its medieval predecessors. It has also abandoned its predecessors' strict hierarchies of inherited privilege and power. The modern U.S. city is already radically altered from that of the eighteenth century. As Foucault might say, we have become a part of its discourse.

The transitional crisis is not now upon us. It has passed us by. Our chore is now to comprehend the new relationship of local state to society and economy. And this will be the result of less posturing and more digging in the evidence, evidence that is from both the past and the present.

APPENDIX   Proportions of Local, State Government Expenditures
           and Receipts (in million of dollars) Accounted for by
           Real Property Taxes and by Interest Payments, 1929-1982

Year		1929	1930	1931	1932	1933
(A)		4543.00	4727.00	4539.00	4424.00	3962.00
(B)		60.01	60.33	58.62	60.50	55.36
(C)		1.55	1.60	4.04	1.83	7.01
(D)		5.10	5.41	7.38	7.38	8.01

	1934	1935	1936	1937	1938	1939	1940
(A)	3907.00	4023.00	4058.00	4162.00	4277.00	4285.00	4407.00
(B)	45.70	44.19	47.03	45.71	44.89	44.41	44.26
(C)	19.45	18.74	8.39	8.39	8.35	10.24	8.61
(D)	6.77	6.04	6.32	5.70	5.26	4.78	5.06

	1941	1942	1943	1944	1945	1946	1947
(A)	4449.00	4397.00	4494.00	4565.00	4642.00	4836.00	5346.00
(B)	42.90	41.57	41.40	41.04	40.05	37.19	34.63
(C)	7.78	8.39	8.68	8.51	7.51	8.52	11.26
(D)	4.58	4.30	4.11	3.61	2.92	5.01	3.81

	1948	1949	1950	1951	1952	1953	1954
(A)	5938.00	6642.00	7143.00	7696.00	8385.00	9096.00	9673.00
(B)	33.54	34.13	33.53	32.83	32.97	33.17	33.30
(C)	11.22	11.45	11.00	10.61	10.40	10.34	10.03
(D)	3.12	2.87	2.77	2.83	2.88	2.97	3.13

	1955	1956	1957	1958	1959	1960	1961
(A)	10448.00	11453.00	12609.00	13764.00	14812.00	16238.00	17580.00
(B)	33.00	32.73	32.77	32.81	31.89	32.55	32.55
(C)	9.85	9.52	10.94	13.45	14.74	13.08	13.42
(D)	3.30	3.46	3.51	3.53	3.80	4.12	4.13

	1962	1963	1964	1965	1966	1967	1968
(A)	18958.00	20245.00	21687.00	23187.00	24535.00	26964.00	29896.00
(B)	32.41	32.02	31.19	30.86	28.93	28.81	27.87
(C)	13.64	14.46	15.00	14.80	16.96	17.00	17.33
(D)	4.25	4.26	4.26	4.18	4.08	3.96	3.92

(continued)

APPENDIX Continued

Year	1969	1970	1971	1972	1973	1974	1975
(A)	32763.00	36674.00	40445.00	43227.00	46355.00	48980.00	53384.00
(B)	27.26	27.08	26.43	24.24	23.77	23.17	22.46
(C)	16.93	18.05	18.96	21.04	20.80	20.79	22.95
(D)	4.08	4.21	4.35	4.57	4.66	4.70	4.76

	1976	1977	1978	1979	1980	1981	1982
(A)	58247.00	63407.00	63984.00	64403.00	68400.00	75100.00	83500.00
(B)	21.75	21.28	19.54	18.34	17.72	18.02	19.10
(C)	22.82	22.66	23.60	22.90	22.99	21.04	19.10
(D)	4.98	5.07	4.99	5.03	5.67	6.16	6.91

SOURCE: U.S. Department of Commerce (1981a: Table 3.3, 128-129, 1981b: Table 3.3, 7, 1982: Table 3.3, 7, *Survey of Current Business*, 1983: Table 3.3, 5).

NOTE: (A) = property tax. (B) = percentage of total receipts from property tax. (C) = percentage of receipts in federal aid. (D) = percentage of expenditures in interest payments.

REFERENCES

ALCALY, R. E. and D. MERMELSTEIN [eds.] (1977) The Fiscal Crisis of American Cities: Essays on the Political Economy of Urban America with Special Reference to New York. New York: Vintage.

ANDERSON, A. (1977) The Origin and Resolution of an Urban Crisis: Baltimore, 1890-1930. Baltimore, MD: Johns Hopkins University Press.

BANNER, L. (1973) "Religious benevolence as social control." Journal of American History 59 (June): 23-41.

BLUMSTEIN, A. J., J. COHEN, and P. HSIEH (1982) "The duration of adult criminal careers." Report to the National Institute of Justice. Washington, DC: Government Printing Office.

CITRIN, J. and F. LEVY (1981) "From 13 to 4 and beyond: the political meaning of the ongoing tax revolt in California," pp. 1-26 in G. G. Kaufman and K. T. Rosen (eds.) The Property Tax Revolt: The Case of Proposition 13. Cambridge, MA: Ballinger.

COOK, P. J. (1983) "Robbery." National Institute of Justice, Research in Brief. Washington, DC: Government Printing Office.

FARLEY, R. (1968) "The urbanization of negroes in the United States." Journal of Social History 1 (Spring): 241-258.

FLANAGAN, T. J. and M. MCLEOD [eds.] (1983) "Sourcebook of criminal justice statistics—1982." U.S. Department of Justice, Bureau of Justice Statistics. Washington, DC: Government Printing Office.

FOUCAULT, T. M. (1979) Discipline and Punish: The Origins of the Prison. New York: Vintage.

GATRELL, V.A.C. (1980) "The decline of theft and violence in Victorian and Edwardian England," pp. 238-370, in V.A.C. Gatrell et al. (eds.) Crime and the Law Since 1850. London: Europa.

GURR, T. R. (1981) "Historical trends in violent crime: a critical review of the evidence," pp. 295-353 in N. Morris and M. Tonry (eds.) Crime and Justice: An Annual Review of Research, Vol. III. Chicago: University of Chicago Press.

HALL, P. A. (1974/1975). "Boston charity: a theory of charitable benevolence and class development." Science & Society 38 (Winter): 464-477.

HARRING, S. L. (1983) Policing a Class Society: The Experience of American Cities, 1865-1915. New Brunswick, NJ: Rutgers University Press.

HOFFMAN, J. (1983) "Urban squeeze plays: New York City crises of the 1930s and 1970s." Radical Review of Political Economics 12 (Summer): 29-57.

HOFSTADTER, R. (1955) The Age of Reform: From Bryan to FDR. New York: Knopf.

IRWIN, D. (1985) "Black males' murder risk 6 times as high as whites." Los Angeles Times (May 6): 4.

JOHNSON, D. R. (1979) Policing the Urban Underworld: The Impact of Crime on the Development of the American Police, 1800-1887. Philadelphia: Temple University Press.

KATZNELSON, I. (1981) Urban Trenches: Urban Politics and the Patterning of Class in the United States. Chicago: University of Chicago Press.

KOLKO, G. (1973) The Triumph of Conservatism: A Reinterpretation of American History. New York: Free Press.

LANE, R. (1979) Violent Death in the City: Suicide, Accident and Murder in Nineteenth-Century Philadelphia. Cambridge, MA: Harvard University Press.

LANGAN, P. A. and L. A. GREENFIELD (1983) "Career patterns in crime." Bureau of Justice Statistics Special Report. Washington, DC: Government Printing Office.

McCLELLAND, P. D. and A. MAGDOVICH (1981) Crisis in the Making: The Political Economy of New York State since 1945. New York: Cambridge University Press.

McDONALD, T. J. (1985) "The problem of the political in recent American urban history: liberal pluralism and the rise of functionalism." Social History 10 (October): 323-345.

———and S. WARD [eds.] (1984) The Politics of Urban Fiscal Policy. Beverly Hills, CA: Sage.

McNEELY, R. L. and C. E. POPE (1981) "Socioeconomic and racial issues in the measurement of criminal involvement," pp. 31-48 in R. L. McNeely and C. E. Pope (eds.) Race, Crime, and Criminal Justice. Beverly Hills, CA: Sage.

MERTON, R. K. (1949) Social Theory and Social Structure: Toward the Codification of Theory and Research. New York: Free Press.

MONKKONEN, E. H. (1984) "The politics of municipal indebtedness and default, 1850-1936," pp. 125-159 in T. McDonald and S. Ward (eds.) The Politics of Urban Fiscal Policy. Beverly Hills, CA: Sage.

———(1981) Police in Urban America, 1860-1920. New York: Cambridge University Press.

MURASKIN, W. A. (1976) "Social control theory in American history: a critique." Journal of Social History 9 (Summer): 559-568.

PIVEN, F. (1977) "The urban crisis: who got what and why," pp. 132-144 in D. Mermelstein and R. E. Alcaly (eds.) The Fiscal Crisis of American Cities: Essays on the

Political Economy of Urban America with Special Reference to New York. New York: Vintage.

————and R. CLOWARD (1971) Regulating the Poor. New York: Pantheon.

PLATT, A. M. (1969) The Child Savers: The Invention of Juvenile Delinquency. Chicago: University of Chicago Press.

ROGERS, D. T. (1982) "In search of Progressivism." Reviews in American History 10 (March): 113-132.

ROTHMAN, D. (1981) Conscience and Convenience: The Asylum and Its Alternatives in Progressive America. Boston: Little, Brown.

SCHULTZ, C. L., E. R. FRIED, A. M. RIVLIN, N. H. TEETERS, and R. D. REISCH-AUR (1977) "Fiscal problems in cities," pp. 189-212 in D. Mermelstein and R. E. Alcaly (eds.) The Fiscal Crisis of American Cities: Essays on the Political Economy of Urban America with Special Reference to New York. New York: Vintage.

SCHUSTER, R. L. (1981) "Black and white violent delinquents: a longitudinal cohort study," pp. 109-128 in R. L. McNeely and C. E. Pope (eds.) Race, Crime, and Criminal Justice. Beverly Hills, CA: Sage.

SEARS, D. O. and J. CITRIN (1982) Tax Revolt: Something for Nothing in California. Cambridge, MA: Harvard University Press.

SHEFTER, M. (1977) "New York City's fiscal crisis." Public Interest 48 (Summer): 98-127.

SILBERMAN, C. E. (1978) Criminal Violence, Criminal Justice. New York: Random.

SMITH, D. A., C. A. VISHER, and L. A. DAVIDSON (1984) "Equity and discretionary justice: the influence of race on police arrest decisions." Journal of Criminal Law and Criminology 75 (Spring): 234-249.

STEINBERG, A. (1984) "From private prosecution to plea bargaining: criminal prosecution, the district attorney, and American legal history." Crime & Delinquency 30 (October): 568-592.

Survey of Current Business (1983) 63 (February): Table 3.3, p. 5.

————(1982) 62 (August): Table 3.3, p. 7.

THERNSTROM, S. (1971) "Reflections on the new urban history." Daedalus 100 (Spring): 359-375.

TRATTNER, W. I. [ed.] (1983) Social Welfare or Social Control? Some Historical Reflections on Regulating the Poor. Knoxville: University of Tennessee Press.

————(1974) From Poor Law to Welfare State: A History of Social Welfare in America. New York: Free Press.

U.S. Department of Commerce, Bureau of Economic Analysis (1981a) The National Income and Product Accounts of the United States, 1929-1976: A Supplement to the Survey of Current Business (Table 3.3, pp. 128-129). Washington, DC: Government Printing Office.

U. S. Department of Commerce, Bureau of Economic Analysis (1981b) National Income and Product Accounts, 1976-1979: Special Supplement to the Survey of Current Business (Table 3.3, p. 25). Washington, DC: Government Printing Office.

WILSON, J. Q. (1983a) "Crime and American culture." Public Interest 70 (Winter): 22-48.

————(1983b) Thinking About Crime. New York: Basic Books.

2

Where Has the Urban Crisis Gone?
How Boston and Other Large Cities
Have Stemmed Economic Decline

ALEXANDER GANZ

□ ALMOST TWO DECADES ago the "urban crisis," which was ushered in by the riots of 1967 following the postwar suburbanization of population and jobs, elicited some curious scholarly "findings" and "solutions." According to one school of thought, our large cities were bereft of social and economic value; they experienced a crisis of function and could be relegated only to the role of pacifying, but not advancing, their concentrations of disadvantaged populations. These findings described "the city as sandbox" and "the city as reservation" (Long, 1971; Sternlieb, 1971). These findings were soon followed by the "solution" of some other scholars: export the poor (Forrester, 1969). Some of these scholars went on to write off the Northeast and its large older metropolitan centers as subject to a regional dynamic that was forever sweeping away employment and population to the newer growth poles of the South and West (Sternlieb and Hughes, 1977).

At the same time, new information on the pervasive emergence of the "services revolution" and new measures of the production and employment role of cities heralded their newly expanding services activity function (Ganz, 1972; Ganz and O'Brien, 1973). Despite the strengthen-

AUTHOR'S NOTE: *This chapter was reprinted from* Urban Affairs Quarterly *(1985) 20, 4.*

ing of services production and employment roles of cities in the 1960s, urban population declined as postwar baby-boom families moved to the suburbs, encouraged by national policies subsidizing suburban housing, infrastructure, and transportation (Stanback and Knight, 1976). In the ensuing two decades, the expanding services production role of cities was accommodated by an extraordinary wave of downtown office and hotel development. And, recently, cities have experienced a new population wave as the postwar babies, now young adults, lead a new era in our national population makeup, forming one- and two-person households and moving back to the city as a result of the attraction of jobs and amenities (U.S. Bureau of the Census, 1983a).

There are two other features of the 1960s that have not changed that much, however. The concentrations of poor and minorities have not been drawn into the mainstream of city economic life and the level of public services in cities has suffered from federal and state funding parsimony and tax limitation legislation (U.S. Bureau of the Census, 1977, 1984a).

In sum, the urban crisis is still with us. It is not, however, a crisis of the cities' role as a provider of places to work and to live. Rather, the crisis is fiscal and also involves barriers to access. These are types of crises with which our society should readily be able to deal.

Another change from the 1960s, important to scholars, is the broad advance in information and analysis on the economic role of cities. For almost a decade now, the U.S. Department of Commerce, Bureau of Economic Analysis, has been publishing information on "place of work" earned income and employment by county and by industry, providing an extraordinary data base on the economy of cities (U.S. Bureau of Economic Analysis, 1984). Using these data, scholars have conveniently dissected the distinctive hierarchy of services activities roles of cities by size (Noyelle and Stanback, 1983).

The analysis that follows presents new information on the cities' "work place" and "place to live" roles, urban poverty and the barriers to access, and the emergence of a new populism aimed at embracing those left behind in the thriving life and prospects of our large city economies. Reference is made to the experience of Boston and other large cities.

LARGE CITIES' EXPANDING ROLE AS
SERVICES ACTIVITY WORK PLACES

The transformation of our national economy, favoring a more rapid rate of growth in a broad range of finance and services activities—

embracing business and professional services, higher education and medicine, communications and money management—in comparison with goods-producing activities, has proceeded inexorably since the end of World War II. The "services revolution" has provided the base for substantial economic growth in our large cities. Highly urbanized New England, drawing on services activity and hi-tech industry, has surpassed the nation as a whole in employment growth since 1976. As a consequence of the rising role of services, Boston and New York City have experienced a notable expansion of employment since 1976, and 1984 was a banner year. In contrast, the primary industrial cities—where obsolescent industry had not been replaced—continued to decline.

Two recent reports on office employment and office construction provide an extraordinary insight into the expanding services activity role of our large cities. An article in the December 1984 issue of *Monthly Labor Review*, a publication of the U.S. Bureau of Labor Statistics, presents (for the first time) statistics on "estimated office employment" by occupations for 1975-1982, which reveal that office employment makes up more than one-third of all jobs in the nation and has increased almost twice as fast as total employment since 1975 (Schloss, 1984).[1] An October 1984 report by Urban Investment and Development Co. (of Chicago) also presents a unique body of information on office space construction in the downtowns of the 30 largest metropolitan areas from 1950-1984 (Urban Investment and Development Co., 1984). This body of information is significant in three ways: the time span, the up-to-date feature of the data, and the coverage of our large cities. Thus we have a fine new data base on the new role of our large cities. We now know that finance and services employment, the most rapidly growing sector of our national economy, is mostly centered in office structures (Brown, 1985) and that half of all office structures in our large metropolitan areas are downtown (Office Network, Inc. 1983).

In the third of a century since 1950, a rising trend of office construction in the downtowns of the 30 largest metropolitan areas mirrored the fundamental structural change breathing new life into old cities. The role of office building construction downtown had erupted in the 1950s following a 30-year lag (after the boom of the 1920s), doubled in the 1960s (in relation to the 1950s), increased a further 50% in the 1970s, and in the first five years of the 1980s more than replicated the previous decade's downtown office growth. The outlook to 1990, based on office construction under way, scheduled, and planned, is for substantial growth. Because about half of all office jobs are clerical and support services, this suggests a potential for training workers from poorer city areas.

In addition to office construction, downtown hotels cater principally to business visitors and convention goers, and the number of hotel rooms in the downtowns of the 30 largest metropolitan areas has doubled since 1960. Thus hotel and convention center development and tourism are other sources of jobs and growth.

Finally, services and finance make up a sizable and growing share of employment in large cities, and the role of the export of services is also large. Taken together, office work, tourism, and finance have expanded employment in the city, counteracting somewhat the decline in manufacturing.

TRANSFORMATION

The expanding role of services activities in our national economy, and their impact on the role of cities, has drawn the attention of scholars who have profiled the transformation in depth. Noyelle and Stanback (1983), in their book entitled *The Economic Transformation of American Cities*, note that for the nation as a whole, employment and gross product originating in services activities increased their share, respectively, from 57% and 63% of the nation's total, in 1947, to 63% and 66% in 1977. Manufacturing employment in the nation has not increased in 14 years, whereas that in finance and services forged ahead. Between 1970 and 1983, manufacturing employment showed no gain; employment for finance and services rose by 65%, thereby raising their share of the total from 21%, in 1970, to 28%, in 1983, whereas the manufacturing share fell from 27% to 20% (U.S. Council of Economic Advisers, 1984).

Employment in highly urbanized New England, riding on a crest of growth in services, finance, and hi-tech industry, has surpassed the national growth rate since 1976, increasing at an annual rate of 1.9% in comparison with 1.8% for the nation (U.S. Bureau of Labor Statistics, 1984a).

For the nation's large cities, the postwar loss of manufacturing has been largely offset by the growth in finance and services. In 1980, the central city counties of the 34 largest metropolitan areas (with more than 1 million population in 1960) accounted for one-third of the earned income (measure of place of work production of goods and services) of the national economy (Brown and Kay, 1983). In the period 1959-1980, the cities' earned income, measured in dollars of constant value, had increased at an annual rate of 3.5%, in comparison with 4.8% for the

TABLE 2.1   Earned Income, by Industry, in the Central City Counties
of Nation's 34 Largest Metros Areas, 1959 and 1980
(dollars of constant value at 1980 prices)

| | 1959 | 1980 | 1959 | 1980 | 1959-1980 |
| | | | (Percentage | | (Percentage |
	(Billions)		Composition)		Change)
Total	300	522	100	100	+74
Manufacturing	92	123	31	24	+34
Transportation					
and communication	28	47	9	9	+68
Wholesale trade	26	46	9	9	+77
Retail trade	32	45	11	9	+41
Finance	22	46	7	9	+109
Services	45	108	15	21	+140
Government	36	75	12	15	$108
Construction	19	32	6	6	+68

SOURCE: Brown and Kay (1983).

NOTE: Earned income is composed of wages and salaries and proprietors' income,
by place of work, and is a proxy for the production of goods and services. The
foregoing analysis is based on special tabulations provided by the U.S. Bureau of
Economic Analysis. In 1980, the earned income of the central city counties of the
34 largest metro areas made up 72% of that of their metro areas and 33% of that of
the United States.

nation. For the cities, the annual rate of growth of key sectors over this
period was 1.6% for manufacturing, 4.9% for finance, and 6.8% for
services. For the nation, these percentages were 3.2% manufacturing,
6.2% finance, and 7.9% services (see Table 2.1).

Boston, San Francisco, and New York are the nation's preeminent
services activity cities. For these three cities, employment in services (in
the large sense including transportation, communication, finance, and
services) accounted for 52%, 51%, and 49%, respectively, of total
employment in 1980, in comparison with 38% for the 34 largest cities
and 31% for the nation as a whole (Perkins and Brown, 1982). These
cities were also large exporters of services, with employment in services
exports (medicine, higher education, business, and professional services) representing 41% of services employment in Boston, 26% in San
Francisco, and 28% in New York.

A 1983 taxonomy of the nation's 34 largest cities, ranking them by
"economic growth and improvement," found the average ranking of 14
broad-based services cities to be 16, that for the 12 sunbelt cities was 17,
and that for the primary industrial cities was 27 (see Table 2.2).

TABLE 2.2   Downtown Indicators Report 1983
            Summary of Rankings, by Type of City

	Downtown Market Strength Rank	Economic Growth and Improvement Rank	Retail Trade Rank	Office Market Rank	Hotel Market Rank	Housing Market Rank
Sunbelt						
Atlanta	16	33	18	13	8	33
Dallas	12	23	14	12	11	36
Houston	13	22	16	6	12	31
Los Angeles	7	4	8	7	7	7
Miami	19	15	23	20	28	19
New Orleans	9	9	7	14	5	11
Phoenix	32	24	33	30	31	29
Sacramento	33	8	32	29	34	24
Salt Lake City	23	11	17	33	18	13
San Antonio	26	14	15	27	15	21
San Diego	25	19	31	26	25	12
Tampa	37	17	36	36	37	26
Average Ranking	21.0	16.6	20.8	21.1	19.3	21.8
Industrial						
Buffalo	30	36	34	37	36	30
Chicago	2	3	3	3	2	3
Cincinnati	18	18	20	25	20	28
Cleveland	24	25	28	18	27	27
Detroit	20	34	24	24	19	23
Indianapolis	29	38	26	28	23	37
Milwaukee	21	32	25	23	24	16
Philadelphia	6	7	6	10	9	5
Pittsburgh	10	28	12	9	21	21
Providence	35	37	35	38	38	18
Rochester	31	35	29	34	35	13
St. Louis	22	27	30	19	17	38
Average Ranking	20.7	26.7	22.7	22.3	22.6	21.6
Broad-Based Services						
Baltimore	17	29	19	16	26	15
Boston	4	5	4	5	6	4
Columbus	27	21	21	21	22	25
Denver	14	16	13	8	13	17
Hartford	28	26	27	22	33	20
Kansas City	34	31	37	31	29	35
Louisville	36	20	22	35	30	34
Memphis	38	30	38	32	32	32

(continued)

TABLE 2.2 Continued

	Downtown Market Strength Rank	Economic Growth and Improvement Rank	Retail Trade Rank	Office Market Rank	Hotel Market Rank	Housing Market Rank
Broad-Based Services (Continued)						
Minneapolis	10	10	10	17	14	9
New York	1	2	1	1	1	1
Portland	15	12	11	15	16	10
San Francisco	3	1	2	2	3	2
Seattle	8	6	9	11	10	6
Washington, D.C.	5	13	5	4	4	8
Average Ranking	17.1	15.9	15.6	15.7	17.1	15.6

SOURCE: *Downtown Indicators, Report 1983*, Urban Investment and Development Co., Chicago.

Boston and New York City have been thriving since the mid-1970s with a substantial growth in employment, which has been largely services-based. Boston gained 80,000 jobs between 1976 and 1984, an increase of 16%, with a growth of 64,000 jobs in finance and services and 38,000 in office employment (Brown and Perkins, 1985). New York City gained 156,000 jobs in the 1950s and 1960s, lost jobs in the 1970s, and garnered 164,000 jobs in the first half of the 1980s (*New York Times*, 1985e). In 1984, the New York City gain of 72,000 jobs was the largest since 1950.

OFFICE EMPLOYMENT AND CONSTRUCTION BOOM

Newly available information on office employment and construction reveal a lot about "where has the urban crisis gone?" at least in terms of transformed economic function and pattern of growth over the last third of a century. According to a recent report of the U.S. Bureau of Labor Statistics (Schloss, 1984), office employment increased from 24.3 million jobs in 1975 to 31.2 million in 1982. This increase made up 35% of the nation's 89.6 million jobs in 1982, and reflected a growth over this period second only to that of employment in finance and services as a whole (a rise of 28% for office in comparison with 35% for finance and services, which include higher education and medicine). A report of the Office Network (1983) on the stock of office space in 23 large metro areas suggests that about half the office space (and office employment) in 1983 was located in the central business district.

Corollary information indicates that almost half of the nation's post-1950 gain in office employment and construction was captured by the downtowns of our large cities. Downtown office construction in the 30 largest metropolitan areas totaled 603 million square feet between 1950 and 1984, according to a recent report of the Urban Investment and Development Corporation (1984). This indicates a gain of about 3 million office jobs in the nation's large cities over this 34-year period (assuming average office space per office worker at 200 square feet), which is equal to more than 40% of the national gain (Torto, 1982).[2] For the large cities, with approximately 30% (27 million) of the nation's jobs in 1984, and office employment estimated at 8 million in that year, the increment of 3 million jobs since 1950 is a fundamental measure of the evolution and takeoff in economic structure (Brown, 1982).

Even more significant is the pattern of downtown office growth over the last 30 years. Of the 600 million square feet of downtown office construction built since 1950, 10% was built in the 1950s, 22% in the 1960s, 33% in the 1970s, and 35% in the 1980-1984 period (Urban Investment and Development Co., 1984). Moreover, space under construction, scheduled, and planned indicates a record total of 340 million new square feet of downtown office construction for the 1980-1990 decade. Looking to 1990 and 1995, long-range projections of the U.S. economy prepared by the U.S. Bureau of Labor Statistics indicate that services activities may be expected to grow more rapidly than the economy as a whole (U.S. Bureau of Labor Statistics, 1984b).

THE PEOPLE ROLE OF OUR
LARGE CITIES—A NEW ERA

Urban restructuring, discerned in the 1960s, blossomed in the decade following 1975. In the meantime, suburbanization increased as a result of the postwar family formation and related baby boom, and subsidies for suburban housing, infrastructure, and transportation. In effect, the large cities were able to strengthen their economic function whereas their people function drained away, leaving a concentration of poor and minorities behind.

This is all changing rapidly. A new era is upon us; its vintage is almost ten years. For almost a decade now, the postwar babies who are now adults have opted for one- and two-person households, nonfamily households, two-worker households with a preference for city living. And there has been a rapidly expanding participation of women in the labor force. Attracted by jobs and amenities, these smaller, young adult households are flooding our large cities where they are contributing to a pervasive housing shortage and raising property values extraordinarily. They are also bringing new life and spirit to our older cities.

Young adults, 25 to 44 years old, increased in number by 13,323,000 between 1975 and 1982, accounting for 73% of the total national population growth in that period (U.S. Council of Economic Advisers, 1984). In contrast, the "under 24" age group rose by only 2,041,000 in this period. By way of comparison, in the 1945-1960 period, the "under 15" age group had grown by 21,949,000, accounting for 53% of the nation's 40,743,000 population increase in that period and spurring suburbanization.

The change in age composition has affected the pattern of household formation, favoring the flow to the cities. From 1970 to 1982, the number of one- and two-person households almost tripled (rising 2.8 times), and made up 55% of all households in the latter year. The total number of households had grown by 32% over the 1970-1982 period. In Boston, one- and two-person households accounted for 66% of all households in 1980. In many Boston neighborhoods, even where population has been declining, the number of households has been expanding with their smaller size (U.S. Bureau of the Census, 1983a).

These young small households are remaking our older cities. Their role was graphically reported in a recent *Newsweek* (1984) cover story on "The Yuppies." The return to the cities also reflects the declining influence of the effects of suburban subsidization—housing subsidies, infrastructure subsidies, and highway transportation subsidies—although they remain important for families.

Our large cities have passed from an era of throw-away housing to one in which housing is scarce, in demand, and has value; these factors produce extraordinary incentives for fix-up. Many formerly run-down neighborhoods are blossoming.

THE URBAN FISCAL CRISIS WORSENS

A constant in the urban equation is the sharpening fiscal crisis. Our cities have fallen victim to federal and state parsimony and to tax limitation legislation. Municipal public services have been cut back. In one month—January 1985—three northeastern governors—Cuomo of New York, Dukakis of Massachusetts, and Kean of New Jersey—felt compelled to jump on the bandwagon and announce tax cuts much to the dismay of some of their mayors and more progressive legislators who are mindful of cities' need for revenue.

Municipal services have been severely reduced in many large cities. For our 30 large cities taken together, municipal employment levels declined by 56,612 (7%) between 1975 and 1983 (see Table 2.3). This overall record even hides the more tragic savaging of public services in many cities, with reductions of 10% in Chicago, 15% in Los Angeles and Philadelphia, 20% in Baltimore, 14% in Washington, D.C., 27% in Cleveland, 25% in Boston, 18% in St. Louis, 13% in Nashville, and 15% in Atlanta. Several sunbelt cities, however, experienced substantial growth in municipal employment. These include Houston, Phoenix, San Jose, and El Paso.

The reduction in municipal expenditure, FY1976 to FY1983, measured in dollars of constant value, was 9% overall for the 30 large cities (heavily weighted by the 22% decline in New York City, in relation to its fiscal crisis year; see Table 2.4). Of the 30 large cities, 10 experienced lower levels of expenditure and 20 had increases. For some, even reduced levels of public service human resources were associated with higher costs.

President Reagan's proposed FY1986 defense-oriented budget bodes ill for the urban economy, with projected expenditure reductions of 47% for housing and urban development programs, 100% for revenue sharing, and 3% for education.

POVERTY AMIDST PROSPERITY

As 1985 began to unfold, paeans of euphoria and optimism were sung on the nation's record of prosperity. News writers had to hark back two and three decades to find comparable rates of increase in economic growth and income. More than that, an economist of the Federal Reserve Bank of Boston, writing in the November/December 1984 *New England Economic Review*, found the current cyclical national economic expansion stronger than average and strongest since the Korean War boom, and cited factors that may be with us for some time: (1) expansionary federal fiscal policy (deficit spending with rising military expenditures more than displacing short-changed social programs); (2) inflation softened by modest wage gains, ample harvests, and a weak energy market; and (3) business investment fed by "the huge increase in economic profits" (McNees, 1984).

TABLE 2.3 City Government Employment, 1975-1982
(full-time equivalent employees)

	1982	1975	Change Number	Change Percentage
New York	335,252	347,686	−12,434	− 3.6
Chicago	43,848	48,799	− 4,951	−10.1
Los Angeles	39,939	46,929	− 6,990	−14.9
Philadelphia	32,228	37,981	− 5,753	−15.1
Houston	19,495	14,258	+ 5,237	+36.7
Detroit	20,063	20,511	− 448	− 2.2
Dallas	13,959	13,320	+ 639	+ 4.8
San Diego	6,926	6,923	+ 2	NC
Baltimore	32,560	40,522	− 7,962	−19.6
San Antonio	10,753	11,068	− 315	− 2.8
Phoenix	8,343	7,363	− 980	−13.3
Indianapolis	10,988	11,474	− 486	− 4.2
San Francisco	20,786	21,555	− 769	− 3.6
Memphis	21,549	21,708	− 159	− 0.7
Washington, D.C.	39,270	45,801	− 6,531	−14.3
San Jose	4,024	3,673	+ 351	+ 9.6
Milwaukee	8,817	9,687	− 870	− 9.0
Cleveland	9,165	12,637	− 3,472	−27.5
Columbus	6,491	6,663	− 172	− 2.5
Boston	18,677	24,895	− 6,218	−25.0
New Orleans	10,116	10,544	− 428	− 4.1
Jacksonville	9,868	10,388	− 520	− 5.0
Seattle	8,434	8,771	− 337	− 3.8
Denver	11,431	12,257	− 826	− 6.7
St. Louis	11,037	13,519	− 2,482	−18.4
Kansas City	7,606	6,506	+ 1,100	+16.9
Nashville	15,686	18,032	− 2,346	−13.0
El Paso	4,212	3,508	+ 704	+20.0
Pittsburgh	5,738	5,557	+ 181	+ 3.3
Atlanta	7,600	8,937	− 1,337	−15.0
Total	794,860	851,472	−56,612	− 6.6

SOURCES: U.S. Bureau of the Census (1976: Table 4, 8-20; 1983b: Table 4, 10-32).

But *other* records were also reported in 1984. These included 900,000 more Americans in poverty in 1983, and the highest poverty rate since 1973. There was more poverty in the nation and its metropolitan areas, and a relative concentration of poverty in the central cities. There were graphic accounts of poverty in New York, Boston, and Baltimore.

TABLE 2.4 General Government Expenditures for 30 Large Cities, Comparison of Trends from FY1976 to FY1983 in Constant FY83 Dollars (millions of dollars)

	FY1983 Expenditures	FY1976 Expenditures	Absolute Change	Percentage Change
New York	$16,412	$20,933	−$4,521	−21.6
Chicago	2,087	1,758	+ 329	+18.7
Los Angeles	1,673	1,539	+ 134	+ 8.7
Philadelphia	1,821	1,774	+ 48	+ 2.7
Houston	1,065	616	+ 450	+73.0
Detroit	1,283	1,068	+ 215	+20.2
Dallas	477	375	+ 103	+27.4
San Diego	342	334	+ 7	+ 2.2
Baltimore	1,262	1,716	− 454	−26.5
San Antonio	354	275	+ 79	+28.6
Phoenix	510	346	+ 164	+47.5
Indianapolis	468	436	+ 31	+ 7.2
San Francisco	1,141	1,035	+ 106	+10.3
Memphis	545	546	− 1	− 0.2
Washington, D.C.	2,337	2,512	− 175	− 7.0
San Jose	262	229	+ 33	+14.3
Milwaukee	393	345	+ 48	+13.9
Cleveland	335	466	− 131	−28.2
Columbus	306	257	+ 48	+18.8
Boston	848	1,270	− 422	−33.2
New Orleans	463	403	+ 60	+14.8
Jacksonville	332	409	− 77	−18.8
Seattle	361	338	+ 22	+ 6.5
Denver	509	560	− 60	−10.6
St. Louis	406	409	− 3	− 0.8
Kansas City	338	357	− 19	− 5.3
Nashville	457	430	+ 27	+ 6.3
El Paso	145	97	+ 48	+49.8
Pittsburgh	271	226	+ 45	+19.8
Atlanta	367	360	+ 7	+ 2.0
Total	37,570	41,431		− 9.3

SOURCES: U.S. Bureau of the Census (1977: Table 5, 9-66; 1984b: Table 5, 6-61).

Professor John Kenneth Galbraith (1984) wrote an article on "The Heartless Society," and the Urban Institute (1984) in a report on "The Reagan Record," found that Reagan's policies helped the affluent but were detrimental to the poor and the middle class.

RISE IN POVERTY

Despite the euphoria in the press about the economic turnaround of cities (*New York Times*, Wallace, 1985c, 1985d; *Boston Globe*, 1985b), there were other types of news headlines. On August 3, 1984, stories in the *Boston Globe* and *New York Times* were captioned, respectively, "Nearly 900,000 More Americans in Poverty In 1983" and "Rate of Poverty Found to Persist In Face of Gains." The *Globe* story reported, "The number of Americans officially in poverty climbed by nearly 900,000 to break the 35 million mark last year, The Census Bureau said yesterday." The *Times* story reported that the poverty rate, the percentage of the population living below the poverty level, had risen from 11.1%, in 1973, to 15.2% in 1983. For blacks, the incidence of poverty over the 1973-1983 decade rose from 31.4% to 35.7%. For Hispanics, the respective poverty rates were 21.9% and 28.4%.

A U.S. Census Bureau Report issued in March 1984, entitled *Characteristics of the Population Below the Poverty Level: 1982*, reported even higher and growing poverty rates in the nation's central cities and poverty areas than in the nation as a whole (U.S. Bureau of the Census, 1984a). Whereas the poverty rate for the nation had risen from 12.3% in 1975 to 15.0% in 1982, that for the central cities of metropolitan areas has increased from 15.0% to 19.9% in the same period. For poverty areas in the central cities, the incidence of poverty grew from 34.9% in 1975 to 45.6% in 1982.

The extent of the new deprivation amidst booming growth is so newly emerging that newspaper reports are so far its best documentary source. Graphic headlines told "tales of two cities"—poverty amidst prosperity—in New York, Baltimore, and Boston, and probing beneath the surface identified the features of this face of the urban crisis. A story in the *New York Times* (1984a) was entitled "Poverty Worsening In City, Study Finds." The story's lead found that

> the poor of New York City have not been helped by the city's recent economic resurgence and are unlikely to be touched by future improvements, according to a sweeping study sponsored by the Community Service Society of Greater New York. For far too many people, the city has been transformed from a place of opportunity and hope to one of want and hopelessness, said the report, which has not yet been issued. While New York remains a city of gold at the top of the ladder, it has become a city of despair for many.

Another story in the same issue of the *Times* was bannered "Poor Quarter Left Behind New York Boom," and reported, "More and more the story of New York's economic resurgence is becoming a tale of two cities. Since January 1983, more than 140,000 new jobs have been created by the booming service and financial industries. . . . But the good times have not trickled down to the other New York. The Human Resources Administration disclosed last week that the number of residents living in poverty had grown by 20 percent since 1979. Today, the income of 1 in 4 New Yorkers is below the poverty line."

An article by Sydney H. Schanberg in the January 22, 1985, issue of the *New York Times*, headlined "The Poverty Divide," said that "New York City is booming economically. More people are hungry and homeless than at any time since the Depression. The city keeps gaining jobs, as the local employment picture brightens. One of every four city residents lives below the poverty line, as the hardship picture darkens."

New Year's tidings were summed up in a January 20, 1985, article in the *New York Times*, bannered "How Many Will Share New York's Prosperity?" The story states,

> For New York City, it is the best of times and the worst of times. . . . More jobs were created in the city last year than in any year since 1950. . . . But the resurgence has not reached all New Yorkers. . . . A report last week added further evidence that New York was becoming a city of extremes. . . . Brooklyn in the decade between 1970 and 1980 lost thousands of manufacturing jobs, its population declined . . . and the economic disparities between white and minority residents grew wider.

The *Washington Post* of November 24, 1984, had a somewhat similar story on Baltimore, with the headline "Is Baltimore Truly Back? New Showcase City Faces Old Problems." The story went on to note, "Few cities have tried so long, so hard or so creatively to reverse their decline as Baltimore. . . . Yet even as more projects are announced and new buildings take their place on the skyline, nagging questions persist about Baltimore's future. . . . An increasing proportion of those who remain in the city are poor."

In Boston, the percentage of families in poverty increased from 11.3% in 1970 to 16.7% in 1980 (O'Brien, 1984). In that year, 20.2 of all households (family and nonfamily) had income below the poverty level. In early 1985, Governor Michael S. Dukakis's "State of the State" address was greeted by these headlines in the *Boston Globe* of January 17: "Dukakis sees jobs for all, expansion of services" and "An Invitation to Paradise in Massachusetts." But Bob Kuttner, writing in the *Boston Globe* of December 14, 1984, assessed the situation a little differently, noting that "lately, the out-of-town papers have been full of stories about the City With No Unemployment—Boston. There are heart-warming tales of bulging ads, high-tech companies stealing each other's engineers, and local retailers going as far as New Hampshire to find sales help for Christmas. But from the perspective of Roxbury or Dorchester (Boston neighborhoods) these stories might as well be about Sweden. Inner-city Boston has the same dreadful youth unemployment rates as Cleveland or Detroit—40 and even 50 percent. The problem is that kids from poor neighborhoods tend to be the least job prepared and the most discriminated against."

A January 24 story in the *Boston Globe* adds the final straw with the story bannered "Study Says the Poor's Tax Burden is Up, the Rich's Down." The story lead, based on a new Brookings Institute book by Joseph Pechman entitled *Who Paid the Taxes, 1966-85*, summed it up: "The total tax burden of the poorest 20 percent of Americans has gone up over the last two decades while that of the wealthiest 10 percent had declined" (*Boston Globe*, 1985a).

In sum, in 1982, when the national poverty rate was 15% and that in the central cities of metropolitan areas was 20%, poor whites in cities numbered 6,757,000 and poor blacks in the cities totaled 5,438,000 (U.S. Bureau of the Census, 1984a). Thus economic growth does not translate into benefits for all and its special nature today seems to increase the urban underclass. For this reason active public policy is still needed to combat the costs of uneven development.

THE NEW POPULISM—DEVELOPMENT WITH FAIRNESS

The last decade's rise in urban poverty amidst prosperity was associated, in part, with the growing concentration of minority population and the increase in the number of female-headed households and elderly in the cities. But the main culprits were (1) national economic policy (which both curtailed social programs benefiting the poor and taxed them more heavily) and (2) barriers to access—discrimination, short-falls in human resources training and education, and the mismatch of obsolescent blue-collar skills and the occupational requirements of white-collar jobs.

In Boston and San Francisco a new breed of modern populist mayors were swept into office on a platform of (1) encompassing everyone irrespective of race, ethnicity, or sexual preference and (2) exacting benefits from development prosperity for lagging neighborhoods and population groups. San Francisco pioneered the way with an ordinance requiring office building developers to provide housing in the measure of the size of the office structure, the employees it would bring in, and the impact it would have on the housing market (Share and Diamond, 1983).

Boston adopted its own version of "development impact project payments" to fund a Neighborhood Housing Trust, but soon added requirements for public improvements and amenities, job training and hiring, and contributions to a neighborhood development bank (McCormack and Bolling, 1983; Boston Redevelopment Authority, 1983a, 1983b; Zoning Commission, 1983). The key to the potential success of this effort is (1) the extraordinary development boom and the eagerness of developers to participate and (2) the ample margin for access of minorities and women to the new office jobs that require large numbers of clerical and support personnel as well as professional, managerial, and technical workers.

A report entitled *Downtown Projects—Opportunities for Boston*, which was issued in October 1984, cited the projected employment table of a current large office development project and revealed that 40% of the jobs would be made up of clerical and support services (Boston Redevelopment Authority, 1984). A related consideration is the potential for increasing the share of jobs held by Boston resident workers; a recent report had shown that suburban commuters held 60% of Boston's jobs. Boston has consequently adopted a policy requiring developers to make a good faith effort to assure that at least 50% of the new jobs go to Boston residents. Another bold plan, "Dudley Square, Strategy for Revitalization," currently in a formative stage, is designed to embrace Boston's principal poor minority neighborhood into the mainstream of the city's thriving economy by constraining downtown office development and inducing it to envelop the Roxbury neighborhood that is a scant two miles away (Boston Redevelopment Authority, 1985).

For Boston's new (self-proclaimed) working-class mayor the objective is "to create a city that works for and cares about everyone" where "economic growth and economic justice are the principles of the future" (Flynn, 1985). Although this is a difficult act to carry out in an era of federal and state parsimony and strained city fiscal capacity, mayoral populism is an important new style of political leadership that might spearhead the solution to current problems of uneven development

(Scharfenberg, 1984). If the barriers to access are lowered for poor whites and poor blacks, it will be largely because it is affordable in the "bottom-line" economics of development. In a time of military expenditure-fed prosperity, the guttting of federal social programs, and the rise in poverty, it will be interesting to see how far grass-roots populism can take us. Americans, with their egalitarian heritage dating back to the Constitution and earlier, are not a people to countenance idly, or for long, growing poverty in the midst of prosperity. The new populism may provide the leadership and the strategy for forging enlightened federal initiatives in partnership with grass-roots public and private sector development roles.

NOTES

1. An earlier study by Regina Armstrong (1979), covering the period 1957-1976, foretold the rise of office employment and its role on the cities' economic base. "Office work . . . represents the most rapidly growing economic activity in the United States. . . . Because office jobs are eminently suited to city centres, they offer a chance to provide a new economic base for deteriorating central cities."

2. An extensive survey of the characteristics of firms occupying office space in Boston, carried out in 1977, found that "Class A and B office space (built since 1960 or renovated to new condition) have a gross leasable square feet per worker ratio of 208 and 203 respectively. . . . The Class C (built prior to 1960) ratio (is) 238 square feet per worker."

Other analysts use a smaller ratio of space per worker (which would yield a higher downtown office employment estimate for the 603 million square feet of downtown space in 30 metro areas constructed in the 1960-1984 period. See Armstrong (1979) (155 square feet per worker) and Downs (1984) (150 square feet per worker).

REFERENCES

ARMSTRONG, R. (1979) "National trends in office construction, employment and headquarters location in U.S. metropolitan areas," in P. W. Daniels, Spatial Patterns of Office Growth and Location. New York: John Wiley.
Boston Globe (1985a) "Study says the poor's tax burden is up, the rich's down." January 24: 7.
———(1985b) "Economic growth in '84 sets 34-year high, U.S. says." January 23: 25, 26.
———(1985c) "Dukakis sees jobs for all, expansion of services." January 17: 1, 30.
———(1985d) "An invitation to paradise in Massachusetts." January 17: 30.
———(1984) "Nearly 900,000 more Americans in poverty in 1983." August 3: 3.
Boston Redevelopment Authority (1985) Dudley Square, A Strategy for Neighborhood Revitalization. Boston: Author.
———(1984) Downtown Projects, Opportunities for Boston. Boston: Author.

————(1983a) Boston Population and Housing by Neighborhood Areas, 1980. Boston: Author.

————(1983b) Boston's Prospective Development and the Linkage to Housing Needs. Boston: Author.

BROWN, J. P. (1985) Boston Employment, Citywide, Downtown, Downtown Office, and Remainder of Boston, 1976-1983 and Projections to 1990 and 1995. Boston: Boston Redevelopment Authority.

————(1982) Boston and Thirty-Three Large Cities' Economic Structure and Trends: Full- and Part-Time Employment by Industrial Sector. Boston: Boston Redevelopment Authority.

————and F. KAY (1983) Boston, Thirty-Three Large Cities and Their Metropolitan Areas: Economic Structure and Trends. Boston: Boston Redevelopment Authority.

BROWN, J. P. and G. PERKINS (1985) Boston Employment, City of Boston, Downtown Boston and Downtown Office, 1976-1983 and 1990 and 1995 Projected. Boston: Boston Redevelopment Authority.

DOWNS, A. (1984) "How much office space will we need in the future?" Money and Real Estate, National Real Estate Investor: 28, 32, 106.

FLYNN, R. L. (1985) Mayor's State of the City Address, Boston.

FORRESTER, J. (1969) Urban Dynamics. Boston: MIT Press.

GALBRAITH, J. K. (1984) "The heartless society: as America becomes more affluent, we increasingly ignore or rationalize the plight of the poor, the economist believes." New York Times Magazine (September 2): 20-24.

GANZ, A. (1972) Our Large Cities: New Light on Their Recent Transformation; Elements of a Development Strategy; A Prototype for Boston. Boston: MIT Laboratory for Environmental Studies, Department of Urban Studies and Planning.

————and T. O'BRIEN (1973) "The city: sandbox, reservation, or dynamo?" Public Policy XXI (Winter): 107-123.

KUTTNER, R. (1984) "Unemployment amid the jobs boom." Boston Globe (December 14): 23.

LONG, N. E. (1971) "Is the inner city doomed? (II) The city as reservation." The Public Interest 25 (Fall): 22-38.

MATRULLO, M. (1979) The Office Industry Survey, Part II: An Analysis of Office Tenant Responses. Boston: Boston Redevelopment Authority.

McCORMACK, E. J., Jr., and B. C. BOLLING (1983) Linkage Between Downtown Development and Neighborhood Housing. Report to the Mayor by Co-Chairman, Advisory Group.

McNEES, S. C. (1984) "The current expansion in historical perspective." Federal Reserve Bank of Boston, New England Economic Review (November/December): 5-11.

Newsweek (1984) "The year of the yuppie (cover story)." December 31: 14-31.

New York Times (1985a) "How many will share New York's prosperity?" January 20: 6E.

————(1985b) " '84 income rise biggest in 2 decades." January 19: 31, 34.

————(1985c) "Poll shows New Yorkers' pride is growing; as pessimism fades, pride grows among New Yorkers in poll." January 19: 1, 24.

————(1985d) "Optimism takes hold for '85." January 15: D1.

————(1985e) "Gain of 72,000 jobs for New York City in '84 sets record." January 1: 1, 30.

————(1984a) "Poorer quarter left behind by New York boom." December 16: 6E.

————(1984b) "Poverty worsening in city, study finds." December 16: 42.

————(1984c) "Rate of poverty found to persist in face of gains." August 3: A1, A5.

NOYELLE, J. and T. M. STANBACK, Jr. (1983) "The Economic Transformation of American Cities. Totowa, NJ: Rowman & Allanheld.

O'BRIEN, M. C. (1984) Diversity and Change in Boston's Neighborhoods: A Comparison of Demographic, Social, and Economic Characteristics of the Population and Housing, 1970-80. Boston: Boston Redevelopment Authority. (draft report)

The Office Network, Inc. (1983) National Office Market Report, Spring/Summer 1983. Houston, TX: Author.

PERKINS, G. and J. P. BROWN (1982) The Boston Economy, Year End 1982. Boston: Boston Redevelopment Authority (December).

SCHANBERG, S. H. (1985) "New York: the poverty divide; one of every four here lives below the line." New York Times (January 22): A25.

SCHARFERNBERG, K. (1984) "Taking stock of Flynn's first year." Boston Globe (December 29): 19.

SCHLOSS, N. (1984) "Use of employment data to estimate office space demand." U.S. Bureau of Labor Statistics, Monthly Labor Review, U.S. Department of Labor, December.

SHARE, L. B. and S. DIAMOND (1983) "San Francisco's office-housing production program: office developers finance local housing costs." American Planning Association, Land Use Law & Zoning Digest (October): 4-10.

STANBACK, T. M., Jr. and R. KNIGHT (1976) Suburbanization and the City Conservation of Human Resource Series. New York: Columbia University Press.

STERNLIEB, G. (1971) "Is the inner city doomed?" (I) the city as sandbox." The Public Interest 25 (Fall): 14-21.

———and J. W. HUGHES (1977) "New regional and metropolitan realities of America." AIP Journal (July): 227-241.

TORTO, R. G. (1982) The Office Market Across America. Boston: American Realty Services Group.

U.S. Bureau of the Census (1984a) Characteristics of the Population Below the Poverty Level: 1982, Current Population Reports, Consumer Income, Series P-60, No. 144. Washington, DC: Department of Commerce.

———(1984b) City Government Finances in 1982-1983, Series GF83-No. 4.

———(1983a) Population Profile of the United States: 1982, Current Population Reports, Special Studies, Series P-23, No. 130. Washington, DC: Department of Commerce.

———(1983b) City Employment in 1982, Series GE82-No. 2.

———(1977, 1984) City Government Finances, FY1976 and FY1983. Washington, DC; Department of Commerce.

———(1976) City Employment in 1975, Series GE75-No. 2.

U.S. Bureau of Economic Analysis (1984) Local Area Personal Income 1965-82 (for all counties and metropolitan areas), and unpublished data for selected years back to 1929. Washington, DC: Department of Commerce.

U.S. Bureau of Labor Statistics (1984a) Published and unpublished information on U.S. employment, by industry (1 Digit S.I.C.) 1970, 1976 and 1983, U.S. Department of Labor.

———(1984b) Employment Projections for 1995, Bulletin 2197, U.S. Department of Labor.

U.S. Council of Economic Advisers (1984) Economic Report of the President, February 1984, Appendix (Table on employment, by industry, by year); (Appendix table on population, by age group, by year). U.S. Superintendent of Documents.

The Urban Institute (1984) The Reagan Record. Washington, DC: Author.

Urban Investment and Development Co. (1984) Downtown Office Construction in Major U.S. Cities. Chicago: Author.

WALLACE, A. C. (1985) "Investing: a wave of euphoria hits Wall St." New York Times (January 27): F10.

Washington Post (1984) "Is Baltimore truly back? New showcase city faces old problems." November 24: A1, A8, A9.

Zoning Commission of the City of Boston (1983) Article 26. Development Impact Projects.

Part II

Case Studies

☐ CASE STUDIES are an important means of monitoring change. Those presented below encompass a diversity of perspectives. John Matzer, Jr., a city administrator, discusses the techniques of planning and management initiated by city officials in the wake of fiscal crisis. Todd Swanstrom, a former employee of Cleveland's Mayor Dennis Kucinich's regime while a doctoral student, reports on his detailed case study of that city and the conditions precipitating its default. Robert Stein, Elizabeth Sinclair, and Max Neiman, three political scientists, analyze the relation between fiscal stress and several determinants of municipal spending in a national sample of 500 cities. Finally, Dennis Judd presents the results of case studies tracing the important political changes that have occurred in some of our largest fiscally stressed municipalities.

Both Matzer and Stein et al. define "fiscal stress" for us but do so in somewhat different ways. According to the former, "strain" is measured by a concrete budgetary situation. It involves the inability of a local government to maintain existing levels of service and infrastructural provision, that is, a failure to meet fiscally the demands of metropolitan growth and restructuring. For the latter, "stress" is more a general operating condition brought on by political factors. It concerns a dilemma forcing local government leaders to make a choice between cutting support for public provision in the aggregate or pursuing revenue-generating policies with high political costs, such as the raising of taxes. The concept of stress developed by Stein et al., though not as clear an objective indicator of crisis as is Matzer's, brings to the notion of stress the larger political processes within local areas that mediate policies in cities facing massive and uncoordinated growth and change.

Matzer documents the multidimensional causes of strain and views its control as largely a function of proper financial management. The threat of crisis presented a challenge to city managers that was met efficiently and rather quickly by the introduction of sophisticated, quantitative management techniques. Some of these techniques that are discussed include financial condition analysis, financial policy frameworks, multiyear financial forecasting, fiscal impact analysis, capital programming, and creative capital financing. Matzer explains these and indicates why they have been successful in placing local governments on a more even fiscal keel. Despite the progressively increasing level of technical rationality that Matzer sees intruding into the budgetary process, he indicates that a disjuncture remains between the instrumental practice of city managers and the political needs of elected officials. At times passionless management techniques must take second place to the political expediency of running cities. Although Matzer merely indicates rather than explores this theme, it is apparently an important area of inquiry for future research on the relation between city managers and local political leaders under conditions of fiscal stress.

The relevance of local political processes to crisis restructuring is also highlighted by Stein et al. They argue that the current fashion of viewing cities as limited and as prisoners of powerful forces operating in the larger exogenous environment has been reinforced by previous studies on fiscal stress management using the factor of total municipal spending. Due to the formidable influence of incrementalism, statistical analysis of public policy determinants over time tends to obscure the effects of compositional factors when only total spending is studied. Instead, the authors argue that a compositional view of city budgets, stressing especially the place of municipal employment expenditures, breaks open the neat picture of the limited city to reveal the active influence of local political processes on adjustments to change. This result reinforces the observation of Matzer that local politics persists as a salient force in crisis management. Controlling stress can never be rationalized fully because the budget is itself a political instrument that remains sensitive to the contingencies of leaders, parties, and separate constituencies locked in political competition over scarce resources.

In rejuvenating an appreciation for the political nature of the budgetary process, however, we should not forget that cities still operate within some well-defined and often harshly invoked structural limits. Of these the most formidable are the constraints imposed on the relative autonomy of the local state by the capitalist class. No better illustration of this reality exists than the case study of Cleveland. Under Mayor Kucinich, Cleveland had a leader attuned to the social needs of a declining frostbelt city. Far from being bankrupt in fixed capital resources, and negotiating the trials of rapid manufacturing decline with some success, Cleveland nevertheless was typical of many cities in becoming weakened by the larger socioeconomic changes afflicting our older metropolitan areas over the past three decades. In this critical state it became highly dependent on the resources of finance capital rather than tax revenues for the floating of city budgets.

As Swanstorm shows, the happy marriage between capital and the public interest advocated by conservatives promoting a "proper business climate" is a myth. When conditions are right and the base of public institutions are weak, capital shows itself as a formidable predator, one that willingly will sacrifice the polity's interest for financial gain. Swanstrom, however, does not surrender to the economic determinism that these facts suggest. He also points out the limits of the "economic structuralism" perspective—Cleveland's default also depended on the actions of Mayor Kucinich in agreeing to play the political game set up by greedy banks. In short, Swanstrom advocates an approach to fiscal politics that appreciates the relation between structuralist determinants and political contingency in the generation of public policy.

Dennis Judd's examination of local politics exposes a different face for the relation between capital and the local state. 1960s militancy and 1970s reforms have brought new constituencies into power in American cities along with a host of minority mayors. Such political change reflects the all but forgotten legacy of the past decades of social activism. The new coalitions representing a broader composition of urban inhabitants also bring to the city new attitudes about development that contrast with those of the past. Judd reports on the nature of these coalitions and their prospects for enacting substantive change within beleaguered cities. In effect, not every city has been handed over to the iron fist of capital following crisis, as is the case for New York. Places like Philadelphia, Chicago, Detroit, Denver, and San Antonio presently possess minority mayors who lead strong constituencies committed to growth, fiscal soundness, *and* social welfare. In a sobering look, Judd examines whether all the new populist coalitions are equally dedicated to these goals. He finds them strung out between different styles of leadership. On the one hand, a kind of neo-colonialism is in place oriented mainly toward downtown interests and growth while mollifying the masses of minority residents. On the other hand, a neoliberalism has been born in cities such as Chicago, where genuine attempts are being made to address long neglected social issues of uneven development.

3

Local Control of
Fiscal Stress

JOHN MATZER, Jr.

☐ LOCAL GOVERNMENTS experienced considerable fiscal strain and stress during the 1970s and early 1980s. "Fiscal strain" is defined in this essay as an inability of a local government to maintain existing service levels, withstand local and regional economic disruptions, and meet the demands of growth and change (Groves, 1980: 2). Serious types of fiscal strain include financial emergencies that have been categorized as local government bankruptcies, defaults on bonds or notes, or a failure to meet other financial obligations such as meeting payrolls, paying vendors, or meeting mandated payments such as pension contributions (Advisory Commission on Intergovernmental Relations, 1985: 2). Examples of financial emergencies are the defaults of New York City; Cleveland; Parlier, California; Saco, Maine. Examples of bankruptcies are those of Bay St. Louis, Missouri; Wapanucka, Oklahoma; South Tucson, Arizona; and San Jose School District, California. New York City, Cleveland, Philadelphia, Boston, Buffalo, Chicago, Detroit, and New Orleans are a few of the cities that have experienced deficits, cash liquidity, tax collection, unfunded retirement, and other financial problems.

There are many causes of fiscal strain and emergencies. The principal cause of financial emergencies is unsound financial management consisting of poor budgeting and accounting practices, unaudited financial reports, abuse of short-term borrowing, issuance of long-term debt, or selling of assets to finance operating deficits, court judgments, and arbitration awards (Advisory Commission on Intergovernmental Relations, 1985: 5-6). Other causes of fiscal strain for local governments include reductions in intergovernmental and other revenues, escalating inflation and unemployment, deteriorating capital facilities, high interest rates, voter disapproval of bond issues, increased citizen demand for services, tax and expenditure limitations, costly labor contracts, tax reform legislation, a growing debt burden, accumulation of unfunded liabilities, declining reserves, natural disasters and emergencies, and intergovernmental mandates.

A National League of Cities survey of city officials on current economic and fiscal conditions in their cities listed the important causes of local fiscal stress as employee salary and benefit demands (95%), public demands for service (90%), pension costs (83%), mandates (77%), cost and supply of energy (75%), reduction in federal aid (75%), and interest rates (74%; Viscount, 1985: iv). The survey also listed the expansion of municipal lawsuits as a major problem affecting cities. In general the fiscal strain confronting local governments involved an interplay of political and economic forces that produced a loss of public confidence in local government financial management and placed a spotlight on the importance of sound financial condition and practices.

Local government officials responded to the financial pressures in varied ways. In some cases the emphasis was on quick fix solutions and unorthodox financial gimmickry utilizing such practices as postponing current obligations to future periods, accruing revenues from a future year to a current year, overestimating revenues, extending the length of the fiscal year, changing the basis of accounting, underfunding pensions, and abusing short-term and interfund borrowing. Other responses were severe service cutbacks, redefined service objectives and priorities, and deferred capital maintenance and improvements. Considerable attention was focused on retrenchment techniques consisting of hiring freezes, across-the-board budget cuts, target service reductions, creation of new revenue sources with a special emphasis on service charges, improved revenue collection efforts, and formation of quasi-governmental agencies for service delivery. Extensive attention has been given to alternative service delivery approaches including purchase of service contracting, franchise agreements, subsidy arrangements, vouchers, volunteer personnel, self-help, and regulatory and other tax incentives (Valente and Manchester, 1984: xvii-xix).

Fiscal stress offered an opportunity for many local government managers to employ creative and innovative financial management techniques. Financial pressures encouraged experimentation and an inventive set of financial management responses in dealing with fiscal strain and managing conflict surrounding budget cutbacks. A major benefit of the era of fiscal strain has been an increased awareness on the part of local government managers of the importance of sound financial management policies and practices. Emphasis began to be placed on the use of modern financial management techniques and on the upgrading of local government financial management systems. Techniques addressed in this chapter are financial condition analysis, financial policy frameworks, multiyear financial forecasting, fiscal impact analysis, capital programming, and creative capital financing. Other techniques being employed consist of aggressive revenue collection methods, revenue surveys, contracting, development of accounting standards, performance auditing, performance measurement, value management, and life cycle costing. These and other financial management techniques represent a positive response to local government fiscal strain.

FINANCIAL CONDITION ANALYSIS

One positive outcome of the fiscal crisis has been the development of diagnostic techniques to predict and identify early warning signals of fiscal stress. Many local government managers began to place a high priority on measuring financial condition in order to determine the fiscal health of their jurisdictions and to be sure resources were being responsibly managed. Financial trend monitoring systems with their related indicators provided a means of gathering insight into the financial condition of local governments. The systems identified the factors that affect financial condition and arranged them in an order that enabled analysis and measurement.

Extensive use began to be made of trend monitoring systems developed by the International City Management Association and Government Finance Officers Association. The International City Management Association developed five handbooks titled *Evaluating Local Government Financial Condition*. The Government Finance Officers Association issued a handbook called *Is Your City Heading for Financial Difficulty: A Guidebook for Smaller and Other Governmental Units*. These handbooks presented financial, economic, and social indicators that measure financial condition. A trend analysis of the factors over a period of years aids in revealing existing fiscal problems and in predicting emerging problems. In many cases the information uncovered problems that were unknown to local officials or showed that problems were worse than they had estimated.

Through use of the trend monitoring systems local governments were able to highlight key fiscal strengths and weaknesses. Trend monitoring assists in identifying trends, determining whether the trend indicates a problem, and assessing underlying causes and possible solutions. With such a predictive tool local officials are able to anticipate potential problems and take corrective action. Use of the systems revealed that financial problems did not develop overnight. In many instances the financial problems were slow in developing and relatively obscure.

The trend monitoring systems employ social, economic and financial indicators. Examples of social indicators include changes in population, age, income, and extent of poverty. Economic indicators consist of unemployment rates, retail sales, building permits, and commercial-residential vacancy rates. Financial management indicators include per capita and intergovernmental revenue, percentage of uncollected taxes, per capita debt, percentage of debt of assessed value, unfunded pension and leave liabilities, and declining maintenance. The ICMA Financial Trend Monitoring System focuses on 12 environmental, organizational, and financial factors that influence financial condition and employs 36 indicators that quantify changes in the factors.

In addition to the use of the trend monitoring systems, local governments began to see the benefits of assessing financial practices. Financial practices serve as the basis for developing indicators and identify the need for financial policies. Examples of poor financial practices include accounting and financial reporting practices, lack of internal financial controls, and absence of audits, purchasing controls, and a capital program. Local concern regarding financial management practices led to a renewed interest in the development of accounting standards, improved financial reporting, more effective internal control systems, improved budgeting systems, and improvements in other financial areas such as purchasing and auditing.

Interest in financial indicators is growing. More local governments are implementing all or portions of the financial trend monitoring systems. The International City Management Association (1981) tested its system in 24 cities including Allentown, Pennsylvania; Auburn, Maine; Spokane, Washington; Walden, New York; Tipton, Iowa; Columbia, Missouri; and Rock County, Wisconsin. Other users of the ICMA trend monitoring system include Fort Collins, Colorado; Newport News, Virginia; Fairfield, California; Santa Ana, California; and Milwaukee, Wisconsin. Users have found the systems to be helpful in documenting the need for additional revenues, improving bond ratings, conducting labor relations, and orienting policymakers and the public to the governmental entity's financial condition. Information obtained from a trend analysis aids in reducing the conflict that is sometimes generated when budget reductions must be made. Policymakers and citizens are made more aware of the need for such cutbacks.

Although financial condition analysis has proved to be an effective device for predicting fiscal stress, it does possess limitations. Financial condition analysis is an art, not a science. Although it identifies fiscal problems, it does not offer solutions. In some instances policymakers did not accept the findings from such an analysis or the findings were used for negative political purposes. Finally, the analysis may be limited by the unavailability of pertinent and current data. Despite the fact that financial condition analysis suffers from some imprecision and a lack of standards or benchmarks, it does provide hard data for evaluating financial condition and formulating financial policies and priorities.

FINANCIAL POLICIES

Financial condition analysis encouraged local government managers to initiate systematic financial planning and to formulate explicit, understandable, and flexible written financial policy statements. Formally adopted financial policies facilitate short- and long-range financial planning, preserve credibility and fiscal integrity, aid in responding to fiscal crises, improve financial practices, increase credit worthiness, and help monitor financial management performance. Well-defined financial policies are an integral part of a formal, long-range financial planning process that includes an analysis of financial condition and formulation and implementation of financial policies. Financial condition analysis identifies gaps, conflicts, and inconsistencies in existing financial policies. Such policies serve as guidelines for coping with and avoiding fiscal stress. Many local governments developed written financial policies as a tool for rejecting financial gimmickry, setting parameters for financial practices, establishing financial accountability, and creating fiscal stability.

Typically, written financial policy statements are prepared as guidelines for handling revenues, operating and capital budgets, reserves, debt, cash management, accounting, auditing, financial reporting, and purchasing. Revenue, operating and capital budgeting, debt, and reserve policies are critical to maintaining financial solvency. Policies relating to emergency, contingency, capital improvement, and equipment reserves provide for temporary financing of unanticipated needs. Debt policies covering the amount of short- and long-term debt, type and purpose of debt, and debt reserves can assist in avoiding a financial emergency. Policies requiring an annual audit, compliance with generally accepted accounting principles, internal controls, and sound financial reporting can be used to monitor and hold accountable financial managers. A policy requiring compliance with the Government Finance Officers Association Disclosure Guidelines for Offerings of Securities by State and Local Governments can lead to improved credit ratings, lower interest rates, and increased competition for bonds. The International City Management Association has issued a handbook that includes seven sample policy frameworks and examples of policy statements that have been adopted and are in use by six local governments (Godsey, 1980).

Long-range financial plans and policies have been adopted by Arlington County, Virginia; Lubbock, Texas; Lakewood, Colorado; Dallas, Texas; White Plains, New York; San Diego, California; Austin, Texas; Milwaukee, Wisconsin; Cleveland, Ohio; Sunnyvale, California; and Fairfax County, Virginia. These and other cities and counties have found that the anticipation of financial problems and the development of financial policies are critical to achieving financial stability (Matzer, 1980: 6). Preparation of financial policies focuses attention on the overall financial condition of the local government. Financial policies can be modified as part of an ongoing evaluation of financial condition. Local governments that have developed financial policies have found that they preserve the fiscal integrity of the governmental unit by demonstrating that thoughtful consideration and deliberation have gone into the management of financial affairs. By reaching agreement on financial policies, local policymakers can help reduce the political conflict that is often produced by fiscal stress. The continuing effectiveness of a policy framework depends upon a system that monitors financial condition, modifies policies in response to new problems and needs, and implements policies that are adopted. Trend monitoring systems and financial policy frameworks are closely interrelated because once problems are identified, policies can be designed to provide corrective action or reduce the intensity of future stress. Inherent in a financial policy formulation process is a thorough evaluation of potential financial problems and the design of plans and strategies to prevent, minimize, or control them.

MULTIYEAR FORECASTING

Another positive response to local government fiscal strain is the movement toward the use of improved multiyear revenue and expenditure forecasting techniques. The fiscal crisis reinforced the need for local government managers to project their revenues and costs into the future. Now there is a greater recognition that local fiscal systems are sensitive to the consequences of recurring economic recessions and sustained inflation (Petersen, 1979: 1). Local officials recognize the need for reliable estimates of future revenues and expenditures in order to predict the fiscal impacts of alternative responses to fiscal strain. Financial trend monitoring systems provide the historical information; multiyear forecasting provides the means of estimating future resources and needs.

Many benefits are associated with multiyear forecasts. They reduce uncertainty and aid in predicting revenue shortfalls. An analysis of policies with long-term implications is facilitated. They assist in estimating the impact of alternative economic scenarios on the budget. Forecasts are used to support the need for new revenue sources and for cutting back expenditures. By documenting the need for budget reductions, forecast information can help reduce the conflict that is associated with budget cuts. Information developed by forecasts aids in making economic development decisions and in estimating the long-range implications of labor agreements. Multiyear forecasts are essential in capital programming and budgeting and in developing contingency plans to cope with a loss of intergovernmental aid. Improvements in credit ratings and the preparation of multiyear operating budgets are also assisted by forecasts.

Multiyear forecasting has been defined as projecting what revenue and expenditures may be expected if a set of consistent and well-defined assumptions hold (Schroeder, 1982: 122). Although many local governments use best guess or simplistic forecasting methods based upon experience, averages, and conditioned judgment, they found such techniques depend solely upon time and the continued presence of the expert, and tended to ignore economic and demographic changes. In order to adjust for such factors, local governments turned their attention to the use of trend analysis and deterministic, statistical, and econometric techniques. Trend analysis depends on time and employs constant percentage or constant absolute changes. The deterministic method uses preestablished formulas involving a base and a rate such as number of employees times salary. This technique assumes a fixed relationship between input and activities and is primarily used in expenditure forecasting. Statistical forecasting techniques permit several independent variables to be used such as personal income, population, prices, and time in forecasting sales and income taxes. This method allows for consideration of the effects of simultaneous changes in several variables on revenue and expenditure estimates.

Correlation analysis, multiple regression analysis, the least squares method, and time series analysis provide a theoretical framework to forecasts. Statistical techniques are especially valuable in forecasting revenues and expenditures that are sensitive to economic conditions. More sophisticated econometric (input-output) models are also beginning to receive some attention. These complex and costly models employ a number of simultaneous equations. Mobile, Alabama, has used such a model for forecasting revenues. The model consisted of fifteen econometric equations (Chang, 1976: 17).

Although the majority of local governments continue to use the expert or best guess technique, many are beginning to experiment with the trend analysis and statistical techniques. One survey of cities with over 50,000 population and counties with over 100,000 population showed that 25% of the cities and 20% of the counties had some form of computer-based expenditure forecasting model with a fewer number having similar capabilities in revenue forecasting (Petersen, 1979: 16). A U.S. Department of Housing and Urban Development (1979: 1) study reported that nine large urban jurisdictions were regularly and systematically preparing and using multiyear revenue and expenditure forecasts. These jurisdictions included Washington, D.C.; Dallas, Texas; Portland, Oregon; San Antonio, Texas; New Orleans, Louisiana; New York, New York; San Diego, California; Montgomery County, Maryland; and Santa Clara County, California. Other jurisdictions who have fully developed multiyear revenue and expenditure models include Overland Park, Kansas; Plano, Texas; San Diego County, California; and Scottsdale, Arizona (Public Technology, Inc., 1980: 8). Vancouver, Washington; Oklahoma City, Oklahoma; Austin, Texas; Columbus, Ohio; Arlington, Texas; Garland, Texas; and Grand Praire, Texas, are also involved in multiyear forecasting.

Those who use the more sophisticated forecasting techniques have encountered problems that have probably limited more extensive local government application. Some of the problems are associated with deciding the variables to use, selecting the proper equation, data availability and quality, changes in rates and bases, and statistical distortions. The techniques are costly, require trained staff, and are time-consuming. Development of a multiyear forecast can be expected to take between 6 and 18 months. A knowledge of economics, statistics, computers and local government financial practices is necessary as is access (in many cases) to a computer. Unavailable, outdated, or inaccurate data often handicap forecasting. In many cases there is a communications problem in that the technicians have difficulty explaining the results, assumptions, and corrective action to be taken.

Despite the problems associated with multiyear forecasting, there is a definite trend among local governments toward more extensive use of three- to five-year revenue and expenditure forecasts. Such forecasts demonstrate prudent management of financial resources and contribute to more effective financial planning, budgeting, and capital programming. Multiyear forecasting and financial condition analysis complement each other. Forecasting aids in determining (1) future gaps between revenues and expenditures, (2) the impact of external factors, and (3) the formulation of financial policies and practices needed to address the problems. The Report of National Workshops held by the U.S. Department of Housing and Urban Development includes several excellent suggestions for local governments considering the development of multiyear revenue and forecasting systems (Public Technology Inc., 1980).

FISCAL IMPACT ANALYSIS

Confronted with fiscal restraints, local governments began to explore the use of fiscal impact analysis to calculate the impact of intergovernmental and private development. The basic purpose of such analysis is to estimate the long-term revenue and expenditure implications of proposed development. Fiscal impact analysis techniques assist in the prediction of costs and revenues associated with residential and non-residential growth. Such analysis is useful in budget planning, capital programming, growth management, evaluating the consequences of alternative policy choices as they affect land use, projecting the economic impact of alternative development proposals, evaluating major zoning or subdivision review plans, and annexation proposals. Local officials are becoming more aware of the interrelationship between land use and financial management.

Six fiscal impact analysis techniques have been identified including the per capita multiplier, case study, service standard method, comparable city method, proportional valuation method, and employment anticipation method (Burchell and Listokin, 1980: 5). The per capita multiplier method applies to residential development and considers an average costing approach. The case study technique projects future costs resulting from specific services required by new development and employs marginal costing strategies. Estimated personnel needs for specific services required by new development is the basis for the service standard method, which uses the average costing approach. The comparable city method estimates the impact of new development by comparing it with the impact of comparable developments on similar communities. Marginal costing strategies are used with this method. The proportional valuation method evaluates the impact of nonresidential development according to its proportion of total property valuation and uses the average costing standard. The employment anticipation technique estimates costs associated with new employees produced by nonresidential development and utilizes marginal costing strategies.

Phoenix, San Diego, Tucson, San Antonio, and Minneapolis-Saint Paul use fiscal impact analysis to evaluate areawide land use alternatives (Stern and Stuart, 1980: 15). Other cities using fiscal impact analysis are Fairfax, Virginia; Tulsa, Oklahoma; San Diego, California; Oxnard, California; Germantown, Tennessee; Carmel, New York; Raleigh, North Carolina; Holden, Massachusetts; and Fairfield, California. Several computerized models have been developed to perform the analysis. The Local Government Fiscal Impact Analysis Model has been used by San Juan Capistrano, Hemet, Anaheim, Orange, Victorville, and Huntington Beach, California. Irvine, California, has used the Fiscal Impact Systems for Communities; Fairfield, California, has employed the Cost Revenue Impact System. Fiscal impact computer models provide a computerized simulation of the real world that can be used by the local government unit to predict the economic consequences of alternative policy choices as they affect land use. The models produce a profile of the local government that ranks land use categories by associated costs and revenues, thereby indicating which land use pays its own way, costs more, or returns higher revenues than it costs. There is a determination of the percentage of revenue generated by each land use category and the percentage of costs attributed to each land use category.

Local government managers have found fiscal impact analysis to be useful in analyzing current or new revenues, operating and capital budgeting, capital programming, and maintaining and providing information on equipment and capital facility inventories. Fiscal impact analysis has not been used more extensively because of a lack of knowledge on the part of many local officials of how to select the correct technique that can be implemented and understood. Users must be able to understand the assumptions and methodology used and the findings. Too often private developers present analyses that mislead policymakers and cause them to make the wrong decision. Pitfalls to be avoided in the use of the various techniques include the following (Stern and Stuart, 1980: 16-17):

(1) making inappropriate assumptions about the ratios of residential to nonresidential land uses;
(2) overestimating or underestimating intergovernmental transfers;
(3) perpetuating the mystique of computerized models;
(4) neglecting to weigh fiscal impacts against other impacts;
(5) not knowing when to use average costing approaches;
(6) using fiscal impact analysis to support exclusionary zoning;
(7) risking the increasing skepticism of public officials by not using standardized methods;
(8) neglecting to devote enough time to the presentation of conclusions.

Local government managers who carefully consider these pitfalls and understand the mechanics of fiscal impact analysis and how it fits into the evaluation of development will benefit greatly. Fiscal impact analysis techniques offer a means of improving the quality of financial management. As local officials search for ways of stimulating development as a means of responding to fiscal strain, they will come to depend on the relevant information provided by fiscal impact analysis as a means of improving their decision making.

CAPITAL IMPROVEMENT PROGRAMMING

Cutback management practices such as deferred maintenance and replacement of capital assets are creating a demand for capital funds and renewed interest in capital programming and budgeting. Estimated costs over the next ten years for the maintenance, repair, and rebuilding of public facilities range from $3 to $4 trillion (Matzer 1984: 129). Local concern over the crumbling infrastructure has focused attention on capital planning and programming as a means to improve capital investment decisions. Capital programming and budgeting provide a systematic approach to determining capital needs, setting priorities, and selecting appropriate methods to meet and finance them. Comprehensive planning and fiscal planning are linked to physical development by capital programming.

A successful capital improvement process provides for the collection of information on the condition of public facilities, the use of evaluative criteria to assess their condition, the preparation of a multiyear program, consideration of short- and long-term costs and benefits, ranking of projects in order of priority, analysis of financing options, and monitoring of projects. Several benefits are associated with capital planning and programming. They serve as an effective public relations tool and relate public facilities to other public and private development and redevelopment policies and plans. Attention is centered on community objectives and financial capabilities. Intra- and intergovernmental projects are better coordinated. More adequate time is allowed for planning and design. Credit ratings can be enhanced and the most economic means of financing can be identified.

Considerable experimentation is occurring in the area of capital inventory and condition assessment practices. The Urban Institute's Guide to Assessing Capital Stock Condition sets forth the elements of a condition assessment system (Godwin and Peterson, 1984: 25). Dallas, Texas, and Kansas City, Missouri, have developed sophisticated inventory systems. King County, Washington; Milwaukee, Wisconsin; and Minneapolis, Minnesota, have developed systems for measuring the condition of roads, sewers, and bridges. Houston, Texas; Denver, Colorado; and Anchorage, Alaska, have implemented water system condition assessment programs. Cities are making more extensive use of engineering measures, service level indicators, and maintenance cost data. All of these efforts help determine the most appropriate method of addressing infrastructure problems and help provide a factual basis for making capital investment decisions.

Progress is also being made in the refinement of systems for the prioritization of projects. Traditional rating techniques such as priority categories, value weighting systems, and rating systems based on a list of questions are being replaced by more sophisticated systems that use numerical points to rank projects against such established criteria as fiscal impacts, health and safety effects, community economic effects, environmental effects, aesthetic and social effects, amount of disruption and inconvenience caused by the project, distributional effects, feasibility, implications of deferring the project, amount of uncertainty and risk, effects on interjurisdictional relationships, and advantages accruing from relationships to other projects (Hatry et al., 1984: 9). Minneapolis rates projects on a scale of zero to fifty points on fourteen factors. Dayton, Ohio; Dade County, Florida; Denver, Colorado; Montgomery County, Maryland; Norfolk, Virginia; St. Paul, Minnesota; Winston-Salem, North Carolina; and King County, Washington, use similar weighting systems. Dayton, Minneapolis, New York City, Portland (Oregon), Saint Paul, and Tulsa provide for extensive citizen participation in their priority setting. Other local governments have experimented with creative group techniques such as the nominal group technique and the use of decision matrixes. None of the priority-setting techniques fails to recognize the fact that priorities are often set by political compromises by local governments. There is some application of private sector capital investment techniques such as payback method, discounted cash flow, and internal rate of return (Chapman, 1983: 55).

The art of capital programming will continue to improve as condition assessment, priority setting, replacement analysis, and capital investment techniques are developed and improved. An Urban Institute report identifies three basic strategies and 30 ideas a local government can employ to reduce its capital investment and facility maintenance problems (Hatry and Peterson, 1984: 2-12). Several local governments are using systematic approaches to capital maintenance planning and budgeting. Dallas; Dayton; King County, Washington; Milwaukee; Minneapolis; Montgomery County, Maryland; New York City; Savannah, Georgia; and Seattle are employing new technologies, materials, procedures, and equipment to optimize their maintenance strategies. An analysis of the local government maintenance practices found eight basic facility maintenance strategies that can be used by local governments (Hatry and Steinthal, 1984: 6). One study has proposed a comprehensive strategy for responding to the infrastructure crisis. This strategy recommends the following (Vaughan, 1983: 5-8):

(1) redesigning engineering replacement standards and improving maintenance procedures;
(2) reducing subsidies to private investment;
(3) improving capital planning, budgeting, and management;
(4) project-specific cost-sharing arrangements with private firms;
(5) charging for public services;
(6) improving bond financing mechanisms;
(7) state assistance to local governments;
(8) increasing public capital investment.

All of these proposals represent a significant improvement in the way local governments are coping with their infrastructure needs.

CREATIVE CAPITAL FINANCING

Deterioration in credit quality, lower bond ratings, high interest rates, unstable market conditions, and tax reform are creating a challenge to local officials to identify alternative and creative capital financing mechanisms and to improve the marketability of their securities (Matzer, 1983: 2). Local governments have responded with a diverse assortment of financing devices and methods for improving the marketability of their securities. One source has identified over 25 alternative methods for financing capital improvements (Goldman and Mokuvos, 1984: 30-36). Innovative financing instruments receiving increasing attention include commercial paper, demand notes, variable rate bonds, bonds with warrants, put option bonds, compound coupon bonds, zero coupon bonds, stepped coupon bonds, and stripped coupon bonds. Extensive use is also being made of a variety of leasing options including operating, capital, and financing leases, sale-leasebacks, and certificates of participation. All of these creative financing techniques have been developed in response to uncertain market conditions and reluctant investors.

Local governments are also increasing their use of special assessment, tax allocation, and industrial development bonds, development fees, and privatization. Because of the large variety of financing alternatives, local governments experience a problem in selecting the most appropriate option. One organized method for evaluating funding possibilities employs a set of criteria that measures each option in terms of applicability, key procedures, adequacy of funding, equity, economic effects, ease of public administration, and legal constraints and opportunities (Association of Bay Area Governments, 1983: 51-69). Generally local governments utilize various combinations of the foregoing techniques.

In addition to experimenting with creative financing techniques, local governments are applying new methods of increasing the marketability of their securities. Among these methods are bond insurance, bond banks, improved disclosure in official statements, small denomination bonds, intensive efforts to raise bond ratings, more extensive use of expert advisors, and use of letters of credit, lines of credit, and third-party guarantees. None of the new innovative financing techniques is meant to be a panacea to local government capital financing problems. Although they are important tools, they are complicated and involve risks, legal issues, and public acceptability. Local government managers can minimize the risks and maximize the potential benefits of the new financing techniques by employing them as part of a comprehensive capital financing strategy that consists of a system for assessing the government's fiscal condition, a framework of written performance goals, a multiyear capital improvements program, a system for ensuring the adoption and maintenance of sound financial management practices, and a system for carefully evaluating the potential impact of the full range of conventional and innovative capital financing alternatives.

CONCLUSION

Local governments experienced a number of forms of fiscal strain and financial emergencies during the 1970s and early 1980s. Although there are many causes of fiscal stress, a principal cause is unsound financial management. Responses to fiscal strain included financial gimmickry, conventional retrenchment techniques, and creative financial management techniques. Fiscal stress presented opportunities for the development and application of improved and innovative financial management techniques.

Many local government managers viewed fiscal stress as an opportunity to upgrade local government financial management systems. They became proactive in initiating improved and new financial management techniques. Furthermore they made a long-range professional commitment to design better early warning systems for predicting fiscal stress and better methods for preventing and handling it.

One important benefit of fiscal stress has been an increased level of professionalization in local government financial management. Chief executives and policymakers have become more cognizant of the critical role of financial management. Financial managers have become more skilled in the development and application of quantitative financial techniques and are assuming more prominent positions as policy advisors. Financial management professional development programs offered by the Government Finance Officers Association, other professional associations, and universities have expanded in response to increased demand. The quality of the literature on local government financial management has shown a marked improvement. Although considerable progress is being made in the application of quantitative financial management techniques, their full benefits are not always being achieved. In some instances political considerations tend to limit the implementation of a more rational approach to local government financial management.

Financial condition analysis, financial policies, multiyear forecasting, fiscal impact analysis, capital programming, and creative capital financing are some of the techniques used to cope with fiscal stress. These and other financial management improvements such as performance auditing, uniform accounting standards, strategic planning, contracting, cost analysis and pricing, more diversified revenue systems, formalized and comprehensive revenue collection systems, and creative purchasing techniques contributed to converting the negative aspects of fiscal stress to positive benefits. By adopting these techniques, local governments found that they could effectively address financial priorities and policies and better manage the conflict surrounding budget cutbacks required by fiscal stress. Local governments will continue to experience periods of fiscal stress; however, experience has shown that they have the professional capability to respond with sound and innovative financial management strategies and techniques.

REFERENCES

Advisory Commission on Intergovernmental Relations (1985) Bankruptcies, Defaults, and Other Local Government Financial Emergencies. Washington, DC: Author.

Association of Bay Area Governments (1983) Renewing Our Infrastructure: Workable Ways to Build and Maintain Public Facilities. Berkeley, CA: Author.

BURCHELL, R. and D. LISTOKIN (1980) The Fiscal Impact Guidebook: A Practitioner's Guide. Washington, DC: U.S. Department of Housing and Urban Development.

CHANG, S. (1976) "Forecasting revenues to municipal government: the case of Mobile, Alabama." Governmental Finance (February): 16-20.

CHAPMAN, R. (1983) "Capital financing: time for a new look at an old idea." American City and County (June): 55-57.

GODSEY, W. M. (1980) Financial Performance Goals: A Guide for Setting Long Range Policies. Washington, DC: International City Management Association.

GODWIN, S. and G. PETERSON (1984) Guide to Assessing Capital Stock Condition. Washington, DC: Urban Institute Press.

GOLDMAN, H. and S. MOKUVOS (1984) "Local government financing: the shirttails or the alternatives." American City and County (March): 30-36.

GROVES, S. (1980) Evaluating Financial Condition. Washington, DC: International City Management Association.

HATRY, H. and G. PETERSON (1984) Guides to Managing Urban Capital: A Summary. Washington, DC: Urban Institute Press.

HATRY, H. and B. STEINTHAL (1984) Guide to Selecting Maintenance Strategies for Capital Facilities. Washington, DC: Urban Institute Press.

HATRY, H., A. MILLAR, and J. EVANS (1984) Guide to Setting Priorities for Capital Investment. Washington, DC: Urban Institute Press.

International City Management Association. (1981) Final Report: An Evaluation of the Financial Trend Monitoring System. Washington, DC: Author.

MATZER, J., Jr. (ed.) (1984) "Capital planning and programming techniques." Practical Financial Management. Washington, DC: International City Management Association.

———(1983) Capital Financing Strategies for Local Governments. Washington, DC: International City Management Association.

———(1980) "Financial policies payoff." Public Management (April): 6-7.

PETERSEN, J. (1979) State and Local Fiscal Forecasting. Washington, DC: Government Finance Officers Association.

Public Technology, Inc. (1980) Multi-Year Revenue and Expenditure Forecasting Report of National Workshops. Washington, DC: U.S. Department of Housing and Urban Development.

SCHROEDER, L. (1982) "Local government multi-year budgeting forecasting: some administrative and political issues." Public Administration Review (March/April): 121-126.

STERN, R. and D. STUART (1980) "Beware the pitfalls in fiscal impact analysis." Planning (April): 15-17.

U.S. Department of Housing and Urban Development (1979) Multi-Year Revenue and Expenditure Forecasting—The-State-of-the-Practice in Large Urban Jurisdictions. Washington, DC: Author.

VALENTE, C. and L. MANCHESTER (1984) Rethinking Local Services: Examining Alternative Delivery Approaches. Washington, DC: International City Management Association.

VAUGHAN, R. (1983) Rebuilding America: Financing Public Works in the 1980's. Washington, DC: The Council of State Planning Agencies.

VISCOUNT, F. (1985) City Fiscal Conditions and Outlook for Fiscal 1985. Washington, DC: National League of Cities.

4

Urban Populism, Fiscal Crisis, and the New Political Economy

TODD SWANSTROM

☐ THE SHIFT AWAY from the purely political explanations of urban politics characteristic of the pluralists and elitists has been a healthy development. In the past ten or fifteen years, however, the pendulum may have swung too far in the opposite direction, as the shift from internal political factors to external economic factors has created its own conventional wisdom, an abstract economic determinism, that requires critical examination.

The basic logic of this new conventional wisdom is simple and elegant: Local politicians require a prosperous economy in order to provide adequate tax revenues for basic services and to retain voter support; the economy will not prosper unless mobile wealth (both capital and residents) is attracted into the city; mobile wealth will not be attracted into the city unless local policies cater to its needs and interests. QED: Local policymaking is tightly constrained by the functional need to serve mobile wealth.

My animus here is not a full-fledged theory but rather a tendency within existing theories to emphasize the impact of economic factors, in a particular way, on urban outcomes. The substance of the argument is economic; the form is structural functional. Policies are not viewed as the result of the intentions of political actors but as the product of the function of the political system in the economy. It does not matter who is in power; in the long run, policy must conform to the needs of the economy. Following Gold et al. (1975: 39), I shall refer to the argument as "economic structuralism." Although it has the logic of a structuralist argument, it should be kept strictly separate from structuralist political theory associated with the French structuralists such as Poulantzas.

One of the intriguing aspects of economic structuralism is that it is endorsed by writers of both the left and the right. Probably the purest expression of the left-wing version of economic structuralism is Fred Block's (1977) "The Ruling Class Does Not Rule," but there are numerous other scholars, working generally from a left or Marxian tradition, who have developed variations on the same theme. (See Molotch, 1976; Goodman, 1979; Bluestone and Harrison, 1982; Friedland, 1983; Kennedy, 1984. None of these writers is guilty of economic determinism as such, but all present, at times, economic structuralist arguments.) What is, above all, characteristic of economic structuralism is that it does not rely upon conscious political organization or manipulation by an elite. In the words of Block (1977: 19), the constraining effects of the business climate originate from purely economic decisions: "Conspiracies to destabilize the [left of center] regime are basically superfluous, since decisions made by individual capitalists according to their own narrow economic rationality are sufficient to paralyze the regime." Whereas Block pitched his argument at the level of the nation-state, many have observed that, logically, the effect will be greater at the local level than at the state or national level because of the greater ease with which capital can cross highly permeable local political boundaries (Piven and Cloward, 1982: 90-91).

The right-wing version of economic structuralism has its roots in neoclassical economic theory, specifically as it has been applied to government in welfare economics. Local governments are viewed as analogous to firms in a competitive market, an approach first developed by Charles Tiebout (1956). Like analysts on the left, analysts on the right emphasize the objective need for cities to adapt their policies to the imperatives of a mobile capitalist economy (see Breckenfeld, 1977; Simon, 1978: ch. V; President's Commission for a National Agenda for the Eighties, 1980; President's National Urban Policy Report, 1982; Hicks, 1982). The difference between the left and right is that whereas the former finds the economic pressures on cities to be understandable but regrettable, the latter finds them both understandable and laudable. Right and left tendencies are synthesized in Paul Peterson's (1981) *City Limits*. Acknowledging a seminal debt to welfare economics and structural Marxism, Peterson argues that rational local policies must conform to economic constraints, yet in the end he calls for redistributive policies at the national level.

I propose here to engage in what Michael Smith (1984: 14) has called "a dialogue between structural logic and historical process." Specifically, I propose to examine the validity of economic structuralism through a detailed study of one city, Cleveland, focusing on that city's fiscal crisis and default that led to the defeat of populist mayor Dennis Kucinich. Although a single case cannot disprove a broad argument like economic structuralism, it can suggest, I believe, ways of combining economic and political factors that acknowledge the insights of economic structuralism without falling into economic determinism.

CLEVELAND: THE POLITICS OF FISCAL CRISIS

When we think of defaults, we think of accountants leaning over calculators adding up long columns of numbers. If the numbers don't add up, if the money isn't there, the city goes into default. In fact, defaults are rarely determined by economic pressures alone; there is almost always room for political discretion. In one of the few historical studies of urban fiscal crisis in the United States, Eric Monkkonen (1984: 150) concludes, based on an analysis of 941 municipal defaults between 1850 and 1930, that, with the exception of the Great Depression, "external economic forces alone did not force default on the cities. Instead . . . most important, the dimensions of local political struggle determine[d] who defaulted and when" (Monkkonen, 1984: 133-134). Essentially, cities chose not to pay back certain debts for political reasons, whether as part of an effort by the mercantile elite to disenfranchise propertyless voters (Memphis) or as the result of a victory of local taxpayers over growth-oriented entrepreneurs (Duluth).

Cleveland's default, only the second by a major city since the Great Depression,[1] confirms Monkkonen's findings on the politicalness of municipal defaults. In this case, however, it was the lenders who precipitated default, not the borrowers. Dennis Kucinich, populist mayor of Cleveland from 1977 to 1979, charges that bankers attempted to blackmail the city into selling a valuable asset for the benefit of private interests. Kucinich, who became embroiled in political conflicts with the city's business establishment, describes a meeting with Brock Weir (chairman and chief executive officer of Cleveland Trust) the day of default this way:

At that meeting, Mr. Weir told me that only if I agreed to sell the Municipal Light System to CEI (Cleveland Electric Illuminating Company, the area's private utility) would he agree to roll the notes. He also offered to raise $50 million in city bonds, but only if the Light System was sold [United States Congress, 1979: 265, Kucinich letter].

According to Kucinich, the banks were involved in a monumental conflict of interest, because they, and financial interests close to them, stood to benefit from the sale of Muny Light. In addition, by forcing Kucinich either to sell Muny Light or default, the bankers were guaranteeing political damage to a mayor they had an avowed interest in defeating.

The most thorough study of Cleveland's default, a staff study for a subcommittee of the Committee on Banking, Finance and Urban Affairs of the United States House of Representatives, came, tentatively, to the conclusion that Cleveland's default was politically motivated:

> The interlocking relationship of Cleveland Trust Company and some of the other banks with much of the corporate community, and the deep animosities and political crosscurrents in which some bank officers became involved, suggest the strong possibility that factors, other than pure hardnosed credit judgments, entered the picture. At a minimum, it is impossible to conclude that key bankers donned green eyeshades, locked themselves in their board rooms, and made dispassionate decisions based solely on computer runs [United States Congress, 1979: 240].

In the next two sections I will present evidence to demonstrate that Cleveland's default was, indeed, political. This contradicts Block's argument that narrowly economic decision making is sufficient to paralyze left-of-center regimes.

MUNY LIGHT AND DEFAULT

In order to comprehend default, it is necessary to understand how Muny Light, a small, dilapidated public utility, became the center of a raging political controversy that precipitated default. Born in conflict during the administration of populist mayor Tom Johnson (1901-1909), Muny Light successfully overcame CEI's strenuous opposition and established itself as a viable competitor, offering consumers in many parts of the city a choice between competing utilities (Johnson, 1911:

192-194). Until the 1960s, Muny prospered, growing to over 58,000 customers and reporting consistent operating profits. In the 1960s, however, Muny began to experience operating problems, such as outages, which CEI took advantage of with an aggressive marketing campaign to attract Muny's customers. From 1906 through 1968, Muny reported profits of $31.5 million as well as significant subsidies to the City's General Fund; from 1969 through 1977, it lost $31.1 million. The General Fund was forced to subsidize Muny.

In 1971, Ralph Perk ran for mayor vowing to save Muny Light. Unable to sell bonds for the ailing plant, however, Perk later reversed his position and in September 1976 announced that an agreement had been reached to sell Muny to CEI. In May 1977, the Council passed an ordinance (18-15) to sell Muny Light.

Meanwhile, Kucinich, who had been elected citywide clerk of courts in 1975, became a vocal opponent of the sale. With challenges in court and before the Federal Power Commission (FPC), Kucinich attempted to block the sale. The SAVE MUNY LIGHT COMMITTEE, which he chaired, gathered 29,758 signatures to put the sale before the voters in a referendum. The Election Board, however, ruled the petitions invalid due to improper language. Kucinich appealed that decision in the courts and challenged the Zoning Board approval of the sale. With a legal cloud hanging over the proceedings, Kucinich was just able to prevent completion of the sale until he became mayor in November 1977. As mayor, Kucinich had the power to block the sale.

One question hangs over the entire Muny Light controversy: Was Muny a drain on the city or was it a public asset? This is not an easy question to answer. Basically, it hinges on whether Muny's huge losses from 1969 to 1977 were due to mismanagement or were caused by predatory efforts of CEI to eliminate its competitor. If the latter is the case, the losses are turned into an asset because, under the nation's antitrust laws, the city can recover triple damages—which in fact it is trying to do in a $150 million lawsuit against CEI, filed in 1975. (The first trial ended in a hung jury; the second ruled in favor of CEI. Currently, the city is appealing the case on the grounds that the judge failed to grant sufficient time for discovery and excluded crucial testimony. The Sixth Circuit Court of Appeals ruled against the city in 1984. The case may go all the way to the Supreme Court.)

Findings issued by the Atomic Safety and Licensing Board of the Nuclear Regulatory Commission (NRC) in 1977 tend to support the city's case. The most serious finding concerned CEI's refusal to allow Muny, which is surrounded by CEI, to purchase outside electricity. Since Muny began purchasing cheaper outside power through its new interconnection, required by the NRC as a condition for CEI's license to operate nuclear power plants, Muny's steep plunge into the red has been halted and the utility has been basically operating in the black. The NRC (1977: 177) also called CEI's conditions for Muny's access to the power generated at the nuclear power plants, which included setting Muny's rates, an "outrageous affront" to the nation's antitrust laws. The NRC concluded that CEI had violated the Sherman Antitrust Act, attempting to eliminate its public competitor through unfair and anticompetitive acts.

Cleveland's financial crisis, which culminated in default, was inextricably bound up with the struggle between CEI and Muny Light. Nine days after Kucinich took office in November 1977, CEI filed a certificate of judgment of lien on lands and property of the city to recover disputed debts owed CEI by Muny. Faced with a General Fund deficit of $10 million, the Kucinich administration lacked the money to pay the debt. When Cleveland Trust refused to roll over $7.8 million in short-term notes in May 1978, the city was forced to purchase its own notes using funds slated for other purposes. Soon after, Standard and Poor's suspended Cleveland's bond rating and Moody's Investor Service downgraded the city's bond rating for the second time. Cleveland was gradually shut out of the national bond market.

More bad news came in August when the national accounting firm of Ernst and Ernst reported that $52 million in bond money for capital projects had been misspent for operating expenses (most during the previous Perk administration). For the first time, the Kucinich administration became aware of the perilous financial condition of the city.

In September, $3.34 million in short-term notes came due and the banks, again, refused to refinance. Kucinich was forced to dip into the city's meager cash reserves. Having narrowly survived a recall election one month earlier, Kucinich this time took the offensive against the banks with a blistering political attack containing the kind of anticapitalist rhetoric generally outside the pale of American politics. Kucinich challenged the banks to come to the aid of Cleveland "even if they can't make the same extraordinary profits as they do elsewhere." He concluded with a political threat:

Unless the banks begin to respond to the needs of Cleveland residents, a tremendous uprising of anger and bitterness will be directed against them.

We must bring democracy to the banks as we have to our political life.

This administration will be in the forefront of a movement to severely hamper normal business operations of area banks if they do not begin to respond to the needs of the city government and city residents. The banks leave us no choice but to fight back to save our city [United States Congress, 1980: 317-20; Kucinich press release].

Ignoring Kucinich's attack, the banks again, in October 1978, refused to roll over short-term notes. The notes were refinanced internally with the few remaining city funds. Meanwhile, a time bomb was ticking in the budget: $14 million of short-term notes, held by six local banks, would come due on December 15, 1978. And the city still owed CEI $5.7 million. A federal district court ruled that, unless the CEI debt was paid by the end of the year, Cleveland's $150 million antitrust suit would be thrown out.

In December, everything came to a head. United States Marshals began tagging city property for CEI's debts. By December 13, about 50 of Muny's repair trucks were impounded. Kucinich was able to squeeze money from operating expenses to pay CEI and keep the antitrust suit alive, but this meant there were no funds to purchase the $14 million in short-term notes due December 15. With the City Council supporting a plan to sell Muny Light and Kucinich rejecting that and offering his own plan, the city was unable to agree on what to do to avoid default. When, at midnight on December 15, before packed chambers, the council rejected the mayor's plan on a procedural vote (17-16), Cleveland officially went into default.

If default was the dramatic climax, the period that followed was the denouement. One week after default, the Council worked out a compromise, passing ordinances that placed before the voters in February both a 50% increase in the income tax and the sale of Muny Light. Kucinich led an effective grass-roots campaign that, according to polls, turned around public opinion on Muny Light (Rice, 1979). The electorate voted to retain Muny Light and increase the municipal income tax—both by almost 2-1 margins. Kucinich began paying off the defaulted notes with the income tax receipts late the next summer, but Cleveland remained technically in default throughout his administration.

THE POLITICALNESS OF DEFAULT

To say that default was political is to say that factors other than immediate economic interests entered into the decisions leading to default. The *Congressional Study* (U.S. Congress, 1979) suggested two factors, "other than pure hardnosed credit judgments," that could have entered into the bankers' decision not to roll over the notes: forcing the sale of Cleveland's public utility to CEI and politically crippling the Kucinich administration. By demanding that Muny Light be sold as a condition for rollover, Kucinich was placed on the horns of a dilemma— with either horn (selling Muny or default) exacting severe political damage.

Definitive proof of the bankers' intentions would require getting into their heads. Sufficient circumstantial evidence exists, however, including statements by the participants and evidence of their material interests, to prove "beyond a reasonable doubt" that the banks had other motives in mind when they refused to roll over the notes beyond simply the ability of the city to repay a loan.

With regard to the sale of Muny Light, there is, first of all, no doubt that CEI had long desired to eliminate its competitor. In fact, that was the first thing admitted by CEI in the antitrust suit (though CEI denied using any illegal methods). Second, strong ties existed between CEI and the banks involved in default, especially Cleveland Trust. (Space permits citing only a small portion of this evidence.) Altogether, five of the six banks (one provided no information) held almost 1,800,000 shares (about 5%) of CEI's total outstanding stock. Also, extensive interlocks existed between the banks and the private utility. Of the eleven directors of CEI during 1978, eight were also directors at four of the six banks. Four directors of Cleveland Trust were also directors of CEI. Cleveland Trust managed CEI's pension fund, served as bond trustee and counsel, and was registrar for CEI's stock. Of the Cleveland banks, four had $72 million in lines of credit available for the utility. Indirect links drew the net of common interests tighter. The six banks had 79 director interlocks with 20 other corporations that also shared one or more directors or officers with CEI. Top officials of CEI also had extensive social ties to bank executives through such associations as the elite Union Club and Growth Association, Cleveland's Chamber of Commerce.

In short, evidence exists of a massive conflict of interest between the banks' loan-making functions and their considerable ties to the private utility, especially their trust holdings. Ever since court rulings, beginning in 1961 (see Cady, Roberts; cited in Herman, 1975: 151), it has been contrary to public policy for trust and commercial departments within a single bank to trade material inside information. As a result, banks have constructed what have come to be known as "Chinese Walls" between their trust departments—which are supposed to act solely in the interest of the institutions or persons whose money they manage—and their commercial loan departments, the purpose of which is to make loans purely on the basis of creditworthiness, so as to protect the interests of bank shareholders.[2]

In this case, at least, there is evidence that the wall broke down—that is, the banks' refusal to roll over the city's notes was influenced by the benefits that would accrue to trust department holdings, as well as to the economic and political interests of bank officers. In the case of Cleveland Trust, suspicions are further aroused when one learns that in October 1979, shortly after Kucinich's verbal attacks on the banks, decisions regarding city debt at Cleveland Trust were removed from the commercial bank level to an executive committee at the holding company level. In other words, the decision not to roll over the notes was made not on one side of the wall but by high-level executive officers sitting atop the "Chinese Wall."

A second alleged ulterior motive of the banks in default, besides forcing the sale of Muny Light, was a desire to damage Kucinich politically, and prevent him from being reelected. Considerable evidence exists of banker hostility toward Kucinich. At least 70 officers and directors of the six banks involved contributed to the campaign to recall Kucinich, including Brock Weir and 17 of 32 directors of Cleveland Trust. (Very few, if any, lived within the city of Cleveland.) A month before default, Claude Blair, chairman of National City Bank, which Kucinich had attacked for obtaining a tax abatement, was quoted on television news as saying, according to confidential sources, that he would not refinance the notes held by his bank because of the "Kucinich administration's antagonism toward the business community" and that he was "willing to accept the consequence to Cleveland as the price to pay to see Mayor Kucinich defeated in next year's election."[3]

Weir, however, was the most visible leader in the banks' conflict with Kucinich. After default, Weir made a number of statements that indicated his intentions toward the Kucinich administration. Perhaps most telling is the following statement made less than a month after default:

We had been kicked in the teeth for six months. On December 15 we decided to kick back [quoted in Weirnek and Geidel, 1979].

In addition, a January 1979 *Boston Globe* article, based on an exclusive interview with Weir, contained the following paragraph:

Although public finances are a mess and virtually all the upper middle class has deserted the city for the suburbs, the business climate remains healthy. Weir said, "The only problem is the little canker downtown" [quoted in U.S. Congress, 1979: 231].

Not only is there evidence concerning the bankers' motives, there is also evidence that they acted on those motives. Conditioning rollover of the notes on the sale of Muny Light stood to benefit the financial interests attached to CEI as well as put the bankers' adversary, Kucinich, on the horns of a political dilemma: either sell Muny Light or default.

Overwhelming evidence exists that this quid pro quo was, in fact, communicated to the city. The crucial meeting between Kucinich, Weir, Maurice Saltzman (president of Bobbie Brooks), and George Forbes (City Council president) on December 15 is where Weir, according to Kucinich, made the corrupt offer. This meeting, however, is bathed in controversy; only a tape recording could settle the issue. Unfortunately, no tape exists. Two participants at the meeting originally backed up Kucinich's version of the story. A few days after default, Saltzman was quoted as saying:

> Brock (Weir) was nice. He said, "Look, Dennis, get this (Muny Light) out of the way. Sell the building, we'll roll over the notes and I personally will help with the $50 million in bonds" [quoted in Hopwood, 1978].

It is unnecessary to prove, however, that the bankers communicated the quid pro quo to Kucinich in person, for it was communicated clearly enough through the media; at the time, all the principal actors assumed that the sale of Muny Light was the sticking point in default. (Space permits citing only a small portion of the evidence, which is summarized in the U.S. Congress, 1979: 219-35.) Certainly everyone in Cleveland who read the newspapers or watched television knew that it was Kucinich's refusal to sell Muny Light that was the cause of the banks' unwillingness to roll over the notes. The *Cleveland Plain Dealer*, for example, linked the sale of Muny Light to rollover of the loans in front page headlines the day before default (see Illustration 4.1).

Significantly, Brock Weir took no action to deny the widespread stories linking the sale of Muny to rollover until eleven days after default.[4] On December 26 in a letter to Cleveland Trust employees, later reprinted as a newspaper advertisement, Weir denied that Cleveland

Dressing the part can run into money

In Living, Page 1-D

Cleveland's rock 'n' roll discovery

In Friday magazine

THE PLAIN DEALER

OHIO'S LARGEST NEWSPAPER

CLEVELAND, FRIDAY, DECEMBER 15, 1978

15¢

Cleveland Trust: Pay up

Bank would relent if Muny Light were sold, Forbes believes

By Joseph L. Wagner and Frederick E. Freeman

Cleveland's hopes for avoiding default were dealt a serious blow last night as Cleveland Trust Co., the city's largest bank, insisted on prompt payment today of $5 million in loans.

The five banks holding the remaining $9 million in notes due at the close of business today will be closely watching City Council — which is meeting this morning — but are apparently leaning toward going along with the city's refinancing plan.

If council and the mayor cannot

agree on a package, the other banks would be likely to refuse to refinance the notes.

Council President George L. Forbes, D-20, why met with bank executives yesterday, said he believes Cleveland Trust "could change its mind if Muny Light were sold." Mayor Dennis J. Kucinich has said repeatedly he will never sell Muny Light.

Saying "I want to save the city from default," Forbes called an emergency council meeting for 9 a.m. today at which time council leaders would push for passage of:

• Enabling legislation for the

50% income tax hike and a $90 million bond issue with specific language that these issues would become effective only after Kucinich sells Muny Light.

• A resolution asking the Ohio Legislature and Gov. James A. Rhodes to establish a multimember board of fiscal control to supervise city financial administration. Kucinich has opposed a board, but has agreed to establishment by .he state of a single fiscal aspect.

Last night, Forbes ruled out any referendum on Muny Light.

In a letter to Finance Director Joseph G. Tegreene, William J.

Clutterbuck, Cleveland Trust vice president for public investment, said the city's bailout plan was deficient. He appeared to leave the door open for new proposals that might affect the loans.

"While we commend the administration's recognition of the need for additional revenue, we still feel that the plan is too reliant on speculative contingencies which are beyond control of the administration.

"If, prior to maturity, you have any other proposal that will deal with alternatives that have more

materially, we will be happy to review them.

Forbes said this was a reference to Muny Light.

"I spoke to the chairman of Cleveland Trust and he indicated he could go with the sale of the Muny Light Plant," Forbes said.

The chairman is M. Brock Weir.

Clutterbuck's message on the notes was officially terse:

"This will advise you of our intention to present our notes for payment at the office of the city treasurer of Cleveland on Decem-

Continued on Page 10-A

• Ohio legislators discuss a bill that would permit Cleveland to hike the municipal income tax.

Page 8-A

• City consultant reports that the Municipal Light Plant will make a profit of nearly $1 million in 1978.

Page 10-A

• Andrew M. Juniewicz, the mayor's news secretary, says local news reporters have sometimes been irresponsible or inaccurate.

Page 11-A

Newmen waited in vain through the day for reports on the city's financial situation.

The Plain Dealer/James A. Hatch

It's Snubsville as suburbs shun save-city session

By W.C. Miller

Dozens of reporters and businessmen flocked to University Heights yesterday, expecting to see an equal number of suburban mayors discussing Cleveland's money problems.

The television cameras whirred at Temple Emanu El. The businessmen listened. But most of the mayors weren't there.

The meeting was scheduled for University Heights City Hall, but was moved to accommodate an expected large turnout.

But only nine of Cuyahoga County's 61 suburban mayors and city managers showed up to hear an ambitious cleaned-up plan presented by University Heights

mirror and solve its own problems.

Even Avery admitted the legality of his plan is questionable.

He asked the suburban Council of Governments to review and develop his proposal and to offer Cleveland's political leaders advice. He also asked Cleveland's business and industrial community to help the suburban council review city finances.

"The time is here for the suburbs and industry to stop sitting as complacent observers while the mother city dies," Avery said. "The time is here to stop playing the deadly game of city vs. suburb."

Avery asked Cleveland's banks to extend, for 120 days, the $14

SOURCE: *Cleveland Plain Dealer.* Reprinted with permission.

Illustration 4.1: Front Page Headlines on Muny Light Sale and Default

Trust had any interest in who owned Muny Light (reprinted in U.S. Congress, 1979: 304-307). What is inexplicable is why Weir did not make his position clear, at considerably less trouble and expense, at the time that it mattered. It would have been a simple matter to call the newspapers and clear up this monumental misunderstanding. The bankers' inaction implicitly confirmed reports that the sale of Muny Light was a condition for rollover. Together with Cleveland Trust's refusal to go along with Kucinich's plan for avoiding default and the approval, in executive committee, of a rival plan that included the sale of Muny, the only reasonable conclusion is that the banks, and especially

Cleveland Trust, wanted the city to know: either sell Muny Light or we will not roll over the notes.

Another way to determine if any political motivations were involved is to examine whether the Kucinich administration was treated differently from other similar administrations or borrowers. First, it is important to note, rollovers are routine in the financial community. Rollover of short-term notes, as in Cleveland's case, is not a decision to lend money but rather a decision to extend in time a line of credit already granted.[5] Rollovers are often granted to private corporations with declining fortunes; in fact, they are a prime tool used to restore them to financial health (U.S. Congress, 1979: 235-236).

Questions are also raised concerning Cleveland's default when it is compared to the other major municipal default in the postwar era: New York. In an article comparing the defaults in Cleveland and New York, John Beck (1982: 214) presents evidence that New York's fiscal crisis was due to abnormally high expenditures on "marginal" social welfare functions. "Although New York may be described as a high-tax/high-expenditure city, Cleveland did not exhibit extreme behavior in this regard." Cleveland was not overtaxed and still had considerable assets; a 1981 Ernst & Whinney audit appraised the city's net worth, including all of its land and buildings, at slightly more than $1 billion (Hopwood, 1981). With the full faith and credit of the city behind the notes, the banks were in little danger of losing their investment. Nevertheless, the banks refused to refinance a relatively small $14 million debt.

By contrast, the New York Legislature, with the implicit approval of the bankers, declared a moratorium on the repayment of $2.4 billion of outstanding notes in 1975. Technically the same as default, New York City avoided the stigma, even though it was more overextended and the banks had much more to lose than in Cleveland's case. In 1975, New York's cumulative deficit was about $8 billion (Auletta, 1975: 96); soon after Kucinich left office, Cleveland's was estimated at $111 million. The difference in treatment raises the question of whether it was related to the fact that Cleveland was governed by an angry populist mayor whereas New York was led by politicians who promoted a new growth partnership between government and business (Berkman and Swanstrom, 1979).

After comparing default in New York and Cleveland, Beck (1982: 215) concludes that the explanation of Cleveland's default lay not in its "distressed circumstances at any point in time but with the *prolonged* mismanagement of its municipal finances" (emphasis added). Mismanagement resulted in a high ratio of short-term debt to own-source revenues. Financial mismanagement, however, actually started during the administration of Republican Ralph Perk (1971-1977), or earlier. Perk practiced sloppy bookkeeping, sold capital assets to pay for operating expenses, and relied heavily on short-term borrowing, yet the banks routinely, and without probing questions, rolled over the notes of the Perk administration.

On many issues, Kucinich was a radical, but on fiscal matters he was basically a conservative. It is difficult to argue that Cleveland's finances deteriorated during his administration. Kucinich added almost no new debt during his two years in office; he was able to pay off, out of operating funds, a sizable Muny Light debt that had accumulated during previous administrations, as well as millions in short-term debt; the payroll dropped from 11,640 to 9,500—by a process of attrition; and, unlike Perk, Kucinich did not succumb to the dubious practice of selling assets to meet operating expenses. Finally, although the informational demands placed on the Kucinich administration by the banks were not unreasonable, given the city's questionable bookkeeping methods, they were clearly much greater than during previous administrations.[6]

Objective evidence indicates that the Kucinich administration was discriminated against compared to its predecessor; there is also the testimony of Weir, who admitted that Kucinich was treated differently than Perk and in explaining why so much as confessed to a political bias.

> We weren't asking the type of questions of them (Perk Administration) that we are asking this (Kucinich) administration. There are a couple of reasons why. First, New York happened. That taught us all a lesson about asking questions. The second reason is the *attitude of the Kucinich Administration*. The Perk Administration was not as antagonistic toward the business community and the banking community as to precipitate a showdown [quoted in U.S. Congress, 1980: 35-36, emphasis added].

In short, the banks treated Kucinich differently than Perk for political reasons.

Evidence also exists that the banks treated Kucinich differently than his Republican successor, George Voinovich.[7] Interestingly, Mayor Voinovich, who has improved Muny's ability to compete with CEI, eventually came to see the same kind of conspiracy against Muny Light that Kucinich saw.[8] In 1984, the Voinovich administration negotiated with CEI to take over all of Muny's private customers in exchange for, among other things, a promise by CEI not to move its over 1,000 employees to the suburbs, as threatened, but to locate them instead in a major downtown development. Voinovich, perhaps fearing a Kucinich comeback, killed the deal saying, among other things, that CEI's decision over where to locate its headquarters should have nothing to do with Muny Light (Lawless, 1984). Indeed, CEI's attempt to link staying in Cleveland with the sale of the municipal utility is another example, like default, of political discretion in investment. Voinovich, who said he never believed the story that the business community offered to prevent default if Kucinich would sell Muny Light, said he wasn't so sure the story wasn't true after the incident described above (Bartimole, 1984: 2).

In summary, there is strong evidence that the bankers had motives for demanding that Cleveland sell Muny Light or go into default; there is incontrovertible evidence that this demand was, in fact, communicated to the city; and finally, there is substantial evidence that Cleveland city government, under Kucinich, was treated differently than other borrowers, other cities, and other administrations. In sum, Cleveland's default was political.

ELITE INTERVENTION IN A
STRUCTURAL CRISIS

The political unity of Cleveland's financial elite in pursuit of its political interests exceeded that which would be predicted by an economic structuralist analysis. Unlike Block's (1977: 19) formulation, "decisions made by individual capitalists according to their own narrow economic rationality" were not sufficient, at least in Cleveland's case, to paralyze the regime. In Cleveland, a financial elite had to override narrow economic rationality in order to manipulate the electoral process, using an instrument of power that goes well beyond the legitimate use of lobbying or campaign contributions: the political allocation of credit.[9]

Cleveland's default, then, seems to fit clearly within the tradition of elite theory (at least in the negative sense of an elite using its control over credit to destabilize a left-of-center regime) rather than economic structuralism. Before concluding that this is a pure example of elite instrumental intervention, however, it is necessary to analyze the conditions that made the exercise of this power possible in the first place.

At root, Cleveland's default is an example of one group acquiring a monopoly over a needed commodity, in violation of market theory, and then exercising political discretion in its decision to withhold that commodity. In order for this monopoly power to operate, four conditions were necessary:

(1) The city had to be shut out of the national bond market and forced to depend on local banks.
(2) The local banks, for their part, had to possess extraordinary unity of political purpose and action.
(3) Forced to deal with a united phalanx of local banks, the city's bargaining relationship with the banks had to be highly unequal.
(4) Finally, the political leadership of the city had to be willing to resist the demands of the banks.

All four conditions were necessary before the instrumental power in question could be exercised. Of the four conditions, the second is clearly in the domain of elite power structure research focusing, as it does, on the intentions and organization of the elite through networks such as interlocking directorates and social clubs. I argue that the first, third, and fourth conditions, however, are rooted in the structures of modern political economy. They result not from the intentional political actions of elites but from the structurally induced decisions of investors motivated by short-term profit.[10]

Power structure research focuses on the second necessary condition listed above, the political cohesion of the economic elite. Little research has been conducted, however, on the organization of economic elites in declining industrial cities like Cleveland. An exception is the work of Richard Ratcliff on St. Louis (Ratcliff et al., 1979; Ratcliff, 1980). Whereas the massive shift of investment out of industrial cities presented obvious problems for the maintenance of elite rule, Ratcliff observes, the metropolitan capitalist class in St. Louis remained highly organized around a core elite. In a study of bank directors in St. Louis, Ratcliff (1980: 136) found "a hierarchical system of stratification which separates and makes distinct a core network of capitalists closely bound together by multiple economic and social ties." Much the same result was found for Cleveland.

In Cleveland a financial elite headed by Cleveland Trust led the fight against Kucinich's urban populism and the threat it posed to the dominance of business values in city government. This financial elite showed remarkable political unity throughout the city's fiscal crisis. The six banks that held the notes formed a tacit agreement that all would go forward together or none would; the highly demanding rule of unanimity was adopted as the principle of political unity. In apparent violation of antitrust laws, Cleveland had the benefit of only one credit judgment, not six.[11]

The political cohesion of the Cleveland banks is not surprising, given the already noted social ties as well as the tight network of interlocking relationships among the banks and between the banks and the private utility. (U.S. Congress, 1979, presents over 150 pages of documentation of these interlocking relationships.) One factor that has not been noted is the economic concentration within the banking community and, within that, the dominance exerted by Cleveland Trust over the entire financial sector. Congressional studies in the late 1960s documented Cleveland's centralized pattern of bank stock ownership and control, calling it "the most alarming of any of the 10 cities under study."

> According to the latest FDIC concentration statistics as of June 30, 1966, the five largest banks in the Cleveland metropolitan area held 91.7 percent of all the commercial bank deposits in the area, one of the highest concentrations in the Nation. . . .
>
> It is clear from the major Cleveland banks' extensive web of stockholder links, more pervasive than in any other city examined thus far, that competition among these banks is bound to be adversely affected [United States Congress, 1967: 948-949].

A year later another congressional study, focusing on trust holdings, found Cleveland to be one of four cities (out of ten examined) where banking was dominated by a few institutions with "permanently entrenched managements."

> All in all, it is clear from the Subcommittee's survey that not only is Cleveland banking from the point of view of commercial bank operations, dominated by the Cleveland Trust Co., but when the additional factor of trust investments combined with interlocking directorships is considered, the Cleveland Trust Co., along with the other banks surveyed in Cleveland, is probably the single most influential element in the entire economy of the area [U.S. Congress, 1968: 633].

The 1979 *Congressional Study* of default confirmed the earlier pattern, concluding that Cleveland Trust "remains by far the dominant financial institution in the city" (U.S. Congress, 1979: 196).

In short, the near monopoly of the major banks in Cleveland, their strong ties to each other and to most major corporations through investments and interlocking directorates, and the intimate social and political connections between key bank executives created a "community of interest" among the major bankers in Cleveland. Led by Cleveland Trust, finance capital in Cleveland showed remarkable solidarity throughout the December default crisis. This is important because if only one bank had broken ranks, Kucinich's hand would have been greatly strengthened and the city might have been able to work out a refinancing plan.

The evidence shows, then, that there was a well-organized financial elite in Cleveland that was ready and willing to represent conservative business interests against an insurgent populist mayor. Without three other conditions being in place, however, this elite never could have exercised the power that it did. These other necessary conditions were not primarily the result of political organization; they were primarily due to deep-seated economic trends.

First, Cleveland had to be forced out of the national bond market, requiring it to rely on the local banks for financing. This occurred in the months prior to default when the two national rating agencies dropped Cleveland's bond ratings below investment grade. Fundamentally, these low ratings were due to the city's long-term financial problems stemming from the suburbanization of its middle class and the disinvestment of its industrial base. Yet, as pointed out earlier, Cleveland's financial situation under Kucinich was little different than it had been under the previous mayor, Perk. Undoubtedly, the refusal of local banks to refinance short-term debt beginning in May 1978 and the discovery of the missing bond funds that summer were the major immediate causes of the lowered bond ratings.[12] Regardless of the reason, by December 1978, the national bond market was unavailable to the city. Having exhausted its cash reserves paying the CEI debt and purchasing notes the banks earlier refused to roll over, the only place Cleveland could turn to finance the existing notes in December 1978 was the local banks that held them.

Forced to deal with a united local banking establishment, the city found itself in a highly uneven bargaining relationship. If default can be thought of as a complex game of chicken, as the *Congressional Study* suggested (U.S. Congress, 1979: 272), then, clearly, the banks were driving the equivalent of a Sherman tank, the city a beat-up Volkswagen. Ironically, the unequal financial situations of the banks and city government were due, in large part, to the actions of the banks themselves. For years, Cleveland banks had diverted mortgage investment from the city to the suburbs. In 1978, for example, local financial institutions invested over $1 billion in housing in the county; only 16% of this went to Cleveland even though Cleveland contained about 42% of the total residential units in the county (Swanstrom, 1985: 185). A study for the Federal Reserve Bank of Cleveland concluded that area banks redlined black and racially mixed neighborhoods in Cleveland (Avery and Buynak, 1981). While Cleveland banks continued to invest in downtown office buildings, they pulled much of their housing and industrial investment out of the city. In 1981, a number of community organizations challenged Cleveland Trust's application for mergers under the Community Reinvestment Act (CRA), claiming that between 1977 and 1979 the bank pulled $156 million in loans out of the Cleveland area, investing the money, among other places, in a $40 million loan to a nonunion southern steel mill (Bartimole, 1981).

Able to tap into a national lending market, the banks involved in default had many places to loan their money. Essentially, the banks were able to exercise political discretion by calling in the notes owed by city government because the Cleveland notes represented such an infinitesimal portion of their assets. In the case of Cleveland Trust, its $5 million share of the notes represented less than 1% of its loans to states and political subdivisions ($689 million) and less than 1/10 of 1% of its total outstanding loans (U.S. Congress, 1979: 195). With such low exposure in the securities of their own city, even a complete write-off would have made only a small dent in the total equity of the Cleveland banks.

While the banks had many places to lend their money, the city had only one place to borrow. Moreover, like many cities of the Northeast, Cleveland was in a perpetual fiscal crisis due to forces beyond its control. In 1978, Cleveland had a desperate need for credit—having to pay the debt immediately meant curtailing basic services and massive layoffs; not paying meant default, with all of its long-run implications for future access to credit. Clearly, the confrontation between the public and private sectors, here, was dramatically uneven.

In addition, one more ingredient was necessary before the banks could exercise political power: a mayor who was willing, even eager, to resist their demands. Urban populism in Cleveland has been interpreted as an expression of a crisis in growth politics (Swanstrom, 1985). For nearly a century, Cleveland enjoyed phenomenal growth as one of the world's premier industrial cities. Government played a limited role during this boom period, providing minimal services and keeping taxes low. Since 1950, however, Cleveland has contracted even faster than it grew, losing more than 40% of its population and over 50% of its manufacturing jobs. Extreme disparities have developed between declining neighborhoods and industry and a burgeoning downtown corporate service sector. In an effort to deal with the growth crisis, Cleveland city government has taken on an expanded role in economic and community development.

Kucinich's urban populism was fundamentally an expression of the frustration and resentment of inner city ethnics stuck in a dying industrial economy and with only a marginal place in the emerging service economy. Playing on the suspicions many ethnics felt about the growing collaboration between the public and private sectors brought on by the growth crisis, Kucinich based his appeal on confrontation politics, attacking big banks and corporations.

Based on my earlier analysis, default would never have occurred if Cleveland's mayor had refrained from attacking the banks and had been willing to sell Muny Light. Given Kucinich's political methods, he may have even desired a confrontation with the banks; more important, however, given that he had staked so much of his career on saving Muny Light, Kucinich had little choice. The result (rare in American politics): An elected chief executive of a major city not only resisted the demands of the banks but publicly attacked them.

Analysis of the four conditions necessary for the exercise of elite power in default (exclusion from the national bond market, a politically united local banking establishment, an uneven bargaining relationship, and a mayor willing to resist the demands of the banks) reveals that all, with the exception of the degree of collusion among local bankers, are closely related to the underlying economic and fiscal crisis besetting Cleveland.

Clearly, Cleveland's growth crisis is not due primarily to directly political investment decisions, as in default. Cleveland's fiscal crisis is rooted in structural changes in advanced capitalism. The strength of the new political economy lies not in its ability to explain local government policy (economic structuralism) but in its ability to expose the contradictions of advanced capitalism that produce the problems and crises of urban politics. Whether it be showing that the benefits of growth are bottled up in the monopoly sector, generating a fiscal crisis in the state (O'Connor, 1973), or showing that market relations generate, by their own logic, extreme uneven development (Hymer, 1971; Bluestone, 1972; Bluestone and Harrison, 1982: 203-204), the new political economy demonstrates that investment decisions, notwithstanding that their intent is immediate economic gain, have profound political effects. In this case, structurally induced investment decisions created the preconditions, both subjective and objective, for the instrumental manipulation of Cleveland politics by a financial elite.

The Cleveland example suggests that there is a kind of dialectic of economic structure and political agency in local politics. Normally, the operations of the credit and investment markets are sufficient to keep local governments within safe bounds; disinvestment or withdrawal of credit will automatically occur if there is too radical an effort at redistribution. Contradictions within the "normal" operations of these investment markets, however, create urban problems and crises. Those who suffer these costs mobilize politically in an effort to shift the burden. Economic crisis creates political crisis.

The economic dominants, in turn, mobilize to deal with the threat to their political hegemony. In Cleveland, this has happened twice in the postwar period: once in response to urban populism of the 1970s and once in response to the black nationalist threat of the 1960s, when business reluctantly bankrolled a black liberal for mayor, Carl Stokes. (Business later withdrew its support when Stokes proved incapable of protecting property during the 1968 Glenville riots; Stokes, 1973.)

THE BUSINESS CLIMATE ISSUE

If it is true that the banks deliberately placed Kucinich on the horns of a dilemma (either sell Muny Light or go into default), it is clear that Kucinich grasped one horn of the dilemma, default, and decided to live with the consequences. What were those consequences? In other words, what was the scope of the political power exerted by the banks?

As stated previously, there were two political goals the bankers had in mind: eliminate Muny as a competitor to CEI and politically embarrass Kucinich, preventing his reelection. On the issue of Muny Light, it is clear, the bankers lost. Voters overwhelmingly opposed the sale in the February election. Muny Light remains in the public sector today.

Equally clearly, the bankers achieved their second goal: Kucinich was defeated for reelection in November 1979 by Republican George Voinovich (56% to 44%). Although it is difficult to determine how many votes default cost Kucinich, there is no doubt that it hurt him politically. Kucinich was damaged both by the general onus of default and by the tax increase he was forced to support to cope with default.

For years, Kucinich had criticized the city's income tax as regressive and in the 1977 mayoral campaign had stated categorically, "Under no circumstances will I ever increase the income tax" (McGunagle, 1977). In December 1978, however, Kucinich had little choice. Given Cleveland's stagnating property tax base, raising the income tax was the only viable course of action. Kucinich used his popularity in the ethnic wards to help carry the income tax increase even though, ironically, under Ohio law, neither banks nor utilities pay any local income taxes at all (Swanstrom, 1985: 172-173).

More than the tax increase, it was the general onus of default, related to the whole issue of the business climate, that hurt Kucinich with the voters. Kucinich's electoral appeal, urban populism, was based on the claim that he could deliver economic benefits to the inner city that other administrations could not. If the argument here is correct (that Cleveland was discriminated against, creditwise, precisely because it elected a populist mayor and chose to retain the municipal light plant), then, at least in the short-run, urban populism meant economic sacrifice, not economic gain.

The particular nature of the banks' power in the case of default should be made clear. The banks exerted power over the size and shape of the local public sector, not over particular allocations. Forced to seek an income tax increase, Kucinich nevertheless controlled the allocation of tax receipts and made the banks wait in line behind the city payroll. By voting with their dollars, however, the banks convinced many voters that keeping Kucinich as mayor would hurt the city economically. The banks did not take over city government, they laid seige to it—a seige, it was implied, that would not be lifted as long as Kucinich was mayor. As one voter in a lower income ethnic ward put it the weekend before the 1979 election:

> There's the business people and the common people. The two got to work together. I'm a straight Democrat, but you can't tell people with money to go to hell [quoted in Judis, 1980: 38].

The business climate issue, then, proved very damaging to Kucinich. I argue, however, that, with the important exception of default, Kucinich's shortlived administration had little impact on capital investment in Cleveland (Swanstrom, 1985). To be sure, Kucinich took actions that were perceived as having a negative effect on the business climate, but this does not mean they actually had a negative impact. Kucinich, for example, killed a tax abatement program for downtown. Existing studies overwhelmingly support the conclusion that local tax abatements have little effect on investment (Due, 1961; Advisory Commission on Intergovernmental Relations, 1967; Bridges, 1969; Harrison and Kanter, 1976; Jacobs, 1979). Indeed, shortly after Kucinich killed tax abatement, downtown Cleveland experienced a building boom (Swanstrom, 1982). In this case, just the opposite of default, there was no investment conspiracy to punish Kucinich for acting against business. Competition created economic space for a populist policy rejecting tax breaks for business.

The impact of the business climate issue, however, is not based soley on objective effect; given the importance of perceptions, it is open to a great deal of political manipulation. Although Kucinich's antiabatement stand was economically successful, it was a failure politically. Kucinich's opposition to abatement was used effectively, along with default, as evidence of his baneful effect on Cleveland's economy. Unlike the banks refusing to lend money to the city, most business people were not in a position to exercise political discretion in their investment decisions. What they could do, at no cost to themselves, was exercise political discretion over the reasons for their investment behavior, distributing praise or blame for ongoing investment trends. When Diamond Shamrock, the nation's 178th largest industrial corporation (*Fortune*, May and June 1979), announced that it was moving its headquarters from Cleveland to Dallas, papers gave front page headlines to the charge of its president that the main reason was "the anti-business attitude on the part of the city administration" (quoted in Kelly, 1979). Overwhelming evidence shows that the move was dictated by economic considerations internal to the corporation (Marschall, 1979; *Northern Ohio Business Journal*, 1979), but this did not allay the impression created in the minds of the voters.

In short, the economic pressures on the political system were mediated in crucial ways by politics. A hostile media fostered the impression that Kucinich was a disaster for the local business climate. For the most part, this was simply not true; local governments have little leverage over private investment. Default, however, was an exception, where investment really was pulled out; default helped to validate the impression that business was boycotting Cleveland because of Kucinich. To a certain extent, it should be noted, Kucinich was a victim of his own rhetoric. His headline-grabbing fights with business played into the theme of a deteriorating business climate, and his lack of a positive economic program meant that he had no way to reassure voters that something was being done about Cleveland's growth crisis.

CONCLUSION: THE SPACE FOR
POPULIST REFORM

Economic structuralism, the argument that external economic fac-tors tightly constrain local policymaking, denies any significant role for political discretion, or agency, in the decisions of either investors or governments. In the case of Cleveland's default, we saw that an eco-nomic elite exercised political discretion in its decision to call in loans. Likewise, local governments can exercise political discretion within the interstices of structural economic determinations. Different public poli-cies may have the same effect on mobile wealth—requiring political discretion to decide between them.[13] In addition, the mobility of capital varies across time and across industries. The economic pressures on cities, therefore, will also vary. In short, the degree of discretion that is available to local governments and to investors must be determined empirically; it cannot be postulated in the theory. Economic pressures are not unimportant for political decision making, but their effects are mediated in complex ways by political variables.

Moving from theory to practice, what does the Cleveland example suggest for the future of populist reform in American cities? The lesson seems to be that it is futile for economic reformers to participate in electoral politics at the local level. After all, here was a mayor whose main accomplishments were negative: ending tax abatements for down-town and preventing the sale of the municipal light plant. Nevertheless, he came under severe attack from business. Led by a financial elite, which precipitated the city's default for political reasons, business suc-ceeded in convincing the electorate that urban populism had poisoned Cleveland's business climate. Little room for electoral reforms exists if finance capital can withdraw badly needed credit for political reasons and use that to brand insurgent mayors as responsible for the city's growth crisis.

There are a number of reasons, however, why this extreme pessimism is unwarranted. First, there is economic space for reform. Even the most depressed industrial cities, for example, are enjoying substantial growth in downtown service employment, which offers opportunities for redis-tributive reforms. Cities do not have to offer tax abatements to attract this investment; they can do just the opposite: Cities can tax this sector to provide funds to ameliorate the problems of uneven development, such as neighborhood decay and a shortage of low-income housing.

The most recent policy innovation for spreading the benefits of the downtown service sector is called "linkage." Linkage requires downtown office developers to contribute to a fund for low income housing. Between 1981 and 1983 San Francisco raised over $19 million for this purpose from office developments. The program has had no visible effect on investment (Werth, 1984). Boston, under the leadership of populist mayor Ray Flynn, is considering a similar fee that, it is hoped, will raise $52 million over the next ten years (Advisory Group, 1983). Although such programs are clearly not commensurate with the scope of the problems, they do provide evidence that economic space exists for redistribution. It is a prime function of scholars, it seems to me, to determine exactly how great that space is.

While the economic constraints leave room for discretion, the Cleveland case highlights the severe political constraints on policymaking. Political constraints are different from economic constraints, however, for they can be altered by policy changes—short of radical restructuring of the economic system. At the most rudimentary level is the political organization of insurgent movements themselves. The nature of Kucinich's political organization, its reliance on confrontation politics, antipathy to political parties, and focus on personal appeal as opposed to grass-roots organization made it vulnerable to destabilization. Strong political organization is necessary to counter the impression, fostered by the mass media, that all redistributive reforms are bad for the business climate.

It is much more difficult, however, to counter default, for here we saw that investment really was withdrawn from city government because of its political coloration. Looking at the four conditions necessary for the exercise of this kind of monopoly power, however, shows that only rarely in American politics does a city possess all four. Most cities, for example, retain access to the national bond market. Direct political allocation of municipal credit is rare. On the other hand, if the fiscal pressures on central cities intensify in the years ahead, if the economy is hit with a deep recession, the number of governments vulnerable to financial blackmail will increase.

It is important to note, however, that these tendencies to fiscal crisis are not rooted in the nature of modern capitalism but are the product of political practices chosen by each society. C. G. Pickvance (1980: 32) argues convincingly that the link between economic crises and urban fiscal crises is weak and that "the occurrence of urban fiscal crises is primarily due to the character of political institutions in a society." In

Great Britain, for example, clearly a capitalist economy, there is no general tendency for urban fiscal crisis.

Ironically, among Western liberal democracies, it is in the United States, where local governments have probably the greatest formal powers, that the political structures and practices most seriously undermine local political autonomy. Unlike most Western European countries, the United States also lacks any coherent policy to counteract uneven development (Sundquist, 1975; Fainstein and Fainstein, 1978). Furthermore, local governments in the United States rely more on locally generated revenues than do local governments in Western Europe. "By not providing capital resources to subnational governments from the central government, the United States stands apart from almost every other advanced capitalist state, even other federal states" (Boast, 1977: 114). Local governments in the United States, therefore, are almost totally dependent on wealthy private lenders. In Western Europe most central governments lend money directly to local governments and in many countries municipalities band together to establish lending cooperatives. Almost every major West German city controls its own municipal savings bank from which it can borrow (International Union of Local Authorities, 1963; Jones, 1979; 172; Heidenheimer et al., 1983; 290-291; Sbragia, 1981: 200-220). In short, many of the economic constraints on local governments in the United States are the result of political choices, especially the political structure of American federalism, not the inevitable result of a capitalist economic system.

NOTES

1. Default literally means the failure of a borrower to make payments on time. Strictly speaking, New York was the first city to default. The New York State legislature, however, declared the failure of the city to meet payments on $2.4 billion in outstanding notes on time in November 1975 a "moratorium" rather than a default.

2. Given major structural and legal impediments to complete separation, as well as lack of any enforcement mechanism, Herman concludes that these "Chinese Walls" are rarely completely effective in practice.

3. Channel 8 read a retraction, exactly as dictated by lawyers for National City Bank on the evening news for the following two nights. The reporter who originated the story, Bob Franken, resigned in protest.

4. In fact, on the day of default, an officer of Cleveland Trust confirmed the newspaper reports linking Muny Light and default. (See Phipps, 1978.)

5. According to Ohio law, cities may borrow for capital projects using short-term notes renewable for up to eight successive one-year periods. Cities are required to pay only

interest for the first five years; after five years, they must begin to amortize the principal. At any time in the eight years, the notes may be converted into long-term bonds, thus enabling a city to time its entry into the bond market. The Cleveland notes in question were still several years short of the five-year limit.

6. In 1977, Price Waterhouse declared the city's books unauditable. Reportedly, Cleveland used a single-entry method of bookkeeping that predated Medici banking.

7. Shortly after Kucinich's defeat, top bankers expressed a willingness to help the new mayor, including raising bond money. Less than a year later, the banks approved, without a major tax increase, a $36.2 million bond issue, at a highly favorable 8 and 7/8% interest rate, that got the city out of default. (See Hopwood, "Business is Ready to Aid Voinovich," *Cleveland Press*, November 8, 1979; Alsop, "Bankers in Cleveland Are Clearly Jubilant City Has New Mayor," *Wall Street Journal*, December 8, 1979.)

8. In 1982, Voinovich charged that CEI was trying to cripple Muny by lobbying in council against needed legislation. "We still have a battle going on," said Voinovich. "They [CEI] are as dedicated as ever to laying away the Municipal Light system" (quoted in Clark, 1982).

9. Cleveland's default, of course, is not the first time elites have used their control over credit to exert political influence. As early as the fifth century B.C., there is recorded the example of a banker taking over the administration of a Persian city in Ionia, Atarneus, in order to collect on a loan (Hillhouse, 1936: 38). Much later, Karl Marx described how the "finance aristocracy" ruled in France during the regime of Louis Philippe (1830-1848) by keeping the state "artificially on the verge of bankruptcy" and how later, in a similar fashion, financiers hamstrung the process of revolutionary change during the tumultuous years, 1848-1850 (Marx, 1968). Otto Kirchheimer, likewise, analyzed the period of mass democracy following World War I as a period of conflict "between public control of government and private control of central banks," showing how the left reformist tendencies of the French electorate in the 1920s and 1930s were held in check by the machinations of the banks (Kirchheimer, 1978). Today, of course, many Third World countries have huge external debts and the International Monetary Fund (IMF) frequently conditions rollover of loans on specific policy changes, such as cutting subsidies of essential foodstuffs.

In the advanced industrial countries today, however, central governments have simply become too big and powerful, exerting too much leverage over foreign commerce and exchange, to allow banks to attach specific political conditions to the extension of credit. In particular, the demise of the cherished doctrine of a balanced budget has left the United States government in a much more independent position vis-à-vis finance capital. At the local level, on the other hand, the situation is different. Local governments cannot run deficits year after year, print money, or engineer inflation to lighten their debt load; like underdeveloped countries, they are much more vulnerable.

10. The following analysis, which attempts to synthesize the valid insights of economic structuralism with the power elite perspective, has similarities to the approaches proposed by Whitt (1979, 1980, 1984), Fainstein et al. (1983: ch. 7), and Friedland (1983).

11. John Gelbach, Cleveland Bank Clearing House president, in a draft of a letter rejecting the city's request to purchase $3.3 million in city notes, wrote: "This decision [to reject the notes] has been reached on an individual as well as on a collective basis." In the final letter to the city, the phrase "on a collective basis" was deleted (U.S. Congress, 1979: 232).

12. No implication is made here that the rating agencies were politically motivated. However, although the agencies refuse to divulge their exact formulas, it is clear that subjective factors are important. From an objective point of view, if Cleveland deserved a below-investment-grade rating in 1978, it also deserved the same rating in 1977 or 1976. For discussion of the subjective factors in bond rating, see Twentieth Century Fund (1974) and Judd (1984: 223-225).

13. "Investor discretion" is a key concept in Charles Lindblom's (1977) *Politics and Markets*. In *City Limits*, Peterson (1981) acknowledges that governments may exercise political discretion over what he calls "allocational policies" but, in my view, he underestimates their importance.

REFERENCES

Advisory Commission on Intergovernmental Relations (1967) State-Local Taxation and Industrial Location. Washington, DC: Author.

Advisory Group (1983) Report to the Mayor on the Linkage Between Downtown Development and Neighborhood Housing. Boston: Author.

ALSOP, R. (1979) "Bankers in Cleveland are clearly jubilant city has new mayor." Wall Street Journal (December 8).

AULETTA, K. (1975) The Streets Were Paved With Gold. New York: Random House.

AVERY, R. B. and T. M. BUYNAK (1981) "Mortgage Redlining: some new evidence." Federal Reserve Bank of Cleveland: Economic Review: 18-32.

BARTIMOLE, R. (1984) "Tired city." Point of View 17: 1-4.

———(1981) "Ameritrust." Point of View 13: 1-4.

BECK, J. H. (1982) "Is Cleveland another New York?" Urban Affairs Quarterly 18: 207-216.

BERKMAN, R. and T. SWANSTROM (1979) "A tale of two cities." The Nation: 297-299.

BLOCK, F. (1977) "The ruling class does not rule." Socialist Revolution 33: 6-28.

BLUESTONE, B. (1972) "Economic Crises and the Law of Uneven Development." Politics and Society 3: 65-82.

———and B. HARRISON (1982) The Deindustrialization of America. New York: Basic Books.

BOAST, T. H. (1977) "A political economy of urban capital finance in the United States." Ph.D. Dissertation, Cornell University.

BRECKENFELD, G. (1977) "Refilling the metropolitan doughnut," in D. C. Perry and A. J. Watkins (eds.) The Rise of the Sunbelt Cities. Beverly Hills, CA: Sage.

BRIDGES, B. (1969) "State and local inducements for industry: part 2," in G. Karaska and D. Bramhall (eds.) Locational Analysis for Manufacturing. Cambridge, MA: MIT Press.

CLARK, G. R. (1982) "CEI fighting Muny legislation, mayor charges." Cleveland Plain Dealer (February 26).

DUE, J. F. (1961) "Studies of state-local tax influences in location of industry." National Tax Journal 14: 163-173.

FAINSTEIN, S. S. and N. I. FAINSTEIN (1978) "Federal policy and spatial inequality," in G. Sternlieb and J. W. Hughes (eds.) Revitalizing the Northeast. New Brunswick, NJ: Center for Urban Policy Research.

FAINSTEIN, S. S. et al. (1983) Restructuring the City. New York: Longman.

FRIEDLAND, R. (1983) Power and Crisis in the City. New York: Schocken.

GOLD, D. A., C.Y.H. LO, and E. O. WRIGHT (1975) "Recent developments in Marxist theories of the state." Monthly Review (October): 29-43.

GOODMAN, R. (1979) The Last Entrepreneurs. New York: Simon & Schuster.

HARRISON, B. and S. KANTER (1976) "The great state robbery." Working Papers: 57-66.

HEIDENHEIMER, A. J., H. HECLO, and C. T. ADAMS (1983) Comparative Public Policy. New York: St. Martin's.

HERMAN, E. S. (1975) Conflicts of Interest: Commercial Bank Trust Departments. New York: The Twentieth Century Fund.

HICKS, D. A. (1982) "Urban and economic adjustment to the post-industrial era," in Hearings Before the Joint Economic Committee, Congress of the United States, Ninety-Seventh Congress, Part 2. Washington, DC: Government Printing Office.

HILLHOUSE, A. M. (1963) Municipal Bonds: A Century of Experience. New York: Prentice-Hall.

HOPWOOD, M. (1981) "Assets of city set at $1 billion, budget balanced." Cleveland Press (May 12).

———(1979) "Business is ready to aid Voinovich." Cleveland Press (November 8).

———(1978) "Why Saltzman gave up." Cleveland Press (December 18).

HYMER, S. (1971) "The multinational corporation and the law of uneven development," in J. Bhagwati (ed.) Economics and World Order. New York: World Law Fund.

International Union of Local Authorities (1963) Municipal Credit Banks. The Hague, Netherlands: Internatioal Union of Local Authorities.

JACOBS, J. (1979) Bidding For Business. Washington, DC: Public Interest Research Group.

JOHNSON, T. (1911) My Story. Seattle: University of Washington Press.

JONES, G. W. (1979) "Local government finance in Great Britain," in J. Lagroye and V. Wright (eds.) Local Government in Britain and France. London: George Allen and Unwin.

JUDD, D. R. (1984) The Politics of American Cities. Boston: Little, Brown.

JUDIS, J. (1980) "Decline and fall." Progressive (January): 36-39.

KELLY, M. (1979) "Diamond Shamrock to leave area." Cleveland Plain Dealer (May 30).

KENNEDY, M. D. (1984) "The fiscal crisis of the city," in M. P. Smith (ed.) Cities in Transformation. Beverly Hills, CA: Sage.

KIRCHHEIMER, O. (1978) "Changes in the structure of political compromise," in A. Arato and E. Gebhardt (eds.) The Essential Frankfurt School Reader. New York: Urizen Books. (originally published in 1941)

LAWLESS, J. (1984) "Voinovich kills deal with CEI." Cleveland Plain Dealer (January 6).

LINDBLOM, C. E. (1977) Politics and Markets. New York: Basic Books.

McGUNAGLE, F. (1977) "Two candidates tax each other in debate." Cleveland Press (October 26).

MARSCHALL, D. J. (1979) "Why did Diamond Shamrock go?" Cleveland Plain Dealer (June 25).

MARX, K. (1968) The Class Struggles in France 1848 to 1850. Moscow: Progress Publishers. (originally published in 1850)

MOLOTCH, H. (1976) "The city as a growth machine: toward a political economy of place." American Journal of Sociology 82: 309-332.

MONKKONEN, E. H. (1984) "The politics of municipal indebtedness and default. 1850-1936," in S. K. Ward and T. J. McDonald (eds.) The Politics of Urban Fiscal Policy, Beverly Hills, CA: Sage.

Northern Ohio Business Journal (1979) "Media distorts reason, purely economic" (June 11).

Nuclear Regulatory Commission (1977) Nuclear Regulatory Commission Issuances, January 1, 1977-March 31, 1977, Vol. 5. Washington, DC: Government Printing Office.

O'CONNER, J. (1973) The Fiscal Crisis of the State. New York: St. Martin's.

PETERSON, P. E. (1981) City Limits. Chicago: University of Chicago Press.

PHIPPS, P. (1978) "Default time arrives as the nation watches." Cleveland Press (December 15).

PICKVANCE, C. G. (1980) "Theories of the state and theories of urban crisis." Current Perspectives in Social Theory 1: 31-54.

PIVEN, F. F. and R. CLOWARD (1982) The New Class War. New York: Pantheon.

President's Commission for a National Agenda for the Eighties (1980) Urban America in the Eighties: Perspectives and Prospects. Washington, DC: Government Printing Office.

President's National Urban Policy Report (1982) Washington, DC: Government Printing Office.

RATCLIFFE, R. E. (1980) "Declining cities and capitalist class structure," in G.W. Domhoff (ed.) Power Structure Research. Beverly Hills, CA: Sage.

———M. E. GALLAGHER, and K. S. RATCLIFF (1979) "The civic involvement of bankers: an analysis of the influence of economic power and social prominence in the command of civic policy positions." Social Problems 20: 298-313.

RICE, J. (1979) "2 issues take lead: pollster finds sizable margins or tax hike, Muny Light sale." Cleveland Plain Dealer (January 23).

SBRAGIA, A. (1981) "Cities, capital, and banks: the politics of debt in the United States, United Kingdom, and France," in K. Newton (ed.) Urban Political Economy. London: Frances Pinter.

SIMON, W. E. (1978) A Time for Truth. New York: Berkley.

SMITH, M. P. (1984) "Urban structure, social theory, and political power," in M. P. Smith (ed.) Cities in Transformation Vol. 26, Urban Affairs Annual Reviews. Beverly Hills, CA: Sage.

STOKES, C. B. (1973) Promises of Power. New York: Simon & Schuster.

SUNDQUIST, J. L. (1975) Dispersing Population. Washington, DC: The Brookings Institution.

SWANSTROM, T. (1985) The Crisis of Growth Politics: Cleveland, Kucinich, and the Promise of Urban Populism. Philadelphia: Temple University Press.

———(1982) "Tax abatement in Cleveland." Social Policy 3: 24-30.

TIEBOUT, C. M. (1956) "A pure theory of local expenditures." Journal of Political Economy 64: 416-424.

Twentieth Century Fund Task Force on Municipal Bond Credit Ratings (1974) The Rating Game (with a background paper by J. E. Peterson). New York: Author.

United States Congress, House of Representatives (1980) Role of Commercial Banks in Financing the Debt of the City of Cleveland. Hearing before the Subcommittee on Financial Insitutions, Supervision, Regulation and Insurance of the Committee on Banking, Finance and Urban Affairs. Washington, DC: Government Printing Office.

————(1979) The Role of Commercial Banks in the Finances of the City of Cleveland. Staff Study by the Subcommittee on Financial Institutions of the Committee on Banking, Finance and Urban Affairs. Washington, DC: Government Printing Office.

————(1968) Commercial Banks and their Trust Activities: Emerging Influence on the American Economy. Staff Report for Subcommittee on Domestic Finance of the Committee on Banking and Currency. Washington, DC: Government Printing Office. (reprinted in Commercial Banks and Their Trust Activities: Emerging Influence on the American Economy. New York: Arno Press and the New York Times, 1969)

————(1967) Control of Commercial Banks and Interlocks Among Financial Institutions. Washington, DC: Subcommittee Print. (reprinted in Commercial Banks and their Trust Activities: Emerging Influence on the American Economy: New York: Arno Press and the New York Times, 1969)

WERTH, J. (1984) "Tapping developers." Planning (January).

WHITT, J. A. (1984) "Structural Fetishism in the New Urban Theory." in M. P. Smith (ed.) Cities in Transformation. Beverly Hills, CA: Sage.

————(1980) "Can capitalists organize themselves?" in G. W. Domhoff (ed.) Power Structure Research. Bevery Hills, CA: Sage.

————(1979) "Toward a class-dialectical model of political power: an empirical assessment of three competing models of power." American Sociological Review 44: 81-100.

WIERNIK, J. and T. GEIDEL (1979) "Weir warm to Rhodes' plan for city." Cleveland Plain Dealer (January 12).

5

Local Government and Fiscal Stress: An Exploration into Spending and Public Employment Decisions

ROBERT M. STEIN
ELIZABETH G. SINCLAIR
MAX NEIMAN

☐ EVER SINCE the de facto default by New York in 1975, the financial health of cities has been a central concern among scholars. The focus of worry has been primarily on the apparent difficulty of older, developed, urban places balancing their public ledgers. In the process a host of sociopolitical factors have been marshaled to explain the fiscal malaise among the nation's older cities. Declining tax base, rapidly growing dependent populations, exploitation by suburbs, unfinanced mandates imposed by states and the federal government, and long periods of stagnation in the economy all have been considered as factors exacerbating the fiscal malaise of the nation's cities.

It is possible to encompass all the manifestations of these financial problems under the notion of "fiscal stress," which we define as a situation in which the political costs of making decisions necessary to support given levels of service are sufficiently high so as to pose the prospect of service declines or even service collapse. Our emphasis on the political barriers to managing fiscal stress highlights several ways in which we believe the concept of fiscal stress can be clarified. Two clarifications are of particular importance. First, by viewing fiscal stress as a problem of policy choice, several ambiguities in the concept of fiscal stress are ameliorated. Second, our definition moves away from seeing fiscal stress as strictly an exogenously produced phenomenon for which localities can only provide adjustments to external stimuli.

A TENTATIVE CLARIFICATION OF STRESS

The matter of fiscal stress is a long-standing issue, often disguised because it is a problem that is manifested in so many ways. Indeed, if one accepts the notion that the revenue and spending decisions of localities have always been problematic, then one might even say that for local governments generally there has rarely been a time when the local public purse has not been a source of high anxiety.

This is not an idle historical observation. After all, in recent decades the term fiscal stress and its conceptual kin have been used as major explanatory variables, applied to a very wide range of behavior, including taxpayer complaints regarding tax levels and waste in government, less affluent citizens demanding extensions of greater services, or local officials working to overcome local fiscal limits imposed by their indifferent or hostile state governments.

What, then, is fiscal stress or strain? Most research measures the notion in terms of a ratio of revenues (expenditures) to resources. Yet clearly this is misleading. After all, communities with a much higher than average level of resources can, because of their even higher than average spending levels, experience strain. On the other hand, a community with lower than average resources might, if its spending level is sufficiently low, experience little stress or strain. The fact of the matter is that any ratio of spending to resources is a measure of some policy output. *The strain or stress lies not in the ratio, of course, but in the institutional and behavioral effects experienced by decision makers.* A high ratio of spending to resources is not a problem if those who pay do not complain or otherwise threaten the political health of officials. The ratio is not a problem if the tax rates necessary to produce the spending levels do not result in other objectionable circumstances, such as loss of business or unwillingness to improve property by landlords. High levels of spending are not a problem if there are sufficient resources forthcoming.

In short, fiscal strain represents a situation much more general, encompassing a much wider variety of circumstances than those surrounding the New York or Cleveland cases. There is a great diversity in the array of factors that can make the fiscal life of communities stormy, and they can afflict the decision makers of many different locales with the ailments of fiscal stress.

Is fiscal stress different from the sound and fury that often emerge during budget allocations? Is the political difficulty in resolving disputes over the budget pie different from the problem of balancing the budget? If a city council or mayor find it politically unpalatable to eliminate a service in the face of declining resources, we call it "fiscal stress." But if a local group demands the initiation of some new program in the face of limited resources and is able to create electoral danger for some officials, then why should we not term the resulting difficulties for decision makers "fiscal stress"?

What of communities experiencing both rapid population growth and concurrently escalating demands for public services? What if a city council in such a community refuses to raise development fees for fear of appearing to be antibusiness and allows services to be stretched and to deteriorate? Is this a situation of fiscal stress? After all, if the money were there, the city council could allow growth to continue, satisfying local commercial interests while supporting the extension of services to older residents.

What we are emphasizing is that the tangle of predicaments that converge on local budgets is made up of a variety of political choices; a variety of political dynamics can all create budgetary dilemmas for officials. Fiscal stress, as it is usually measured, does not necessarily inform us of the traits of the locale experiencing it; and when measured largely as a ratio of spending to resources, as is the case in most of the literature (see Clark and Ferguson, 1983), it is inadequate.

FISCAL STRESS AND THE DEPENDENT CITY

Although it is a matter of considerable debate (Munns, 1975), one recurring theme in the literature of urban politics and policy is that of the "dependent city" (Wirt, 1985). In this view cities are weak institutions, with little capacity to ward off externally produced threats to their well-being. Thus factors exogenous to local politics are believed to be the prone determinants of policy. Paul Peterson (1981: 4), for example, makes the vulnerability of local systems a central theme:

Because cities have limits, one explains urban policy by looking at the place of the city in the large socioeconomic and political context. . . . It is these city interests, not the internal struggles for power within cities, that limit city policies and condition what local governments do.

Following Peterson, the increasingly common view is that local circumstances are becoming less relevant respecting the development of local policy. Regarding financial problems, the "dependent city" perspective suggests that fiscal stress is the result of major social and political factors over which localities have little control, such as the following: federal and state program mandates and conditions of intergovernmental aid, unintended consequences of state and federal policies, regional and interregional migration patterns, national—even international—economic conditions, and technology. Yet even scholars who find that local governments are primarily mediators between the larger sociopolitical environment and local populations understand that there are sources of local autonomy. There are some decisions that reflect local factors and local will. Thus a switch to the "dependent city" perspective endangers the inquiry into the relevance of local political processes in the determination of policy.

In the following pages we assert that the overemphasis in the literature on total expenditures as an indicator of policy choice accounts, in part, for the view of the city as merely an object of externally generated forces. By contrast, reliance on alternative measures that are more theoretically justified as indicators of policy choices, rather than reflecting oscillations in aggregate resource levels, are more likely to reveal the importance of local factors on local policymaking. The focus on local policy in this study is public employment and related spending (e.g., wages), which, for theoretical reasons discussed below, are believed to be better indicators of budgetary determinants and which reflect the power of local political forces.

THE RESEARCH ON FISCAL STRESS

Studies of municipal fiscal stress and its impact on the policy decisions of municipal governments have not produced a uniform set of conclusions. On the one hand, there is the traditional work of incremental budget theorists (Davis et al., 1966; Crecine, 1969; Larkey, 1975), who maintain that government responses to fiscal scarcity are not significantly different from expansionary budget strategies. Lewis

(1984) found changes in revenue patterns were not significantly related to changes in spending patterns for fiscally stressed cities, with the exception of capital spending. Prior spending and not the level of fiscal scarcity appears to be the best single predictor of current municipal expenditures during this period.

Levine et al. (1981) and Levine (1980) find that the policy effects of fiscal stress are not likely to be immediate and that responses to stress can proceed through a number of stages before significant nonincremental budget decisions are made. Moreover, there is reason to believe that at the point where major policy changes are made in managing fiscal stress a number of local variables might alter the relationship between fiscal stress and government adaptations. Highly particularistic patterns of state-local relations, varying patterns of intergovernmental aid, and local circumstances will complicate the capacity to generalize about the manner of adjustment to fiscal stress. So despite the literature that documents the important relationship—even dependency—that exists between municipal policy outputs and state and federal influences (Fossett, 1984; Gramlich, 1977; U.S. Advisory Commission of Intergovernmental Aids [ACIR], 1978; MacManus, 1983), local political forces will complicate any assessment of the direct effects of stress on the policy responses of localities.

With respect to local contingencies affecting the management of fiscal stress, three factors appear to be important: (1) change in urban constituencies; (2) the role of city administrations in adapting the local revenue base to the declining yields from traditional local revenue sources; and (3) the role of intergovernmental transfers designed to ameliorate fiscal stress by incorporating formulae. These factors are our sources for the independent variables in this analysis.

POPULATION CHANGE, ELECTORAL COALITIONS, AND POLICY CHANGE

The classical formulation regarding fiscal stress goes something like this: Because of both push and pull factors, great numbers of affluent residents of the older, developed portions of the nation's metropolitan regions have migrated to the suburbs and the exurban fringe (Hirschman, 1970; Hutcheson, 1982). As a consequence, cities have lost revenue, jobs, and the civic activism of the middle classes. As cities attempt to maintain services in the face of declining revenue sources, they experience greater fiscal stress, which in the face of general economic decline or stagnation might push individual communities to the brink of financial collapse.

This view is problematic in several respects. It assumes that the problem of budget stress is solely the problem of older, developed communities; yet the study of rapidly growing communities indicates that they also experience their share of budget problems. More fundamentally, the classic formulation is too deterministic; by adopting the "dependent city" perspective, this conventional view of fiscal stress suggests an inexorable pattern of decay and collapse. As the local governments within the older metropolitan centers try to raise taxes from a relatively smaller resource base, they reduce their attraction to residents and businesses, who avoid the redistributive spending patterns of central cities (Tiebout, 1956). Consequently, the condition of the older urban places deteriorates further, leaving behind an increasingly homogeneous, dependent population.

However, in some communities the flight of businesses and middle-class residents has resulted in (1) the cutting of social services and other programs designed to assist the less affluent, and (2) the replacement of these services by policies that encourage business and that maintain—if not increase—the proportion of more affluent residents. Judd (1984) refers to this response as "the redevelopment strategy."

The fact that population shifts do not seem to have uniform effects on localities has inspired a number of scholars to consider systematically the ways in which local population composition might affect local policy. Clark and Ferguson (1983), Sullivan (1973), and Fisher (1976) suggest that diversity in the local demography implies greater diversity in citizen tastes, thereby complicating greatly the ability to minimize distress over what government does.

Moreover, Shefter, both in his study of the fiscal crisis in New York in the early 1970s (1977) an in his theory of urban coalitions (1978), has argued for a reciprocal relationship between community diversity and official policy. As elected officials compete for votes, the diversity of social groups in the community and changes in the composition of local groups provide opportunities for coalition building. Consequently, public policy can reflect the relative influence of coalitions associated with the ruling administration. Indeed, as Bish and Ostrom (1976) argue, increased diversity and competitiveness among social groups produce instability in ruling coalitions.

Ever fearful that potential and actual opponents can seize the opportunity to threaten reelection bids, officials in highly diverse and competitive political environments like New York's try to embrace emergent groups into their coalition, trying to retain current coalition members simultaneously. The result is ever more complex coalitions, which, in the language of games, require escalating payoffs. Unlike Detroit, in which a powerful black electoral majority was able to impose a redistributive local tax, in New York great reliance was placed on the issuance of debt to meet program and operating costs. Detroit and New York indicate, in short, that local political factors can be important in affecting the onset, as well as shaping the management, of fiscal stress, although it is doubtful that these factors alone caused New York City's real crisis, as Shefter once maintained. The following analysis will explore the relation between political constituency changes and fiscal stress.

ADAPTATION OF LOCAL REVENUE SOURCES TO FISCAL STRESS

Research indicates that since the 1960s local governments have moved toward greater use of user fees and charges, a trend that accelerated after the imposition of revenue constraints during the outbreaks of tax revolts throughout the country in the late 1970s (Mushkin and Vehron, 1981). Indeed, as Chapman (1981: 21) points out, "charges that do not exceed the cost of providing the services were one of the few revenue sources left to cities after the passage of an expenditure limitation measure in November, 1979."

There are also political benefits in such revenue sources, especially during periods of fiscal stress. Citizens are more likely to tolerate fees and charges attached to the receipt of particular benefits. Moreover, such fees and charges give an air of greater choice to citizens who believe that if they do not choose to consume a particular public good or service, then they do not have to pay. This contrasts with the popular view among citizens that taxes are primarily devoted to other people's well-being, a view that must of necessity be true in some important way.

Of course, user fees and charges are not a budgetary panacea. Some public goods cannot be packaged as individualized services for which unit prices can be attached and assigned to particular beneficiaries (e.g., patrolling by police). There are also equity considerations, in that user fees for such services as parks and libraries are likely to reduce access among lower income citizens. Our analysis, therefore, measures the effect of changes in local revenue sources on stress.

FEDERAL AND STATE AID AND EFFECTS ON STRESS

The amount of federal and state aid received by localities is often importantly influenced by the socioeconomic conditions that exist in the communities (Pelessero, 1984; Stein, 1981, 1982; Morgan and England, 1981: Dye and Hurley, 1979). State aid policies have been shown to be more sensitive to a variety of local features that presumably indicate the social needs of communities (Dye and Hurley, 1979; Stein, 1981). In many places, the nonrestrictive conditions of state aid (ACIR, 1981) have allowed cities to substitute state aid for what would otherwise have to be extracted from local sources. In contrast to the average state aid system, federal aid tends to stimulate municipal spending rather than create opportunities to substitute federal aid for locally raised revenues (Nathan, 1983).

Over time federal and state aid systems can contribute to fiscal stress as well as to the manner in which localities try to manage it. Many cities develop extreme dependency on intergovernmental aid, with many fiscally stressed locales having nearly 50% of their budgets dependent on such aid (Fossett, 1984). In 1980, federal aid was cut, and fiscally dependent cities confronted dire fiscal circumstances. Forced to cut services or increase taxes, city officials were cross-pressured by citizens who favored increasing taxes to maintain spending and by a taxpaying public opposed to tax increases to replace federal aid. Depending on the response of officials to each group, therefore, *the loss of federal aid may have either a stimulative or substitutive effect on municipal spending during periods of fiscal decline.*

Stein (1984b), Fossett (1984), MacManus (1984), and Hall (1979) have shown that most cities seek to avoid excessive aid dependency and its risks by using federal assistance for nonbasic capital activities. Stein (1984a), however, maintains that once municipal officials believe that the flow of federal aid money is secure, they succumb to the political benefits of shifting these funds to noncapital basic functions, treating federal aid money as if it were raised from their own resources. For these communities a cut in federal assistance can result in serious political conflict and/or deterioration in their fiscal condition.

Limitations on local revenue systems by states can also represent significant obstacles to a city maneuvering in the storms of an erratic economy and plummeting tax base (Stonecash, 1981; MacManus, 1983; Stein, 1984b). Moreover, many states impose policy mandates on their municipalities, requiring them to provide specific goods and services, often without providing the revenues necessary for producing these goods and services (ACIR, 1977). Neiman and Lovell (1981, 1982) and Stein (1982) show that these mandates have a disruptive effect both on the spending levels of urban governments and the scope of their functional responsibilities. (See Table 5.1.)

MEASURING THE EFFECTS OF STRESS: DISTINCTIONS BETWEEN SPENDING AND EMPLOYMENT

When choosing an operational measure of local government policy, researchers have consistently favored spending measures (Clark and Ferguson, 1983). There are, however, other policy measures that are more relevant to the concern of political analysts and more revealing about the political nature of local government policy choices. For example, public employment and its associated spending (wages, salaries, and pensions) represents an important, yet neglected, component of municipal policy.

Previous research on public employment has been dominated by econometric studies, which largely ignore politics (Ehrenberg, 1972; Gustely, 1974). Municipal public employment and its associated costs are the fastest growing component of municipal spending (ACIR, 1982).

TABLE 5.1   Hypothesized Relationships Between Selected
Independent Variables and Municipal Policy
Outputs by Level of Fiscal Stress

	Spending		Employment	
Variable	Healthy	Stressed	Healthy	Stressed
P.C. Taxes	−/*	+/**	NS	NS
Debt	NS	+/**	NS	NS
Elast	−/*	+/**	NS	NS
Fed. Aid	+/**	−/*	+/*	+/*
State Aid	−/**	−/**	+/*	+/*
Hetero	NS	+/*	+/**	+/**
Fiscal	NS	NS	+/**	+/**
Annex.	−/*	−/*	−/**	−/**
Mandates	+/*	+/*	+/**	+/**
Func.	−/*	−/*	+/**	+/**

*Secondary determinant.
**Dominant determinant.
+/−Direction of relationship.
NS = not significant.

Moreover, the study of public employment seems an appropriate means for assessing the influence urban politics has on this policy area.

Students of local government have long recognized the political role of public employment. The venerable, colorful history of the political machine was intimately connected with the manipulation of public employment for partisan and material ends (Callow, 1966). Indeed, the political use of public employment and other government goods and services continues in various guises (Wolfinger, 1974; Mladenka, 1984), although social scientists have yet to develop any general interest in the political use of such goods and services in contemporary settings. Perhaps only the studies dealing with the response of local governments to urban unrest in the mid to late 1960s represent systematic study of the political use of local resources (Wikstrom, 1974; Levine, 1980).

Despite its relative neglect, there are a number of reasons to focus on public employment, both as a policy and political tool. In the context of fiscal stress, elected officials may lack the revenues to support expanded spending programs that are believed to be necessary to win support from large and diverse constituencies. Yet it is not altogether clear whether a pork barrel spending strategy is effective in urban areas because the scope of municipal functional responsibility is not associated with many individualized private benefits. Many goods and services in the large urban environments manifest characteristics of public goods; they suffer the risk of trivialization of individual benefits when the good or service is shared or consumed by large numbers of other urban dwellers. The provision of public jobs, however, allows incumbents to target private consumed benefits, enabling officials to develop the desired patron-client relationship. There is empirical evidence to support their view that public employees reciprocate with signficantly higher rates of electoral participation and support for current officeholders, an anticipated effect of new public employment (Courant et al., 1979).

The emphasis on the political gains from public employment is not intended to be cynical or suggest that there are not substantive policy goals and gains from increasing public employment. The skillful use of public employment levels and wage rates provides cities a measure of control over their city's public welfare not normally present in other policy arenas (e.g., social services), which are often financed and heavily directed from Washington, D.C., and state capitols. Even though labor costs are often the fastest growing and largest component of local budgets, this is not an unalterable condition. Utilization of part-time labor, for example, provides city officials a great deal of latitude. Part-time or temporary workers are not normally unionized, not eligible for costly benefits and pensions, and not usually covered by civil service laws.

OPERATIONAL MEASURES AND FRAMEWORK FOR ANALYSIS

Because we hypothesize that, due to incrementalism, total spending is not as revealing about the genesis or management of stress as is the compositional measure of employment, the following seeks to compare the two with regard to the factors discussed above. Two lines of inquiry are involved in the following analysis. First, we address cross-sectional differences in the effects of fiscal stress and scarcity on municipal governments. Second, we concentrate on changes in spending and employment decisions as they are related to changes in the dependent policy measures. In this sense the analysis shifts from being cross-sectional to having longitudinal implications. Data limitations prevent a full-blown time series application; however, we can assess whether the changes in municipal policy are linked to changes in stress, scarcity, intergovernmental forces, and political factors between two points in time, 1974 and 1982. (See Table 5.2.)

Included in the study are all cities over 50,000 in population (N = 504), with the time period under study being 1974-1982. Missing data for some of the cities (N = 95) reduce the size of the sample and introduce a potential bias to the findings. A number of tests were conducted to determine the extent of bias due to the loss of cases, and even though no such bias was indicated, we remain cautious in view of the missing data.

Based on the extant literature and research on the subject of fiscal stress and the politics of local budgets, we select the following variables and factors for operationalization as predictors of local spending policies: fiscal stress, fiscal scarcity, social diversity, intergovernmental relations, and state-local relations. We then compare the effects of these factors on two separate dependent variables: total municipal spending—the factor used most in fiscal stress research—and municipal spending for public employment—a factor that we feel is related in more telling ways to changes in our independent variables. Our variables and the operationalization of their respective measures is provided in Appendix A at the conclusion of this discussion.

FINDINGS

The results of the analysis are presented in the following order. First, the cross-sectional findings for the total spending and employment

TABLE 5.2 Concepts and Operational Measures

Concept	Operational Measure	Source	Variable Name
Fiscal stress	Standardized composite score including: unemployment; dependent persons (i.e., under 18 and over 65 years); housing value; change in population; and per capita personal income	U.S. Dept. of Commerce, U.S. Bureau of Census, *County and City Data Book, 1970; 1980*	Stress 70, 80
Elasticity of revenue system	Percent total own-source revenues raised from user fees and utility charges.	U.S. Dept. of Commerce, U.S. Bureau of Census, *City Government Finances in 1974, 1982*	Elast 70, 80
Fiscal scarcity (a) Tax effort	Per capita taxes as a percentage of per capita personal income	*City Government Finances, 1974, 1982, County and City Data Book, 1970, 1980*	P.C. Taxes 70, 80
(b) Short-term debt	Per capita short-debt issued	*City Government Finances, 1974, 1982*	Debt 70, 80

Intergovernmental			
(a) Federal aid	Per capita federal aid	*City Gov't Finances*	Fed Aid 70, 80
(b) State aid	Per capita state aid	*City Gov't Finances*	State Aid 70, 80
(c) State-local relations			
(1) Fiscal discretion	Scale score ranging from 0-6	ACIR (1976)	Fiscal 70, 80
(2) Functional discretion	Scale score ranging from 0-5	Hill (1978)	Funct 70, 80
(3) Annexation auth.	Scale score ranging from 0-5	Hill (1978)	Annex 70, 80
(4) Mandated activities	Scale score ranging from 0-100%	ACIR (1978a)	Mandates 70, 80
Social diversity	Positive measure of the percentage of population that differs on six n-chotomous demographic traits: length of residence; home ownership; occupation; personal income; race; and college education.	*City and County Data Book, 1970, 1980*	Hetero 70, 80
Wages	Monthly wages for full-time equivalent workers	*City Government Finances, 1974, 1982*	Wages 70, 80
Policy output			
(1) Spending	Per capita total expenditures[a]	*City Government Finances, 1974, 1982*	Spending 70, 80
(2) Public employ.	Full-time equivalent workers per 1,000 population	*City Government Finances, 1974, 1982*	Employ 70, 80

a. Minus intergovernmental aid transfers.

policies are presented. Second, the change in both these policies for the 1974-1982 period is discussed. Because we are discussing total spending first and then municipal employment, we wind up with a total of four cases. (See Table 5.3.)

Tables 5.4 and 5.5 report the results of the cross-sectional regression analysis for both the pooled and partitioned sample of cities. A basic thesis in the extant research is sustained by these results in that revenue-enhancing factors, including intergovernmental aid and debt, are the major determinants of total per capita own-source spending. In contrast, however, our results differ for the cases in which municipal employment is the dependent variable. Here the degree to which states impair local revenue production and the level of community diversity both dominate the public employee model.

Our conclusions regarding the findings on local public employee policy, however, are tempered by two limitations. First, the explanatory power of the employment model is modest and leaves open the possibility that we have not correctly specified all the determinants of public employment. Second, and potentially more interesting, is the effect fiscal stress has on urban policy output. We could not detect any significant and consistent interactive effect among stress, other independent variables, and total municipal spending. We did, however, identify significant variation in the regression estimates of municipal

TABLE 5.3 Mean Variable Values for Selected Socioeconomic: 1974, 1982 (constant 1972 dollars)

| | All Cases | |
Variable	1974	1982
Fiscal strain	−.522	−.591
P.C. tax	144.77	135.82
P.C. short-term debt	47.6	44.9
Elasticity	.343	.847
P.C. fed aid	97.50	109.26
P.C. state aid	85.58	113.47
Heter	.417	.321
Func	2.54	NA
Mandates	55.6	NA
Annex	3.47	NA
Fiscal	2.18	NA
TOTPC	210.21	206.02
FTE/1,000	1.37	1.45

TABLE 5.4 Regression Estimates for per Capita Spending by Level of Fiscal Stress: 1974, 1982 (T-values)

| | 1974 | | | | | 1982 | | | | |
| | | Stressed | | | Healthy | | | Stressed | | | Healthy |
Variable	All Cities	1	2	3	4	All Cities	1	2	3	4
Intercept	-184	248	103	-193	14.3	-115	139	-1394	-123	199
	-1.33	-1.56	.477	-.999	.048	-.579	.429	-3.06	-.642	.819
Stress	-.652	NA	NA	NA	NA	6.14	NA	NA	NA	NA
	.767	NA	NA	NA	NA	1.62	NA	NA	NA	NA
P.C. tax	.999*	.765*	.738*	.955*	.599*	1.03*	.908*	2.32*	.24*	1.13*
	22.38	8.42	3.55	9.14	5.02	19.7	10.05	8.21	16.27	14.00
Debt	.048	.006	.252	-.058	-.237*	.266*	.124	.265	.922*	-.001
	.815	.123	.857	-.490	-1.91	5.69	1.18	.744	12.65	9.70
Elast	53.90	89.76*	52.07	64.85	-14.81	22.5*	-25.81	126.58*	2.59	13.44
	1.49	2.04	.924	1.45	-.197	1.97	-1.73	4.47	.216	.967
Fed aid	.436*	.670*	.584*	.237*	1.06*	-.017*	-1.65*	-1.65*	.753*	1.65*
	7.03	4.27	4.58	4.34	6.35	-.266	4.33	-4.70	4.52	9.98

(continued)

125

TABLE 5.4 Continued

State aid	-.111*	.855*	.622*	-.040	-.530	.345*	.006	.093	.221*	-.134
	-4.62	4.67	2.92	-.760	-1.55	5.03	.032	.907	2.35	-1.07
Hetero	236.1	391	-336	143	111	148.7	-37.19	1909	660	-1150
	.890	1.33	-875	.369	.173	.328	-.046	1.87	1.54	-1.86
Func	9.71	3.22	6.81	16.21	7.87	11.87	.108	85.87*	-20.17	25.93
	1.33	.394	.649	1.65	.450	.738	.0003	2.50	-1.28	1.30
Mandates	1.76*	1.29	.965	1.82	.418	2.69*	1.06	11.08*	.652	2.94
	2.32	1.80	.843	1.43	.229	1.79	.543	3.49	.454	1.29
Annex	-13.58*	-7.62	-16.92	3.90	-13.91	-12.7	-7.48	-42.52	-16.75	-48.73*
	-2.03	-.990	-1.98	.430	-1.02	-.940	-.377	-1.51	-1.32	2.64
Fiscal	10.95*	3.97	11.97	-9.80	12.03	-13.56	-24.96*	-2.99	-8.67	.120
	2.04	.785	1.77	-1.26	.757	-1.43	2.29	.888	-.902	.006
R^2	.965	.999	.925	.980	.981	.966	.963	.993	.980	.922
N	419	105	104	106	104	419	104	106	104	105

*T significant at .05 level.

126

TABLE 5.5 Regression Estimates for Full-Time Equivalent Municipal Employment (in 1,000s) by Level of Fiscal Stress for 1974, 1982 (T-values)

| | 1974 | | | | | 1982 | | | | |
| | | Stressed - - - - - - - - - - Healthy | | | | | Stressed - - - - - - - - - - Healthy | | | |
Variable	All Cities	1	2	3	4	All Cities	1	2	3	4
Intercept	-5.46*	-4.7*	-8.5*	-9.2*	-4.0*	-3.11*	-4.7*	-4.7*	-2.23*	-2.56*
	-6.97	-2.02	-4.09	-4.95	4.12	-5.51	-2.64	-3.41	-2.19	-3.45
P.C. tax	.000	.000	.001	.000	-.000	-.001	.004	.001	.000	-.000
	.430	.512	.500	.517	-.588	-.116	-2.80	1.43	.515	-.524
Debt	.000	.000	.001	.001	.000	.000	.001	-.000	.000	.000
	.924	.265	.586	1.07	.267	1.00	1.65	-.009	.719	1.67
Wages	-.000	-.002	-.003	-.002	.000	-.000	.000	-.000	-.001	.000
	-1.29	-.905	-1.63	-1.28	.933	-.538	.161	-1.22	-.878	.313
Elast	-.058	.163	.406	.367	-.550*	.011	.017	.033	.040	.003
	-.280	.251	.770	.826	-2.10	.336	.209	.361	.632	.877
Fed aid	.000	-.000	-.000	.001*	.000	.000	-.003	-.001	.001	-.000
	.957	-.454	-.392	7.01	2.96	1.15	-1.39	-1.27	1.25	-.435

(continued)

127

TABLE 5.5 Continued

State aid	.000*	1.26	.005*	.001	-.002	-.000	-.001	.000	.000	.000
	2.10	.214	1.96	1.40	-1.46	-.018	-1.70	.734	.580	1.29
Hetero	7.15*	5.70	11.87*	12.90*	6.31*	4.98*	7.30	4.83*	4.83*	6.41*
	4.76	1.35	3.22	3.40	2.94	3.83	1.68	1.64	2.12	3.44
Fiscal	.288*	.345*	.278*	.324*	.226*	.312*	.304*	.429*	.226*	.205*
	6.96	2.92	2.82	3.33	3.94	6.85	1.98	4.19	2.64	3.36
Mand	.035*	.036*	.040*	.054*	.016*	.016	.027	.034*	.011*	-.001
	8.17	3.54	3.76	4.46	2.74	3.94	2.53	3.54	1.47	-1.38
Annex	.150*	.066	.192*	.154	.181	.256	.414*	.107	.163*	.343*
	405	.604	2.38	1.78	4.06	6.91	3.87	1.28	2.41	6.00
Func	.33	.321	.355*	.424*	.372	.168	.142*	.214*	.212	.232*
	11.10	4.44	5.58	5.68	7.16	6.30	2.41	3.53	4.16	4.13
R^2	.590	.476	.689	.673	.783	.503	.517	.588	.501	.654
N	419	105	104	106	104	419	104	106	104	105

*T significant at .05 level.

public employment when controlling for both level and change in municipal fiscal stress. This particular finding is discussed in light of the original assertion regarding the politicized nature of municipal public employment because it bears out the principal contention of this article, namely, that attention to endogeneous aspects of local politics as reflected in municipal employment levels and structural changes is a prime and neglected means of understanding stress genesis and management.

Results for the cross-sectional and longitudinal analyses are reported, each with regard to a comparison in predictability for our two dependent variables—total spending and municipal employment.

CROSS-SECTIONAL REGRESSION ESTIMATES:
CASE I—TOTAL PER CAPITA SPENDING

By far, the strongest determinant of total own-source spending (net of intergovernmental aid transfers) is per capita taxes. For all cities this coefficient is nearly 1.00 and does not vary significantly from this level in either year studied. Not surprisingly, city spending rises in a linear fashion with increases in per capita taxes. This finding should not be taken as theoretically trivial. The fact that own-source taxes (net of user fees and charges) closely matches per capita spending suggests that cities are constrained in their spending decisions by the availability of own-source revenues.

As hypothesized, federal and state aid have significant though substantively different effects on municipal spending. In 1974 federal aid had a significant stimulative effect on spending, increasing own-source per capita outlays $.43 for every $1.00 of federal aid. By 1982, however, this stimulative effect was diminished to a fiscally neutral effect on own-source spending. The reduced influence of federal aid is due in part to the Reagan budget cuts (see Nathan and Doolittle, 1983) and increased efforts by local governments to resist the distortionary effects of federal aid requirements (Nathan, 1983).

State aid had a substitutive effect in 1974, reflecting the nonrestrictive requirements associated with these aid transfers. Every dollar of general state assistance actually reduced own-source spending by $.11. Interestingly, however, this effect is reversed in 1982. Cities that received $1.00 more in per capita state aid spent $1.34 in own-source outlays. This stimulative effect is not reflective of any change in the conditional character or level of state aid to cities. Although state aid during this period increased in real dollars, most state aid continued to carry few if any significant program conditions (ACIR, 1978). This finding may represent the effect of a declining revenue base and the need to use state aid to support operating budgets rather than for tax relief. The use of short-term debt to finance city spending not only increased dramatically between 1974 and 1982; this increase had a significant impact on distinguishing cities on total spending in 1982, a condition not observed in 1974: In 1982 cities issuing $1.00 of per capita debt had $.20 higher per capita spending levels.

Greater reliance on inelastic user fees and charges is positively related to higher levels of spending in 1974 and 1982. The size and direction of these coefficients suggest that revenues raised from user fees and utility charges may have exceeded the costs associated with the provision of goods and services. In 1974 cities with a 1% higher reliance on inelastic revenues had a $53.90 higher level of per capita spending. In 1982, however, this effect is significantly reduced (B = $22.50). This change suggests that cities were less able to divert user fees and utility charges to tax relief, reflecting rising costs of production and/or dwindling tax revenues.

State-local relations had a slightly stronger influence, at least in 1974, on municipal spending than originally expected. The provision of greater fiscal discretion to local governments significantly distinguished cities on spending levels. In both 1974 and 1982, the flexibility to raise revenues without prior state approval or restrictions was positively related to spending levels. As expected, the authority to annex adjacent land and population is negatively related to per capita spending in 1974 and 1982, suggesting that this authority is exercised and does net some economies in spending programs. As hypothesized, state mandates have a significant and positive effect on total per capita spending. This effect is significant in both years and actually increased in magnitude in 1982.

The diversity of a city's population had no significant effect on per capita spending in either year. As expected, this measure of the city's population and its composition is not likely to have any demonstrative impact on gross outlays. The fiscal health of a city does not have a significant and independent effect on total spending levels.

The results of the regression analysis for per capita spending are only slightly altered when controlling (by quartile) for the level of fiscal stress. The same revenue variables—per capita taxes, intergovernmental aid transfers, debt, and reliance on user fees and charges—dominate the explanation of per capita spending, independent of the level of fiscal health. With minor exceptions, state-local relations have no significant independent effect on spending when controlling for a city's level of fiscal health. This is a reversal of our findings for the pooled sample, and suggests that stress may have a modest effect on spending. In spite of the general congruence between the structure of our full and partitioned regression models, there are some noteworthy deviations between the two analyses.

In 1974 federal aid had a greater stimulative effect on fiscally healthy rather than stressed cities. We had expected stressed cities to substitute federal monies for own-source revenues, but there is only scant evidence of this occurring in 1982. In 1982 we observe a distinct difference between the fiscal behavior of stressed and healthy cities. Stressed cities spend $1.65 less with each additional dollar of federal aid compared to between $.75 and $1.65 higher levels of spending per dollar of federal aid received by fiscally healthier cities. Stress clearly has a strong and negative effect on these cities' use of federal aid. Greater stress provides a strong incentive to resist the distortionary requirements associated with many federal aid programs. This finding is empirically consistent with case studies of the Reagan budget cuts, particularly among cities already suffering from the effects of a national recession (Nathan and Doolittle, 1983).

Controlling for fiscal stress produces an unexpected 1974 state aid coefficient. Stressed cities were significantly more likely to have experienced a stimulative rather than the expected substitutive effect from state aid transfers. In 1974 the most stressed cities had between $.62 and $.85 higher levels of own-source spending for every additional dollar of state aid they received. Fiscally healthier cities experienced either a neutral or stimulative state aid effect, again a finding that was contrary to our original hypothesis. In 1982 only cities in the second highest category of fiscal health experienced a stimulative aid effect. All other state aid coefficients were insignificant. This finding may reflect in part the inability of stressed cities in 1974 to avoid using state aid to maintain levels of own-source spending rather than for tax relief. Conversely, fiscally healthier cities found own-source revenues adequate for their spending needs and used state aid for tax relief.

CROSS-SECTIONAL REGRESSION ESTIMATES:
CASE II—FULL-TIME EQUIVALENT EMPLOYMENT

As hypothesized, the structure of the model for full-time municipal employment differs significantly from the findings for per capita spending. The dominance of revenue factors in the spending model is replaced in the employment model by local political conditions (i.e., social diversity) and state-local relations. Among revenue variables, only the 1974 state aid coefficient was significant. No other revenue measure, including federal aid and wage levels, was significantly related to the level of public employment. This latter finding is particularly surprising, given previous research that has shown that public employment is strongly influenced by wage rates (Gustley, 1974; Ehrenberg, 1972). In part this finding can be explained by more recent work on public employment (Stein, 1984a), which has shown that negative wage effects on employment levels (i.e., an implicit budget constraint) have declined over time due to earlier distortionary effects of federal aid and the substitution of cheaper part-time workers for full-time workers.

The dominant determinant of municipal public employment is the social diversity of a city's residential population. Cities with a 1% higher level of social diversity have seven more workers per thousand population than their more homogeneous counterparts. Although this effect is diminished slightly in 1982 (B = 4.98), diversity remains the dominant determinant of municipal employment in the 1982 regression model. Greater local autonomy from state-mandated activities and regulations has a strong and positive impact on the level of municipal public employment. Moreover, this effect is substantially stronger in 1982 than 1974. As the national recession continued, restrictive state regulations and mandates effectively curbed cities from expanding their public work forces.

Controlling for the level of fiscal stress does not radically alter these findings. The diversity of the city's population and state-local relations continue to be the dominant determinants of public employment, independent of the level of municipal stress. There is, however, one important deviation in the magnitude of these coefficients across levels of fiscal stress. Diversity has its strongest effect on employment levels in the fiscally healthiest cities. This trend is less obvious in 1974; it is quite pronounced in 1982 (B = 6.41). An inspection of Table 5.5 shows that the social diversity coefficients for moderately stressed cities (category 2) dropped significantly in 1982, suggesting that during the period of a national recession, stressed cities were less responsive to the public employment demands of socially heterogeneous populations. The same trend, however, is also observed for the analysis of the pooled sample.

Our next two cases are summarized in Table 5.6, which reports the regression analysis for change in public employment and spending. All change scores, both dependent and independent, are expressed in con-

TABLE 5.6 Regression Estimates for Change in per Capita Spending and Full-Time Equivalent Employment by Change in Fiscal Stress: 1974-1982 (T-values)

| Variable | Δ PER CAPITA SPENDING | | | | Δ FULL-TIME EMPLOYEES | | | |
| | Change in Fiscal Conditions | | | | Change in Fiscal Conditions | | | |
	All Cities	Worsen	No Change	Improvement	All Cities	Worsen	No Change	Improvement
Intercept	16.09	55.02	45.36	12.45	.615	-.160	.940	.300
	1.05	.140	.750	.321	3.62	.550	.211	.350
Stress 1970	6.45	13.21	3.85	9.17	.012	.011	.017	-.019
	1.69	1.27	.822	.865	2.17	.529	2.74	-.968
Δ P.C. taxes	.999*	.562*	1.03*	1.43*	.000	.000	.000	.000
	14.57	5.24	4.78	12.80	.189	.188	.453	.056
Δ Short debt	.244*	.479*	-.022	-.327*	.000	-.000	.000	.000
	3.49	1.99	-.184	-2.21	.547	-.797	1.53	.923
Δ Elasticity	14.40	21.02	.430	15.90	-.034*	.016	-.050*	-.023*
	1.67	1.28	.034	.878	-2.57	-.471	-2.98	-2.69
Δ Fed aid	1.04*	1.25*	1.58*	.775*	.000	-.003	-.000	-.000
	12.36	3.89	10.83	4.39	.123	-.510	-.854	-.532

(continued)

TABLE 5.6 Continued

	1	2	3	4	5	6	7	8
Δ State aid	.915*	.716*	1.81*	.837*	.000	.000	-.000	-.000
	23.2	4.36	9.57	14.9	1.08	.042	-.640	.071
Δ Hetero	-711	869.5	-1456	-250.8	-.291	-6.45*	3.32*	4.87*
	-1.34	.758	-1.75	-.327	-.356	-2.77	2.95	-2.60
Func	-15.0	-.568	-12.72	-6.75	-.053*	-.037	-.015	-.052
	-1.19	.013	-.627	-.386	-2.74	-.440	-.566	-1.56
Mandates	-.462	2.07	-.076	-1.92	-.009*	-.012	-.007*	-.006
	-.366	.566	-.041	-.935	-4.88	-1.60	-2.98	-1.60
Annex	6.60	-1.04	13.00	13.47	-.021	.035	-.055*	-.041
	.606	-.037	.813	.817	-.126	.638	-2.51	-1.31
Fiscal disc	-2.38	11.81	-12.7	21.13	-.117*	-.068*	-.156*	-.056*
	-.253	.580	-.815	-1.36	-8.10	-1.76	-7.36	-1.86
Δ Wages	NA	NA	NA	NA	-.101	-.000	-.000	-.000
	NA	NA	NA	NA	-.683	.020	.097	.087
R^2	.988	.966	.992	.993	.588	.430	.536	.382
N	405	95	206	104	405	95	206	104

*T significant at .05 level.

stant 1972 dollars. In addition, the lagged value for each dependent variable as well as the lagged stress score were included in the original analysis in order to detect (and correct for) any regression effects (see Campbell and Stanley, 1966; Schrodt and Ward, 1981). With the exception of the lagged stress score, no significant coefficients were observed for any of the lagged dependent measures. The analysis reported in Table 5.6 includes only the lagged stress score for 1970.

REGRESSION ESTIMATES FOR
CHANGE IN SPENDING: CASE III

Changes in per capita spending are driven by the same revenue-based factors that dominated the cross-sectional model (see Table 5.6). Changes in intergovernmental aids, per capita taxes, and short-term debt account for virtually all of the variance in change in real per capita spending. Consistent with the cross-sectional findings, federal aid has a modest stimulative effect on changes in own-source spending. An increase of $1.00 in federal aid was associated with only a $1.04 increase in own-source spending. This effect is considerably smaller than other researchers have observed in earlier periods (ACIR, 1982; Whitman and Kline, 1978). In part, the diminished stimulative effect of federal aid is due to more aggressive resistence to federal aid initiatives. Locales have developed an effective style of implementing federal aid programs, enabling them to avoid some of the more distortionary fiscal requirements attached to federal aid programs (Ingram, 1977).

Consistent with its nonrestrictive character, state aid has a substitutive effect on changes in own-source spending. A $1.00 increase in state aid was associated with only a $.915 increase in local spending, indicating that $.085 of every dollar of state aid was used to reduce or at least stabilize changes in tax and other revenue collections. Increases in short-term debt are positively related to increasing spending, yet this relationship is far from efficient. A $1.00 increase in short-term debt nets only a $.244 increase in spending outlays, indicating that the bulk of this indebtedness goes toward servicing the debt issue. Although the coefficient for change in debt is significant, the cross-sectional debt coefficient is not significant, suggesting that cities have increasingly come to rely on this form of revenue to support operating expenditures. No other variable in the model had a statistically significant effect on change in per capita spending.

Controlling for change in fiscal stress does not alter the thrust of these findings; changes in revenue sources continue to be the dominant determinant of changes in spending across all categories of change in fiscal conditions. The magnitude and in some instances even the direction of these revenue effects vary markedly with the level of change in fiscal conditions. In cities experiencing an improvement in their fiscal conditions a $1.00 increase in own-source taxes was associated with a $1.43 increase in total spending. Declining fiscal conditions raised municipal spending by only $.562 for every additional dollar raised from own-source taxes, indicating a significant degree of tax relief for citizens in these fiscally hard-pressed cities. Spending changes in cities that experienced no change in their fiscal status were associated with a near equal (B = 1.03) rise in per capita taxes.

Change in the use of short-term debt is positively related to change in spending among fiscally declining cities, yet negatively related to spending changes in cities that experienced an improvement in their fiscal condition. For this latter category of cities, increased issuance of short-term debt is positively related to change in spending among fiscally declining cities, yet negatively related to spending changes in cities that experienced an improvement in their fiscal condition. For this latter category of cities, increased issuance of short-term debt is unrelated to increased operating expenses. The negative coefficient indicates that short-term debt in fiscally improving cities was more likely to be used to cover specific cash flow problems arising from differences in the timing of tax collections and spending obligations. This obviously is not the case for fiscally declining cities, who are allocating $.479 of every dollar of short-term debt issued to their operating budget.

Federal aid has an unexpected effect on spending changes when controlling for changes in fiscal stress. Federal aid coefficients were largest and positive in cities experiencing no change in the fiscal health of their community, increasing own-source spending by $1.52 for every additional $1.00 of federal aid received between 1974 and 1982. Moreover, in cities experiencing a declining fiscal climate, the federal aid coefficient was positive (B = 1.25) though smaller in magnitude. Only those cities that experienced an improvement in their fiscal health were able to substitute federal aid monies for own-source spending and revenues successfully, increasing their spending only $.775 for every additional dollar of federal aid received over the ten-year period. A meaningful interpretation of these findings is obscured by our lack of information regarding the specific federal aid programs each category of cities used. Different aid programs are associated with different performance requirements. Consequently, the fiscal effects of aid programs vary as a function of the structure of each program (Oates, 1974). More data are needed on program usage for each city before we can attempt an adequate interpretation of these findings.

Controlling for changes in fiscal health produces significant differences in the relationship between change in state aid allocations and local spending. Moreover, the magnitude and sign of these coefficients are contrary to earlier hypotheses. Cities that experienced any change in their fiscal status (either improvement or decline) substituted state aid monies for own-source spending, doing so at about the same rate (B = .716, B = .837). Cities experiencing no change in the status of their fiscal health, however, increased own-source spending as a result of increased state allocations during the period 1974-1982. Moreover, the state aid coefficient for this category of cities shows that these communities increased their own spending by $1.81 for every additional $1.00 of state aid received. The insignificant coefficient for the lagged 1970 value of fiscal stress rules out the possibility that this population of cities was unusually stressed in both years, possibly accounting for the stimulative effect of state aid. It is possible that these cities received significantly larger amounts of conditional state aid during this period (ACIR, 1982; Morgan and England, 1981). Again, without more detailed data on participation in individual state aid programs, this explanation remains moot.

REGRESSION ESTIMATES FOR CHANGE
IN PUBLIC EMPLOYMENT: CASE IV

As hypothesized and indicated in Table 5.6, the determinants of change in public employment are driven by factors empirically unrelated to changes in spending levels. The regression model for all cities, however, shows that state-local relations or mandates and functional and fiscal discretion have a strong and negative effect, respectively, on the growth of the municipal work force. Cities afforded greater discretion from their states experienced lower levels of growth in the size of their work force, a finding that is counter to our original hypothesis. Those cities prevented (or at least limited) by their states from raising revenues and/or expanding services may use higher employment levels as an alternative strategy for addressing public demand without increasing either revenues or spending. This can be achieved by substituting part-time workers for full-time workers. Part-time workers generally do not receive costly benefits and pensions, keeping the cost of their employment well below that of a full-time worker. Unfortunately our data on employment do not permit us to test this explanation. However, other work (Stein, 1984a) suggests that this strategy is widely used by munici-pal governments. Whether it results in a lower costs-per-worker remains an unexplored empirical question.

Although the cross-sectional coefficient for diversity has a strong positive effect on the level of employment, change in social diversity for the pooled sample is not related to rising employment levels. This raises the possibility that change in diversity is related to changing employ-ment levels only when the fiscal environment provides the proper condi-tions (i.e., fiscal improvement). As cities draw a significantly higher percentage of their revenues from user fees and utility charges, the size of their work force declines. This finding suggests that many of the func-tional activities associated with user fees may be non-labor-intensive (e.g., utilities, licensing operations) and do not drive up the size of a city's labor force as the city expands its use of fees and utility charges.

Controlling for change in fiscal stress alters the structure of our employment model, especially the effect social diversity has on changing employment levels. Increases in social diversity along with a declining fiscal condition are associated with a significant drop in the size of the urban public work force. Growing diversity of a city's population drives up the size of the city's labor force when fiscal conditions have improved or at least remained unchanged. Thus the political effects of growing social diversity on employment are reversed when fiscal conditions are declining. This would suggest that social diversity operates as an implicit control on excessive growth motivated by the political ambitions of incumbent officeholders. Moreover, it is important to note that change in a city's fiscal well-being and not the absolute level of fiscal conditions at a specific point in time mutes the expansionary effect social diversity has on employment levels.

DISCUSSION

The above findings confirm our main thesis: Public employment is closely related to the social composition of a city's electorate and more importantly to changes in the electorate. Although spending decisions are driven by revenue factors that possess both intra- and intergovern-mental sources, employment policy is largely independent of these fiscal considerations. Moreover, state-local relations play a much greater role in structuring municipal employment practices than spending policy, albeit in an unexpected fashion. The fact that the determinants of these two policy measures differ lends further support for our view of urban policy as multifaceted.

Fiscal stress appears not to be a significant factor in shaping municipal spending decisions. This is not to suggest that cities suffering from fiscal stress do not alter their spending decisions, but rather that stress does not alter the basic determinants of spending (i.e., revenue-based factors) or their dominance of this policy output. Stress does, however, have a significant though intervening effect on municipal public employment. Cities will expand their work forces when the changes in the composition of the population and electorate create political uncertainty, but only when the fiscal climate is not declining. The generally weak fiscal condition for most of the cities studied muted the expansionary effect of increasing social diversity on municipal employment. In many of these cities out-migration of middle-class whites (due in part to the deteriorating conditions of the city) propelled black and other minority voters into a position of political influence. Unfortunately, the influence of these groups was not translated into higher public employment levels for blacks because the same forces that impelled blacks and other minorities to a position of political power (i.e., white flight) had also depleted the city of the revenue base necessary for expanding the public work force.

Implicit in our political explanation of public employment has been a high degree of flexibility available to city officials in the use of public workers. The substitution of part-time workers for full-time workers and the savings this strategy might provide has not been empirically tested in this chapter. Future research needs to examine this form of strategic behavior and its linkage with overt political interests.

The political content of municipal public employment has received strong support. It suggests that both the causes and management of stress may be reflected here rather than in measures of total spending due to the effects on the latter of incrementalism. Further refinements and tests should concentrate on (1) detecting a municipal public employment cycle corresponding to competitive municipal elections, (2) the actual degree of substitution of part-time for full-time workers, (3) the resulting savings (if any) in wages, pensions, and benefit packages, and (4) the interaction between determinants of public employment.

APPENDIX A
OPERATIONALIZATION OF MEASURES

Fiscal stress. Five macro socioeconomic conditions define stress: change in population size (1970-1980), unemployment (percentage of total work force), dependent population (percentage of population below 18 and over 65 years of age), per capita personal income, and median owner-occupied home value. Each indicator was standardized and summed for each city and year. As noted earlier, stress operates as a control variable and cities were grouped for analysis by their quartile ranking on the standardized stress score (or change in stress) by year. A wide range of stress measures have been advanced in the literature (see Ross and Greenfield, 1980). Our goal was to operationalize stress in such a way as to (1) distinguish it from the effects of stress (i.e., diminished tax base and increased indebtedness) and (2) draw upon the widest interpretation of the concept. Our own conceptualization is closest to the Nathan and Adam's (1976) hardship index, which defines stress in terms of declining population and its consequent effects.

Fiscal scarcity. Two measures of scarcity are examined: per capita municipal taxes and per capita short-term debt. The former is a widely studied determinant of urban policy outputs, and tests the degree to which local policy outputs are driven by resources indigenous to the city. As noted earlier, the issuance of short-term debt may be just a means of adjusting the cash flow difference between the collection of revenues and expenditure outlays. A positive, and over time, increasing debt coefficient would suggest that short-term debt is used for operating expenditures and not merely as a temporary means of reconciling differences between tax and spending cash flows.

Social diversity. Social diversity is defined in terms of the composition of a city's resident adult population (i.e., those over 18 years of age). Lieberson (1969) has devised a diversity-in-population measure that is interpreted in probability terms because it represents the proportion of characteristics on which a randomly selected pair of individuals from the same city will differ on a set of n-chotomous traits. The measure, constructed for each city, is based on the following computation formula:

$$A_w(\text{Diversity}) - 1 - P(Y^2)$$

Where:

Y = The proportion of the population falling into a given group

Y = The number of groups

P = The total number of categories within all groups

Obviously the choice of group traits is critical to defining social diversity/heterogeneity. Six group traits are identified as relevant to city politics. They include length of residence in the city (less than five years and more than five years), occupation (manufacturing, sales and retail, government, health, and self-employed), home ownership, education (some college, no college), race (white, black, and hispanic) and personal income (five income categories defined in terms of constant 1972 dollars).

Intergovernmental measures. The inclusion of state and federal aid in the same analysis of urban policy outputs poses a potential measurement problem. State aid allocations include federal aid monies that are passed through to municipal governments. Regression estimates might be biased by the inclusion of state assistance with federal monies. Though this would be a real threat if we were studying special districts and county governments, it is of minimal importance in the study of general purpose municipal governments. The ACIR's (1980) analysis shows that state aid passed through to substate units of government go almost exclusively to school districts and county governments (for highways and welfare) and not general purpose governments.

State-local relations. Four scale scores of state-local relations are included in our analysis: local, functional, fiscal and annexation authority, and the number of state-mandated service activities. Each local authority scale is a positive measure of local discretion and is based on individual state statutes. The sources for these data are Hill (1978) and ACIR (1977). An ACIR (1978) survey of state governments identified 77 mandates currently employed in the 50 states. The percentage of total state mandates was calculated for all cities within each state.

Dependent measures. The dependent measure of municipal spending is expressed as per capita own-source expenditures (i.e., net of all intergovernmental transfers). Employment is measured in terms of full-time equivalent city workers per 1,000 population. This measure combines both full-time and part-time city workers. The regression equation for full-time equivalent city employment also includes the average monthly paycheck per worker. Previous research on public employment has identified the operation of a budget constraint between wages and employment levels. Cities either reduce their wage rates to maintain a growing work force or reduce the size of the work force to increase wages. Evidence of a negative wage coefficient supports earlier descriptions of the political and fiscal flexibility associated with public employment.

Change scores were calculated for all measures except state-local relations scales. The 1977 status of these state statutes was employed in the analysis of changes in urban policy outputs. Other researchers (MacManus and Thomas, 1979) provide data that show that during the period studied little if any significant change occurred in the status of these state laws. All fiscal change measures (both dependent and independent) were deflated to constant 1972 dollars.

REFERENCES

BAHL, R. (1984) Financing State and Local Government in the 1980s. New York: Oxford University Press.

———(1969) Metropolitan City Expenditures: A Comparative Analysis. Lexington: University of Kentucky Press.

BISH, R. and C. OSTROM (1976) Understanding Urban Government: Metropolitan Reform Considered. Washington, DC: American Enterprise Institute.

BROWN, L., J. FOSSETT, and K. PALMER (1984) The Changing Politics of Federal Grants. Washington, DC: Brookings Institute.

CALLOW, A. (1966) The Tweed Ring. New York: New York University Press.

CAMPBELL, D. and J. STANLEY (1966) Experimental and Quasi-Experimental Designs for Research. Chicago: Rand McNally.

CHAPMAN, J. (1981) "Fees and charges, rule, use, and land development in post Proposition 13." The Urban Interest 3: 13-21.

CHO, Y. H. (1972) "Tax structure and municipal debt in large Ohio cities," pp. 56-94 in J. Gargan and J. J. Coke (eds.) Political Behavior and Public Issues in Ohio. Kent, Ohio: Kent State University Press.

CLARK, T. (1981) "Urban fiscal strain: trends and policy options," in Norman Walzer and D. Chicoine (eds.) Financing State and Local Governments in 1980: Issues and Trends. Cambridge, MA: OGH.

———and L. C. FERGUSON (1983) City Money. New York: Columbia University Press.

COURANT, P., E. GRAMLICH, and D. L. RUBENFELD (1979) "Public employee market power and the level of government spending." American Economic Review 69: 806-817.

CRECINE, J. P. (1969) Governmental Problem Solving. Chicago: Rand McNally.

DAVIS, O., A. H. DEMPSTER, and A. WILDAVSKY (1966) "A theory of the budgetary process." American Political Science Review 10: 529-547.

DORSETT, L. (1972) "The city boss and the reformer: a reappraisal." Pacific Northwest Quarterly 63: 150-154.

DYE, T. R. and T. L. HURLEY (1979) "The responsiveness of federal and state governments to urban problems." Journal of Politics 40 (February): 196-207.

EHRENBERG, R. G. (1972) The Demand for State and Local Government Employees. Lexington, MA: D. C. Heath.

FISHER, C. (1976) The Urban Experience. Chicago: Harcourt Brace Jovanovich.

FISHER, G. (1981) "The changing role of property taxation," pp. 35-60 in N. Walzer and D. Chicoine (eds.) Financing State and Local Government in the 1980s. Cambridge, MA: OGH.

FOSSETT, J. W. (1984) Federal Aid to Big Cities, The Politics of Dependence. Washington, DC: Brookings Institute.

GRAMLICH, E. M. (1977) "Intergovernmental grants: a review of the empirical literature," pp. 219-240 in W. E. Oates (ed.) The Political Economy of Fiscal Federalism. Lexington, MA: Lexington Books.

GUSTELY, R. D. (1974) Municipal Public Employment and Public Expenditure. Lexington, MA: D. C. Heath.

HALL, J. S. (1979) The Impact of Federal Grants on the City of Phoenix (Washington, DC. U.S. Department of Labor and Commerce, Report MEL 79-25(3). October 1979, p. 61.

HILL, M. (1978) State Laws Governing Local Government Structure and Administration. Athens, GA: Institute of Government.

HIRSCHMAN, A. O. (1970) Exit Voice and Loyalty. Cambridge, MA: Harvard University Press.

HUTCHESON, J. (1982) "Fight, flee, or acquiesce? Responses to urban discontent." Journal of Urban Affairs 4: 1-19.

INGRAM, H. (1977) "Policy implementation through bargaining: the case of federal grants-in-aid." Public Policy 25: 499-526.

JUDD, D. (1984) The Politics of American Cities: Private Power and Public Policy. Little, Brown.

LARKEY, P. (1975) Evaluating Public Programs: The Impact of General Revenue Sharing in Municipal Government. Princeton: Princeton University Press.

LEIBERSON, S. (1969) "Measuring population diversity." American Sociological Review 34: 850-862.

LEVINE, C. (1980) Managing Fiscal Stress. Chatham, NJ: Chatham.

———I. W. RUBIN, and G. G. WOLOHOJIAN (1981) The Politics of Retrenchment. Beverly Hills, CA: Sage.

LEWIS, G. (1984) "Municipal expenditures through thick and thin." Publius 14: 31-39.

MacMANUS, S. A. (1984) Federal Aid Dependency in Houston. Washington, DC: Brookings Institute.

———(1983) "State government: the overseer of municipal finance," pp. 145-185 in A. Sbragia, The Municipal Money Chase. Boulder, CO: Westview.

———(1979) "The impacts of federal grants on the city of Houston." Washington, D.C., U.S. Departments of Labor and Commerce, Report MEL 79-25(2), November 1979, p. 27.

———and R. THOMAS (1979) "Expanding the tax base: does annexation make a difference?" Urban Interest 1: 15-28.

MLADENKA, K. (1984) "Implementing urban services," in G. Edwards (ed.) Public Policy Implementation. Greenwich, CT: JAI.

MORGAN, D. and R. ENGLAND (1981) "Analyzing urban stress among large U.S. cities." Presented at the 1981 meeting of the Southwest Political Science Association, Dallas, Texas.

MUNNS, J. (1975) "System models and urban policy." Western Political Quarterly 28: 112-135.

MUSHKIN, S. and C. VEHRON (1981) "User fees and charges," pp. 213-222 in C. Levine (ed.) Managing Fiscal Stress: The Crisis in the Public Sector. Chatham, NJ: Chatham.

NATHAN, R. (1983) "The behavior of state and local governments under federal grants: toward a predictive theory." Political Science Quarterly 99: 102-118.

———and C. ADAMS (1976) "Understanding central city hardship." Political Science Quarterly 91: 47-62.

———and F. DOOLITTLE (1983) The Consequences of Cuts. Princeton, NJ: PUURC.

NEIMAN, M. and C. LOVELL (1982) "Federal and state mandating: a first look at the mandate terrain." Administration and Society 14: 343-372.

———(1981) "Mandating as a policy issue: the definitional problem." Policy Studies Journal 9: 667-681.

————(1980) "Federal and state requirements: impacts on local governments." Urban Interest 2: 45-52.

OATES, W. (1974) Fiscal Federalism. New York: Harcourt Brace Jovanovich.

PELESSERO, J. (1984) "State aid and city needs: an examination of residual aid to large cities," Journal of Politics 46: 916-934.

PETERSON, P. E. (1981) City Limits. Chicago: University of Chicago Press.

ROSS, J. and J. GREENFIELD (1980) "Measuring the health of cities," in C. H. Levine and I. Rubin (eds.) Fiscal Stress and Public Policy. Beverly Hills, CA: Sage.

SCHRODT, P. A. and M. D. WARD (1981) "Statistical inference in incremental and difference equation formulations." American Journal of Political Science 25 (November): 815-832.

SHEFTER, M. (1978) "Party and patronage: Germany, England and Italy." Politics and Society 7: 403-445.

————(1977) "New York's fiscal crisis: the politics of inflation and retrenchment." Public Interest 48: 98-127.

STEIN, R. M. (1984a) "Municipal public employment: an examination of intergovernmental influences." American Journal of Political Science 28: 636-654.

————(1984b) "State regulation and the political consequences of urban fiscal stress." Publius 14: 41-54.

————(1982) "The political economy of municipal functional responsibility." Social Science Quarterly 63: 530-548.

————(1981) "The allocation of federal aid monies." American Political Science Review 75 (June): 334-343.

STONECASH, J. (1981) "State policies regarding local resource acquisition: disorder, compensatory adjustment or coherent restraint." American Politics Quarterly 4: 401-425.

SULLIVAN, J. L. (1973) "Political correlates of social economy and religious diversity in the American states." Journal of Politics 35: 70-84.

TIEBOUT, C. M. (1956) "A pure theory of local expenditures." Journal of Politics 37: 392-416.

U.S. Advisory Commission of Intergovernmental Relations [ACIR] (1982) Federal Grants: Their Effects on State-Local Expenditures. Employment Levels, Wage Rates. Washington, DC: Government Printing Office.

————(1980) Recent Trends in Federal and State Aids to Local Governments. Washington, DC: Government Printing Office.

————(1978) State Mandating of Local Expenditures, Washington, DC: Government Printing Office.

————(1977) The State and Intergovernmental Aids. Washington, DC: Government Printing Office.

————(1976) Pragmatic Federalism. Washington, DC: Government Printing Office.

WHITMAN, R. D. and R. KLINE (1978) The Fiscal Impact of Revenue Sharing in Comparison with Other Federal Aid: An Evaluation of Recent Empirical Findings. Washington, DC: Urban Institute.

WIKSTROM, G., Jr. (1974) Municipal Government Response to Urban Riots. San Francisco: R & E Research Associates.

WIRT, F. M. (1985) "The dependent city? External influences upon local control." Journal of Politics 47: 83-112.

WOLFINGER, R. E. (1974) The Politics of Progress. Englewood Cliffs, NJ: Prentice-Hall. Prentice-Hall.

6

Electoral Coalitions, Minority Mayors, and the Contradictions in the Municipal Policy Agenda

DENNIS R. JUDD

THE COMPELLING NATURE OF THE
DOWNTOWN DEVELOPMENT AGENDA

Entrepreneurial strategies constitute the heart of the municipal policy agenda of the 1980s. Virtually all municipal public leaders consider economic development to be the linchpin that supports every activity undertaken by local government. As an administrative assistant to Denver's Mayor Federico Peña stated in a 1984 interview, "We probably will be criticized by some for focusing too much on downtown. People will ask, 'What does Saks Fifth Avenue have to do with the neighborhoods?' The answer is that downtown retailing has everything to do with the neighborhoods. The city needs the revenue" (Gougeon, 1984).

Federico Peña is one of the new crop of aggressive, generally young, somewhat unconventional mayors of the 1980s. What makes them unconventional is that many of them engage in populist rhetoric, and they have been elected with the support of new coalitions composed of minority voters, whites who have become disaffected from the two-party system, first-time young voters, traditional liberals and yuppies, and, in some cities, feminists and gays. In most cases the downtown-oriented civic establishment has greeted their election with nervous anticipation or even outright alarm, fearful of a Dennis Kucinich-style assault on civic business-as-usual.[1]

What makes these mayors conventional is their acceptance—once elected—of the necessity to subsidize private sector activity in their cities. Coleman Young is as likely as any big city mayor to have pushed for programs of redistribution as well as growth. He was a Marxist labor organizer in the 1950s who was blacklisted by both the United Auto Workers and the auto companies. But since being elected as Detroit's first black mayor in 1973, he has aggressively pursued corporate investment. The Renaissance Center has been supported with millions of dollars in tax abatements and federal subsidies. In the early 1980s Detroit engaged in one of the nation's most controversial urban redevelopment projects, involving the clearing of 465 acres of land in a working-class, ethnic, and black area known as Poletown, in an attempt to keep a General Motors Cadillac plant in the city. Young has fully accepted a logic of growth that makes clearance and subsidy projects inevitable:

> Those are rules and I'm going by the goddamn rules. This suicidal outthrust competition . . . has got to stop but until it does, I mean to compete. It's too bad we have a system where dog eats dog and the devil takes the hindmost. But I'm tired of taking the hindmost [Greider, 1978; in Swanstrom, 1985: 3].

Mayor Young's attitude is hardly unique. Almost every American city is trying to outbid its neighbors in pursuit of its share of national, regional, and economic growth. A complex assortment of weapons is being used in these wars, including tax abatements and rollbacks, tax increment financing, sales tax exemptions, guaranteed loans, industrial bond financing, free industrial sites, and so on. Despite the fact that the Reagan Administration proposal for urban enterprise zones has not been passed by Congress, these zones are becoming more widely used year by year. At the beginning of 1984 nine states had enacted zone legislation and there were 180 designated zones (Sabre Foundation, 1983: 1). Nearly half the states had passed enterprise zone legislation by the end of 1984.

These policies are based on false premises. The scholarly consensus is overwhelming that tax incentives offered by local governments do not materially influence investment decisions (e.g., Wasylenko, 1981; Schmenner, 1980; Maxwell and Aronson, 1977; Peirce et al., 1979; Moriarty et al., 1980; Vaughan, 1979). Taxes are low on the list of business expenses as a factor of production (U.S. Department of Commerce, 1975), and there seems to be no relationship between tax levels among states and growth rates in manufacturing or service employment (Swanstrom, 1985: 142-145). In a study of business location studies conducted since the 1920s, Michael Wasylenko (1981: 155) concluded that "taxes and fiscal inducements have very little if any effect on industrial location decisions. Thus, state and local policies designed to attract business are generally wasted government resources."

Economic development incentives need not be effective to be favored by urban political leaders. Mayors are caught between opposing forces: They are expected to find solutions to their cities' problems, but they also frequently command diminishing resources with which to implement effective policy responses. As Theodore Lowi (1979: 47) has pointed out, "Most cities [find] themselves literally too small to handle their policy problems but politically too weak to resist trying." In such a circumstance, public officials find that economic growth policies carry important symbolic value, giving the voting public the impression that aggressive, creative leadership is being applied to the municipality's problems—even if, in the short run, city services and budgetary problems remain largely unchanged.

Even if a mayor were to challenge the idea that tax abatements and subsidies were the cure-all for the city's ills, national policy would stand in the way. The Reagan Administration has sharply reduced federal urban aid, proclaiming that "the private market is more efficient than federal program administrators in allocating dollars" (U.S. Department of Housing and Urban Development [HUD], 1982: 2, 23). According to the administration, the fortunes of individual cities will be determined by their success at adapting their local economies to national economic changes. Thus urban political leaders are instructed to become entrepreneurs who promote their jurisdictions to the private sector: "State and local governments will find it is in their interests to concentrate on increasing their attractiveness to potential investors, residents, and visitors" (HUD, 1982: 14).

Long before the new federal pressures, mayors felt that pursuing economic development was an urgent priority. But no big city mayor, however politically conservative, can ignore the fact that one of the central tasks of local government is also managing conflict. This is especially obvious to those "new-breed" mayors who have put together electoral coalitions that may be impatient for the benefits of growth to trickle down. Thus there are tensions in the current growth strategies. How the conflicts between economic growth and the need for social cohesion will be managed is the most important issue for American cities in the 1980s.

THE DEVELOPING CONTRADICTIONS

By 1985 there were nineteen black mayors in cities with populations over 100,000. Baltimore remains the only city of this size with a majority black population that has not elected a black mayor. Black mayors govern in four of the ten largest cities—Chicago, Detroit, Los Angeles, and Philadelphia. Three big cities, Denver, San Antonio, and Miami, have elected Hispanic mayors.

Of course, a minority mayor may not necessarily push for a new municipal agenda. Coleman Young and Andrew Young, for example, preside over conventional, old-style downtown-growth politics in Detroit and Atlanta (Young, 1981; Davis, 1984). Lionel Wilson, the mayor of Oakland, California, has led a fight to cut municipal expenditures and to bring more business investment to that city. Wilson Goode campaigned for the mayoralty of Philadelphia in 1983 on a classic reform platform, promising to streamline city bureaucracies, build a convention center, improve the port, and promote economic development (Davis, 1984: 36). Indeed, because the coalitions that elect them are usually so tenuous, minority mayors probably feel that it is necessary to be cautious about any controversial policy initiatives. A major recent study, in fact, found that black urban officials expressed attitudes and followed policies not distinctly different from white urban leaders regarding levels of city taxation and indebtedness (Clark and Ferguson, 1983: 144-148).

However, it seems certain that pressures on black leaders to advocate progressive policies are accelerating. The Jesse Jackson presidential campaign, with its unprecedented successes at mobilizing new voters, played on massive dissatisfaction with the current two-party system and with traditional policy prescriptions (Muwakkil, 1985: 2, 6; James and Phillips, 1984). For more than twenty years public opinion polls have documented a wide gap between black and white attitudes on social welfare spending and government services (Karnig and Welch, 1980; Clark and Ferguson, 1983). The preference by blacks for higher spending levels has remained remarkably stable over time (Welch and Combs, 1983). Possibly because the general preferences of blacks have not changed much for a long period, there is more agreement between the policy views of black public officials and black voters, regardless of social class, than between white officials and the white electorate (Karnig and Welch, 1980: 11).

The first black mayors of major American cities—Richard Hatcher in Gary, Indiana, and Carl Stokes in Cleveland—successfully pushed for more spending for health, education, housing, and job training programs, and increases in federal grants (Levine, 1972; Nelson and Meranto, 1976). Subsequent studies have confirmed that cities with black mayors and council members have a higher proportion of social welfare expenditures (Karnig and Welch, 1980). A brilliant study that measured the degree of incorporation of blacks and Hispanics into the politics of ten California cities concluded that political incorporation was associated with policies desired by minorities. Further, in several of the cities "Political incorporation was responsible for dramatic changes in bureaucratic decision rules in many policy areas" such as city hiring and contracting procedures (Browning et al., 1984: 251).

The California study also found that federal employment and social programs had the effect of stimulating "demand-protest and electoral mobilization by increasing the resources available to minorities and the cadre of minority leaders committed to mobilization" (Browning et al., 1984: 252).

Now that the federal government has broken its 20-year alliance with the civil rights movement and also slashed urban and social programs, a new politics is certain to appear in cities with large minority populations. Voter registration drives have created urban constituencies strongly opposed to federal cutbacks, and have vastly increased black and Hispanic participation in city elections (James and Phillips, 1984). The mobilization of new voters has sharpened the pressure on local elected officials, as civil rights and community organizations focus attention away from the federal government and toward states and localities. States and cities have, as a result, opposed the federal government on a variety of issues, including the civil rights retreat launched by the Justice Department (Pear, 1985: 1, 13).

Thus, it seems likely that most minority mayors will either favor progressive policies to begin with or be forced to move in that direction. Nearly all black mayors win office by gaining an overwhelming proportion of black votes, usually more than 95%, and a relatively smaller percentage of white votes—typically 10% to 20%. The key to victory is a combination of huge black majorities and heavier-than-usual turnout. For example, Wilson Goode received 97% of the black vote in the Philadelphia primary election held on May 18, 1983, while attracting 23% of the vote in white areas (*New York Times*, 1983a: I, 21A). In Chicago's general election of April 12, 1983, Harold Washington received 98% of the black vote, 58% of the Hispanic vote, and 18% of the white vote (*New York Times*, 1983b: I, 13A). When black candidates run for office, voting divides along racial lines (Karnig and Welch, 1980; Watson, 1984). Even in their reelection campaigns, black incumbents rely on racial bloc voting by the black electorate to keep them in office, though turnout and voter interest does decline from the first campaign (Watson, 1984).

Political pressures do not dictate a policy response—they only provide a context for action. The variety of policy responses to the contradictions between downtown-oriented growth policies and demands for neighborhood development, jobs, and social welfare programs can best be discovered through case studies of individual cities. By mobilizing distinctly populist electoral coalitions, two big cities have recently elected minority mayors: Denver and Chicago. In both cities, mayoral candidates Federico Peña and Harold Washington ran campaigns that promised new policy initiatives responsive to neighborhoods and minority constituencies. But the postelection policies have been completely different. Denver is a city in the process of repackaging the old downtown-growth policies into a bright new wrapper more palatable to minorities and neighborhoods. Chicago's mayor, on the other hand, has redefined the city's growth priorities to create local jobs, assist small businesses and cooperatives, and rejuvenate neighborhoods—all in the context of bitter opposition from entrenched city bureaucracies and the remnants of the old Democratic machine.

DENVER: REPACKAGING THE DOWNTOWN DEVELOPMENT AGENDA

Economic growth, not decline, would seem to be at the heart of many of Denver's problems. Over the past few years, some of the dominant issues in Colorado have included air pollution, urban sprawl, water shortages, and traffic congestion. Denver has participated in the region's growth: In the 1980s a forest of skyscrapers has shot up. In and near downtown, luxury condominiums have been replacing run-down commercial or residential uses.

The Denver metropolitan area's 34% employment increase ranked second only to Houston's job growth from 1970 to 1978 (Gladstone and Associates, 1978: 3). Between 1970 and 1980, per capita income increased by 27%, retail sales grew by 12.6% annually, and the unemployment rate increased by only 0.46% (Denver Regional Council on Governments [DRCOG], 1983: vi). Economic experts in 1980 predicted "continued economic expansion for the Denver metropolitan area economy for at least the next decade" (Gladstone and Associates, 1978: 3). Coping with growth that supported such optimism and protecting the quality of life appeared to be the greatest challenge for the region and for the City of Denver as well.

But the energy boom was short-lived. The national recession of 1981 and falling oil prices worried Denver's urban leadership. Optimism about sustained regional growth had fueled a burst of downtown office construction that far exceeded demand once the recession hit. In 1984 Denver had the highest downtown office vacancy rate in the nation at 28.1%—more than double the average for the nation (Wilkinson, 1984: D1). A new language of economic decline entered Denver's mayoral race in 1983. By the time the newly elected mayor, Federico Peña, delivered his first State of the City address in July 1984, he had thoroughly adopted the view that Denver had to seek new downtown investment:

> We are in jeopardy of losing our place as the dominant center of commercial activity in the metro area. If we cannot succeed in expanding the economic base of our city by creating new jobs, increasing retail sales and adding new development, we will be unable to avoid cutbacks in services, meet the need of our disadvantaged, or reinvest in our neighborhoods at a level sufficient to insure their continued health [Peña, 1984a].

CITY LEADERSHIP DURING THE 1970s

Growth policies in Denver always have been narrowly targeted toward downtown projects (Judd, in Fainstein et al., 1983). During the years when Denver's central business district changed from older, red-brick and sandstone commercial buildings to a forest of skyscrapers, William H. McNichols served as mayor.

"Mayor Bill," as many Denverites affectionately called him, was first elected in 1968. McNichols was a cigar-chomping, progrowth Democrat who applied much of his authority and time toward encouraging private sector initiative and development downtown. During the 1970s a new art museum was built, along with a new sports arena, an expanded sports stadium, and a higher education campus next to downtown. McNichols succeeded in getting over $400 million in bonds approved for public improvements, a feat that earned him the nickname, "Bill the bondsman"(Kelly, 1974: 259). Through the Skyline Project, the Denver Urban Renewal Authority (DURA) presided over the reconstruction of a 27-block area in downtown Denver. By the fall of 1984 nearly a billion dollars of public and private funds had been spent on construction in the Skyline Project (DURA, 1984).

A NEW ELECTORAL COALITION

On June 21, 1983, 36-year-old Federico Peña defied the political odds-makers and captured the mayor's office. His campaign manager exulted, "Taking someone with a five percent name recognition who happens to be Hispanic in a city with an 18 percent Hispanic population—that has got to be something of a major political event in the city's history, if not the state and region" (Delsohn, 1984: 15A). Peña's election was, indeed, a unique event, marking the first time that a Hispanic mayor had been elected in a major U.S. city that was not itself predominantly Hispanic.

The coalition that put Peña into office included thousands of liberals who had consistently voted for Representative Patricia Schroeder and Senator Gary Hart, but who had never been motivated to vote in large numbers in local elections. The disparate group included blacks and Hispanics, labor, gays, some leading business figures, women's groups, environmentalists, neighborhood activists, the handicapped, and even three of the candidates that Peña had defeated in the primary election.

To build this electoral coalition, Peña ran an issue-oriented campaign under the campaign theme, "Imagine a Great City." In a series of issue papers distributed as part of his campaign literature, he advocated new policies on air pollution, airport expansion, neighborhood planning, Denver's financial future, economic development and job creation, and planning for and managing the physical development of the city. He promised to open city hall to neighborhood groups, minorities, and others who had previously been shut out of city government. And he stressed the need for economic development and long-term planning. Peña charged that McNichols had cut back the city planning staff and almost eliminated neighborhood planning, policies he vowed to reverse.

In contrast to the campaigns in Chicago and Philadelphia that same spring, the campaign and election in Denver were notable for their lack of overt racism. Peña's Hispanic background was seldom mentioned in public. He managed to avoid the topic almost entirely. Peña believed, "When I have a chance to meet people and talk to people the last thing they think of is I'm Hispanic" (Yack, 1983: 7B). Peña has persisted in downplaying his minority status while in office. He repeatedly turned down offers to participate in nationwide Hispanic political forums. He also avoided the spotlight during the Hispanic delegates' movement to abstain on the first ballot at the 1984 Democratic National Convention in protest over the Simpson-Mazzoli immigration bill.

Peña consistently maintained that Denver had "gone beyond questions of ethnic background" (Walker, 1983: 15A). The election results revealed Peña successfully had brought together a complex electoral coalition. An intensive voter registration failed to achieve its goal of 16,000 new Hispanic voters before the primary. Fewer than one-fourth of that number had registered (Delsohn, 1983a: 1B). It turned out that Peña did not have to rely on new Hispanic voters to win the May 17 primary. Peña finished first in a field of seven candidates. McNichols came in third. Peña's challenger for the general election was former District Attorney Dale Tooley, who attempted throughout the campaign to characterize Peña as too liberal and inexperienced.

On June 21, 1983, a record 71.5% of the registered voters went to the polls. Peña won by a narrow margin, 51.4% of the total vote, to Tooley's 48.6% (Delsohn, 1983b: 1A). Peña had sealed the victory by adding more than 5,000 new voters to the rolls in the heavily minority-populated western and northern districts of the city. He won the northeast districts (52% black and 21% Hispanic) by four to one. New voters, blacks, and Hispanics, together with the other groups in his electoral coalition, put Peña over the top.

THE DOWNTOWN GROWTH IMPERATIVE

Federico Peña captured the mayor's office on the strength of a coalition composed of diverse groups that had never before had much influence in local politics. The new mayor moved immediately to follow through on many of his campaign promises. He pledged to open city government leadership positions to women and minorities. With regard to the neighborhoods, Peña had pledged that they would "have a partner, rather than an adversary" in the mayor's office (Peña, 1983: 3). To gather information from neighborhood groups he initiated "town meetings" in each council district. Peña increased the size of the neighborhood planning staff from three to eight people and ordered a traffic mitigation study of the one-way streets running through the neighborhoods toward downtown.

Neighborhood groups had strenuously lobbied against the one-ways but had met with firm resistance from the McNichols Administration. In the summer of 1984, Denver Planning Director William Lamont announced that some of the one-ways would definitely be converted into two-way streets (Delsohn, 1984: 18A). A year later this had still not been accomplished.

It would be misleading to concentrate on Peña's symbolic overtures to the neighborhoods. In fact, economic development has become the administration's first priority.

The Peña Administration's overall economic development strategy is borrowed directly from the 1979 Economic Development Program and other plans previously adopted by the McNichols Administration. Peña's economic development team feels that "while some refining and elaboration of this work is needed . . . this should not be the main concern of a City economic development program at this point. Instead, the City should focus on the proposed new initiatives which are directed at implementing or *doing* economic development, not further planning for it" (City and County of Denver, 1984: 1). The principal objective of the city's program is enhancement of the city's economic condition:

> Unless the City's revenue base substantially is enhanced, further reductions in service delivery and increases in taxes will be required. Such actions could easily make Denver less attractive for both residential and business locations which would further aggravate the City's economic condition. This is the single most compelling reason for the City to undertake a strong economic development program [City and County of Denver, 1984: 1].

Denver has enlisted in the competitive race to attract new investment, sales, and jobs. Peña has consolidated the Planning Office, the Zoning Office, and the Community Development Agency under a new director of Planning and Development. An Economic Development Office has been placed within the Planning and Development Department to coordinate the city's economic development initiatives and to oversee such programs as industrial revenue bonds, the city's proposed foreign trade zone, neighborhood business revitalization activities, business information services, and public relations for the city.

Several economic development projects have been proposed. For example, Peña has been working fervently to develop a new convention center as "the major economic development project Denver undertakes in this decade" (City and County of Denver, 1984: 6). According to the mayor, the existing convention facilities are inadequate for large national conventions. A new convention center and better marketing of the cultural attractions downtown are considered essential for attracting more visitors.

Another initiative illustrates the Peña Administration's economic development priorities. On July 8, 1984, Peña announced that his administration and the downtown business development corporation, the Denver Partnership, would cooperate in drawing up a new downtown master plan. The plan, to be completed by early 1986, is designed to direct and promote development in and around the central business district. A 27-member panel serves as the steering committee for the project.

Some neighborhood groups were concerned that downtown interests were overrepresented on the committee. Five Denver Partnership members were included, compared to three seats for neighborhood leaders. The Denver Partnership provided 75% of the initial funding and two-thirds of the staff for the eventual $3 million planning project. William Fleissig, Denver's downtown planner hired in 1984, explained that the Partnership has a dominant voice in the downtown plan because "We just didn't have the core staff or the money to do it ourselves" (Flynn, 1984: 16).

The Peña Administration asserts that other development priorities must follow the revitalization of the central business district. Very substantial subsidies are being offered, in the form of below-market rents, to attract a major national retailer downtown. Big-name retailers are considered pivotal to revive the image of downtown and to increase sales tax revenues. According to Mayor Peña, "If in a major city like Denver you have a downtown which is not full of people and where people are literally gone at 5:30 in the afternoon, then you begin to have questions about how exciting that city is" (Flynn, 1984: 25).

RESPONSE FROM THE NEIGHBORHOODS AND MINORITIES

Soon after his election, Federico Peña attended a symposium for recently elected mayors at Harvard. Peña was surprised to hear the new mayors complain that the main obstacle to governance in their cities was animosity between the central business district and the neighborhoods over development priorities. Most of the new mayors, including Peña, had been elected on platforms advocating more influence for neighborhoods. But following their elections they faced the problem of heightened expectations and inadequate public resources. Peña did not sense this kind of conflict in Denver, and wondered why (Parr, 1984).

Part of the explanation may be that Peña has successfully invoked the symbols of open and responsive government even while not changing the substance of development priorities. Peña was careful not to make specific promises that he could not keep. He promised openness, and proceeded to hold town meetings. He promised representation, and began appointing minority and neighborhood representatives to a variety of posts. Perhaps most important, Peña promised to go to work to improve the city's economic condition and to ensure the vitality of its neighborhoods. It appears that he has successfully persuaded most political groups that his downtown-centric development program is the way (eventually) to accomplish both goals.

Some, however, are beginning to feel impatient with the mayor: "He does listen, and we finally have an ear in the mayor's office. But sometimes an ear is not all you need. You still need some implementation.... We need to get beyond the listening stage" (Jones in Delsohn, 1984: 14A). Perhaps responding to such concerns—and mindful that several candidates have announced an interest in running against him in the next election—Peña emphasized "quality of life" issues over economic development in his State of the City address of July 10, 1985. He announced a $10 million program for low- and middle-income housing near downtown, an $11 million small business loan program, and new park acquisitions and neighborhood improvements (Broderick, 1985: 8). After the address, the mayor's aides complained that the media were responsible for the perception that Peña had neglected the neighborhoods. His top aide then went on to explain that the mayor would have to make it a point to persuade city residents that "big ticket" downtown projects such as the convention center were closely tied to city and neighborhood services:

> Even if you never go to the convention center in your entire life, it affects you because it allows us to clean up City Park, tear down a condemned building that's an eyesore in your neighborhood or get quicker response from the police.... We can only do these things if we have the money to do them [Broderick, 1985: 8].

CHICAGO: REDEFINING
ENTREPRENEURIAL POLITICS

An important struggle is taking place between remnants of Chicago's machine organization and a broad coalition of blacks, Hispanics, and white reformers who elected Harold Washington mayor on April 12, 1983. It is not only a battle between two factions that seek to control city government, and it is not a fledgling political machine replacing a tired old one. Harold Washington campaigned on a reform platform emphasizing more efficient government and an end to patronage; he also promised open government, a redistribution of power and benefits away from downtown to the neighborhoods, and job-oriented economic development. What is at issue in Chicago's political struggle is the definition of the municipal agenda.

An important political experiment is being tried in Chicago. Its three main elements include (1) a redistribution of power and resources away from downtown; (2) the mobilizing of previously inactive groups; and (3) "a substantial downward redistribution of benefits towards the many blacks who occupy the lower rungs of the socioeconomic ladder" (Grimshaw, 1984a: 8; Sampson, 1984: 12). These were the central themes of Washington's campaign, summarized by one scholar as the premise that "power and resources had too long been concentrated in City Hall and in the CBD, which has long been seen by many as either the handmaidens of City Hall or as the key component in city government with City Hall as the handmaiden" (Sampson, 1984: 129).

In April 1983, about two weeks before the mayoral election, the Research and Issues Committee of the Washington campaign released a 52-page document called *The Washington Papers*. These position papers defined city policy priorities in entrepreneurial terms, but populist principles guided the proposed entrepreneurial strategies. *The Washington Papers* constituted the philosophic and strategic underpinning for the lengthy, detailed *Chicago Development Plan* published in May 1984 under the title "Chicago Works Together." The five development goals of the new plan and their respective policies are as follows (City of Chicago, 1984: 3):

Goal I: Increase job opportunities for Chicagoans
- Targeted business investment in support of job development
- Local preference in buying and hiring
- Skilled labor force development
- Infrastructure investment for job development
- Affirmative action

Goal II: Promote balanced growth
- Balanced growth between downtown and neighborhoods
- Public private partnerships
- Strengthened tax base
- Equitable distribution of the tax burden

Goal III: Assist neighborhoods to develop through partnerships and coordinated investment
- Neighborhood planning
- Linked development

Goal IV: Enhance public participation in decision making
- Increased citizen access to information
- Increased opportunities for citizen involvement

Goal V: Pursue a regional, state, and national legislative agenda

The appointment of Robert Mier as acting commissioner of the Department of Economic Development confirmed the new policy directions. Formerly the director of the Center for Urban Economic Development at the University of Illinois, Chicago, Mier is a rare breed: a specialist on neighborhood economic redevelopment in a profession in which most people are oriented to downtown development. According to Mier (1984), under previous administrations his department had been addicted to "blockbuster" downtown projects involving large amounts of money and real estate. Only one small business deal had ever been processsed through the department in its history.

Under the machine virtually all development money not allocated to downtown projects had been distributed to neighborhood chambers of commerce, in proportion to the powers and electoral successes of the ward committee members (Moe, 1984). It may have been labeled "development money," but everyone knew it was patronage. Now the money was going to be distributed to neighborhood redevelopment corporations, cooperatives, and private businesses. By 1987 the Economic Development Department plans to create ten to twelve neighborhood corporations through which it will allocate grants (Mier, 1984).

A successful distribution of money in this manner would undermine the machine's patronage system and at the same time create a new political coalition in the city centered in the neighborhoods. Thus intense battles between the City Council and Mayor Washington are being waged over the new programs (Sampson, 1984: 14).

The *Chicago Development Plan 1984* (City of Chicago, 1984: 5) outlines a formidable number of programs designed to bring recovery to

the city's economy. For the year beginning with the plan's publication—
May 1984—the list of job creation "targets" is extremely ambitious:

- Create or retain over 8,000 direct and indirect jobs through financial
  assistance for business expansion and start-up;
- Provide technical assistance to more than 4,000 businesses;
- Establish public-private task forces for at least two Chicago industries;
- Increase City of Chicago local purchasing from 40% of total pur-
  chasing to approximately 60% or by about $80 million; and increase
  private sector local purchasing by 5% or an estimated $2500 million;
- Generate 1,500 direct and 2,000 indirect jobs through targeted local
  purchasing;
- Increase City of Chicago purchasing from minority and women-
  owned firms to 25% of total purchasing, or $100 million;
- Train 12,000 persons in employment skills, which will result in the
  placement of 8,000 trainees in jobs; and
- Enhance the employment skills of 17,000 youth.

Some of the programs that are supposed to create all these jobs include
the following:

The Department of Economic Development's *Financial Assistance for
Business Development* program. Assistance includes loans for working
capital, fixed assets and real estate, and industrial revenue bond financing
for new construction and expansion. This $24.3 million program will
leverage an estimated $95.3 million in private investment in the coming
year. . . .

A *Direct Micro-Loan* program provides low interest loans of $5,000 to
$12,500 to small neighborhood businesses. . . . Another program provides
co-venture and entrepreneurial equity investment to trigger private
financing for buyouts, acquisitions, [etc.]. . . .

Under the *Technical Assistance to Economic Development Organizations* program, neighborhood business and development organizations
are funded. . . .

A "Buy Chicago" program for which an interim goal of $240 million or
60 percent of City of Chicago purchasing will be targeted to local businesses [City of Chicago, 1984].

Also included in the list are business incubators (low-rent space in
designated areas), tax increment financing, "linked development" (agreements on local hiring, affirmative action, and local purchasing in
exchange for assistance on loans), and enterprise zones.

Neighborhood organizations are encouraged to review programs and submit requests. Capital improvement programs are to be reviewed and implemented through the Neighborhood Infrastructure Renewal Task Force. All city contractors and businesses receiving financial assistance from the city will be expected to participate in an aggressive affirmative action program. Twenty-five percent of city purchasing is to be targeted to companies owned by minorities and women; this will be overseen by the Purchasing from Minority and Women-Owned Firms program.

Several programs are designed to stimulate citizen participation and neighborhood institution-building. The philosophy guiding these programs is that

> successful neighborhood planning cannot be a "top-down" process. It must be based on an awareness that neighborhood problems and assets are best known to neighborhood residents and the local organizations devoted to the betterment of their neighborhoods [City of Chicago, 1984: 14].

A plannng document with such ambitious goals is almost certain to create high expectations. Failure to implement its programs is likely to create immense cynicism. This is a significant danger.

Many observers have described Harold Washington's basic style as cautious and deliberate: "He tends to hold back commitments, listen to all parties, then make a decision" (Moberg, 1983: 175). This style is appropriate for someone who wants to accomplish fundamental reform. But his failure to deliver jobs and favors to his supporters will create problems with his constituency (Grimshaw, 1984a, 1984b, 1984c, 1984d; Moberg, 1983). He has refused to strike deals with his opponents in the City Council for a division of the spoils, thus assuring a collision with the established order.

National news coverage has focused almost exclusively on Harold Washington's clashes with the machine-run Board of Aldermen. There are frequent clashes with Edward Vrdolyak, the Cook County Democratic chairman and the real leader in the Chicago City Council, and with Alderman Edward Burke, who chairs the Council's powerful finance committee. The antagonism is bitter and often racial. One member of The 29, a coalition of 29 aldermen led by Vrdolyak and Burke (the "evil cabal," Jane Byrne once called them), was apparently habituated to referring to the mayor in The 29's secret meetings as "that f _____ nigger" (Moberg, 1983: 175). There is undeniable racial conflict, but racial fears are also manipulated as a handy device to organize opposition to the mayor's policies.

There is a common perception that the Washington Administration has become bogged down, that the rhetoric of political change has been exceeded only by the ineffectuality of implementing programs. Some writers have noted a common perception that Washington "is disorganized and lackadaisical, an ineffective administrator" (Kelly, 1985: 204). A sympathetic observer blames his appointees: "Washington's staff is not organized for a big breakthrough, and its ineptitude sometimes descends to surprising depths: phone calls are not returned, letters go unanswered, the mayor misses meetings" (Lens, 1985: 22).

Even with the best organized staff imaginable, it would be difficult to bring about rapid change. Potential saboteurs work right at the heart of the Washington Administration. In every city department a few Washington appointees, often only two or three, occupy the top positions. The vast majority of employees were there long before the latest mayoral election, and they are secure in their jobs. According to the mayor, some of these employees are outright saboteurs: "We get reports of people calling in to ask a question and getting a snotty answer, on purpose. Or they'll say, 'You don't like it? The Mayor did it. You elected him,' and hang up. Or some inspector will harass someone and say it's on orders of the Mayor. We're weeding it out, but we can't control it" (Kelly, 1985: 206).

Of course, any mayor who attacks the established order will meet resistance. As in other big cities, Chicago's bureaucracies have evolved over a long period. In Chicago's case, the usual bureaucratic inertia is compounded by the way city agencies are accustomed to delivering services. Under Mayor Daley, the bureaucracies were administrative arms of the machine. Many city employees participated actively in precinct-level work on and before election day. The everyday delivery of services was also political. Loyal Democratic wards received the most careful attention in basic services such as street sweeping, road repairs, and utilities improvements. Chicagoans have always been aware that their city government was thoroughly political, and that the Democratic party controlled politics.

Mayor Washington's reforms were designed to change the machine's way of running city government. Only by effectively purging old employees could new programs be quickly implemented to facilitate the sympathetic consideration of citizen complaints and coordination with neighborhood groups—including perhaps especially the neighborhoods in black and Hispanic wards.

Harold Washington was denied even the usual housecleaning. For fourteen years before the 1983 election, Michael Shakman had led a fight through the federal courts trying to get the courts to declare the patronage system illegal. Despite the legal challenge, the Democratic party had been able to keep 8,000 patronage employees off the civil service rolls. But just weeks before the mayoral election, Federal District Judge Nicholas Bua handed down a landmark decision: Only 250 appointments, plus department heads, could henceforth be exempted from civil service.

The inability of the Washington Administration to appoint more people dealt a devastating blow. As of 1985, fewer than 200 top management appointments had been made (Kelly, 1985: 182). Under the judge's supervision, hiring procedures are slow and cumbersome; an open position may take months to fill. In all the departments and agencies there is a sprinkling of Washington appointees. According to a top administrator, "It is like trying to win a reform war with someone else's army" (Moe, 1984).

Mayor Washington has been trying to promote a national urban development agenda to other mayors and to the National Democratic Party. In June 1984, just in time for the U.S. Conference of Mayors meeting and the Democratic National Convention, the mayor's office printed 5,000 copies of a slick booklet under the title, "Mayor Harold Washington: A Federal/Urban Partnership to Renew Our Cities." The document outlined a full employment jobs program, a federally assisted effort to build capital infrastructure, and a federally funded housing program. The strategies promoted by Washington are all "entrepreneurial," a concept that provides the unifying theme for the booklet: "We believe that the cities, with the necessary help of the federal government, can become a dynamic entrepreneurial force which can strengthen local and national economies and increase fairness and equity at the same time" (Washington, 1984: 5). The key new programs advocated include the following: a national Production and Jobs Board "that develops industrial policies in coordination with similar local economic development bodies"; a Community Renewal Employment Act; a National Capital Investment Bank to "provide a revolving fund at lower than private interest rates for local capital investment," to be matched by locally raised capital; and a Capital Investment Council to "advise governments on national resource allocation and local investment planning." But the Chicago delegation's efforts to promote these programs at the Democratic National Convention failed. One well-known progressive mayor who attended the Democratic Convention, George Latimer of St. Paul, could not recall any lobbying by the Chicago delegation, and felt that the booklet they distributed had the earmarks of a single politician's pet project (Latimer, 1984).

Whether Chicago's current programs of economic development catch on elsewhere is an interesting and important question. There is much reason to suppose that a constituency exists to support a redefinition of growth as a divisible public good—a set of strategies to promote affirmative action, small business development, neighborhood institution-building, and local job creation.

Mayor Washington says that it will take six years to "change the system" in Chicago enough to institute many programs. Meanwhile, he believes, "The level of awareness in this city has been raised. People are becoming more relaxed with us. The change is slow but perceptible" (Kelly, 1985: 207). The new policies he advocates, however, are opposed not only by the machine and its local employees but by much of the local business community and by the Reagan Administration's policies. It is doubtful that one city, in isolation, can radically redefine the purposes of municipal government. According to Sidney Lens (1985: 22), it will require a national movement: "To transcend the policy of moderation, [Washington] would have to mobilize poor and disenfranchised Chicagoans for mass activity and join hundreds of other mayors to challenge the American Establishment."

THE EMERGING URBAN CRISIS

Current political conditions in American cities are strikingly similar to the political context that preceded the urban riots of the 1960s. Then, as now, issues of economic growth and downtown redevelopment dominated the municipal agenda. Working closely with a coalition of corporations, real estate and merchant interests, and metropolitan dailies, progrowth mayors pronounced economic decline as the principal issue of city politics. In city after city, these coalitions "engineered a massive allocation of private and social resources" for the cities, reclaiming urban land through huge slum clearance, highway construction, and downtown redevelopment projects (Mollenkopf, 1978: 140).

These projects were the main cause of community turbulence during the 1950s and 1960s. They removed low-income housing, increased racial tensions, tore apart working-class ethnic communities, and put urban officials in frequent conflict with city residents (Mollenkopf,

1973; Mollenkopf, 1983; Stone, 1976). Clearance projects that destroyed homes and neighborhoods made a dramatic statement about political winners and losers: Far from benefiting all the city's residents, renewal made higher profits and living space available for a few "desirable" businesses and residents, at the expense of many city residents.

Most of the growth strategies of the 1980s have not been as divisive as the urban renewal clearance programs. Tax abatements, industrial development bonds, tax increment financing, enterprise zones, loan programs—all seem to be economic and not political in character. In most cases they involve quiet, behind-the-scenes transactions between a public authority and private institutions. Discussion of their merits and mechanisms usually proceed in a market language—for example, their effect on interest rates or investment. And most of the time, voters know little about them. It is indeed true that these policies have been located in development agencies that are neither public nor private, and rarely fall neatly within the jurisdiction of a single city. Thus the institutions that promote economic development have changed venue and enlarged their territory. Often this has occurred as a result of conscious decisions: "Cosmopolitan capital tries to ensure that important decisions are made at levels of government at which it has more influence" (Molotch and Logan, 1984: 493).

Most urban officials and their electoral coalitions have come to believe that growth is the only viable answer to local public problems. The federal government's policies also have exerted an important effect: "The Reagan Administration's cuts in urban aid have stimulated localities to intensify their search for . . . investments. . . . Under desperate conditions, the mere possibility that subsidies may work is apparently enough to prompt politicians to offer them" (Molotch and Logan, 1984: 494).

But the new methods of stimulating growth by redistributing tax burdens from business to city residents will not remain outside the political arena for long. Growth policies utilized by cities are local versions of supply-side economics, and much of the electorate is aware that economic policies over the last few years have redistributed tax burdens downward. Urban political leaders and their constituencies also have been often reminded that economic decisions carry huge political consequences. Plant closings and the fact or threat of disinvestment by mobile national and international corporations have become the focus of community protest (Bluestone and Harrison, 1983). A burgeoning literature documents a lack of local and national patriotism by corporations. Plant closing legislation was advocated in the 1984 Democratic Party platform.

It is also essential to note that the objective social conditions that spawned the urban rebellions of the 1960s have, on the whole, worsened. As carefully documented by Philip Meranto and others, unemployment levels for minorities—and for whites, too—are far higher than in the 1960s, and remain at depression levels for young black males (Nelson et al., 1984; Dunbar, 1984). The rate of poverty has increased precipitously since 1980. These statistics are almost certainly associated with rising suicide and crime rates. Deep cuts in social service programs have exacerbated these problems, so that "it becomes clear that the quality of urban life for millions of Americans is worsening" (Nelson et al., 1984).

The mobilization of new urban constituencies will repoliticize economic development policies. The promises that accompany local versions of supply-side economics will not deter minority electorates from demanding that economic development be directly targeted to providing local jobs, social programs, housing, health facilities, and community physical improvements.

The exclusion of racial minorities from holding important electoral offices in big cities has only recently been ended, beginning with Carl Stokes's election as mayor of Cleveland in 1967. As Rod Bush (1984: 4) has pointed out, the first generation of black mayors confronted a dilemma: They wanted to implement policies to promote their constituents' material interests, but they faced declining local economies and tax bases, crumbling infrastuctures, white flight, and deteriorating neighborhoods. By the late 1970s and accentuated under the Reagan Administration, all minority mayors must also cope with federal cuts in city programs and social services. In response, many of these mayors capitulated to the demands of the local corporate sector: "Increasingly, black mayors were placed in a quasi-neocolonial posture: they depended upon black votes to guarantee their success at the polls, but once elected, they often implemented public policies that contradicted their constituency's material interests" (Bush, 1984: 4). Of course, these observations may apply equally to Hispanic mayors and to any progressive mayor who identifies with the urban underclass.

As convincingly demonstrated by the Jesse Jackson presidential campaign, a new electoral politics is being created in America, centered in its industrial cities. The Jackson campaign provided an electoral voice for millions of blacks, Hispanics, and progressive whites who reject the politics of privilege embraced by both the Democrats and Republicans. This new electorate will place new demands upon the second generation of black mayors and upon the first generation of Hispanic mayors. These mayors are caught between "two 'faces' of politics" (Jennings, 1984: 290). The one face is the old executive-centered, downtown coalition that has presided over growth politics since World War II. The other utilizes a new electoral coalition that favors policies to redistribute wealth and power broadly throughout the urban community.

> As conditions for blacks continue to worsen, we will see more clearly the two faces of urban politics. While one kind of black politician will seek accommodation with corporate America, other black politicians will become more vociferous *and* sophisticated in their challenges to the powerful. It is the latter face of black and urban politics that will be able to mobilize the masses of blacks and the poor in the electoral arena [Jennings, 1984: 300].

This generation of black and Hispanic urban leaders will find it increasingly difficult to pursue the conventional growth politics, however successful they may be in providing window-dressing for neocolonial corporate policies.

NOTE

1. More detailed case studies of Denver and Chicago appear in Judd and Ready (1986). The original field studies were conducted for The Urban Institute. Randy Ready researched and wrote an earlier draft of the Denver study.

REFERENCES

BLAIR, J. P. and D. NACHMIAS [eds.] (1979) Fiscal Retrenchment and Urban Policy. Volume 17, Urban Affairs Annual Reviews. Washington DC: Brookings Institution.

BLUESTONE, B. and B. HARRISON (1982) The Deindustrialization of America: Plant Closings, Community Abandonment, and the Dismantling of Basic Industry. New York: Basic Books.

BRODERICK, C. (1985) "Peña speech shifts focus to 'quality of life.'" Rocky Mountain News (July 12).

BROWNING, R. P., D. MARSHALL, and D. H. TABB (1984) Protest is Not Enough: The Struggle of Blacks and Hispanics for Equality in Urban Politics. Berkeley: University of California Press.

BUSH, R. [ed.] (1984) The New Black Vote: Politics and Power in Four American Cities. San Francisco: Synthesis.

City and County of Denver (1984) Economic Development Action Program. Denver: Author.

City of Chicago (1984) " 'Chicago works together': 1984 Chicago development plan." (May) Chicago: Author.

CLARK, T. N. and L. C. FERGUSON (1983) City Money. New York: Columbia University Press.

Committee to Elect Harold Washington Mayor of Chicago (1983) The Washington Papers: A Commitment to Chicago. A Commitment to You. (April) Chicago: Author.

DAVIS, T. (1984) "Black mayors: can they make the cities work?" Mother Jones (July).

DELSOHN, G. (1984) "Leaders say big problems not attacked." The Denver Post (June 10): 1, 14A.

———(1983a) "Registration of Hispanics short of goal." The Denver Post (April 26): 1B.

———(1983b) "Peña's early coalition a winner." The Denver Post (June 22): 15A.

Denver Regional Council of Governments [DRCOG] (1983) Profiles of 1970-80 Socio-Economic Change by County and Census Tract. Denver: Author.

Denver Urban Renewal Authority [DURA] (1984) Denver Urban Renewal Authority Skyline Project: Summary of Developments. Denver: Author.

DUNBAR, L. (1984) Minority Report: What Has Happened to Blacks, Hispanics, American Indians, and Other Minorities in the Eighties. New York: Pantheon.

FAINSTEIN, S. S., N. I. FAINSTEIN, R. C. HILL, D. R. JUDD, and M. P. SMITH (1983) Restructuring the City: The Political Economy of Urban Redevelopment. New York: Longman.

FLYNN, K. (1984) "Downtown retailers could be costly." The Denver Post (April 1): 15-16.

GINGENBOCH, K. (1984) Personal interview with staff person at Brothers Redevelopment, Inc., August 2. Randy Ready, interviewer.

GLADSTONE and Associates (1978) Economic Impact and Implications of the Transit-way/Mall. Denver: Regional Transportation District and downtown Denver, Inc.

GOUGEON, T. (1984) Personal interview with administrative assistant to Denver Mayor Federico Peña, July 17. Randy Ready, interviewer.

GOVE, S. K. and L. H. MASOTTI [eds.] (1986) Chicago Politics in Transition. Urbana: University of Illinois Press.

———(1982) After Daley: Chicago Politics in Transition. Urbana: University of Illinois Press.

GRIEDER, W. (1978) "Detroit's streetwise mayor plays key role in city's turn around." Cleveland Plain Dealer (July 3).

GRIMSHAW, W. J. (1984a) "Is Chicago ready for reform? or, a new agenda for Harold Washington," pp. 127-140 in M. G. Holli and P. M. Green (eds.) The Making of the Mayor. Grand Rapids, MI: William Eerdmans.

———(1984b) "The election of mayor Harold Washington: reconciling race and reform," in S. K. Gove and L. H. Masotti (eds.) Chicago Politics in Transition.

———(1984c) "Class, culture, and race in Chicago politics," in S. K. Gove and L. H. Masotti (eds.) Chicago Politics in Transition. "The new voter registration strategy."

———(1984d) Personal interview with Associate Professor, Illinois Institute of Technology, July 25.

JAMES, H. and M. PHILLIPS, with D. HAZEN (1984) "The new voter registration strategy." Social Policy (Winter): 2-9.

JENNINGS, J. (1984) "Blacks and progressive politics," pp. 199-314 in R. Bush (ed.) The New Black Vote: Politics and Power in Four American Cities. San Francisco: Synthesis.

JUDD, D. R. and R. READY (1986) "Entrepreneurial cities and the new politics of economic development," in C. Lewis and G. Peterson (eds.) Reagan and the Cities. Washington, DC: Urban Institute.

KARNIG, A. K. and S. WELCH (1980) Black Representatives and Urban Policy. Chicago: University of Chicago Press.

KELLY, B. (1985) "Harold Washington's balancing act." Chicago (April): 180-207.

KELLY, G. V. (1974) The Old Gray Mayors of Denver. Boulder, CO: Pruett.

LATIMER, G. (1984) Personal interview with the major, July 27.

LENS, S. (1985) "A mayor's dilemma." Progressive 49 (June).

LEVINE, C. H. (1972) Racial Conflict and the American Mayor: Power, Polarization, and Performance. Lexington, MA: D. C. Heath.

LOWI, T. J. (1979) "The state of cities in the second republic," pp. 43-53 in J. P. Blair and D. Nachmias (eds.) Fiscal Retrenchment and Urban Policy. Washington, DC: Urban Institute.

MAXWELL, J. A. and J. R. ARONSON (1977) Financing State and Local Governments. Washington, DC: Brookings Institution.

MIER, R. (1984) Personal interview with the commissioner, Department of Economic Development, City of Chicago, July 24.

MOBERG, D. (1983) "The man who wants to break the mold." Chicago (October): 170-182.

MOE, K. (1984) Personal interview with the assistant commissioner, Policy, Planning, and Research, Department of Economic Development, City of Chicago.

MOLLENKOPF, J. H. (1983) The Contested City. Princeton, NJ: Princeton University Press.

———(1978) "The post-war politics of urban development," pp. 134-139 in W. K. Tabb and L. Sawers (eds.) Marxism and the Metropolis: New Perspectives in Urban Political Economy. New York: Oxford University Press.

———(1973) "On the causes and consequences of neighborhood political mobilization." Presented at the annual meeting of the American Political Science Association, New Orleans, September 4-8.

MOLOTCH, H. and J. LOGAN (1984) "Tensions in the growth machine: overcoming resistance to value-free development." Social Problems (June): 483-499.

MORIARTY, B. M. et al. (1980) Industrial Location and Community Development. Chapel Hill: University of North Carolina.

MUWAKKIL, S. (1985) "Black leadership down, but not out." In These Times (January 16-22).

NELSON, W. E., Jr. and P. J. MERANTO (1976) Electing Black Mayors: Political Action in the Black Community. Columbus: Ohio State University Press.

NELSON, W. E., Jr., L. MOSQUEDA, and P. MERANTO (1984) "Reaganomics and the continuing urban crisis in the black community," pp. 15-32 in M. F. Rice and W. Jones (eds.) Contemporary Public Policy Perspectives and Black Americans. Boulder, CO: Greenwood.

New York Times (1983a) "Mayoral nominee works hard at being Goode." (May 19): 21A.
———(1983b) "Chicago election makes a dream come true." (April 13): 13A.
———(1983c) "Defection of white democrats may hinder Washington." (April 23): 13A.
PAAR, J. (1984) Personal interview with the director, Center for Public-Private Cooperation, University of Colorado at Denver, July 19. Randy Ready, Interviewer.
PEAR, R. (1985) "States are found more responsive on social issues." New York Times (May 19).
PEIRCE, N. R., J. HAGSTROM, and C. STEINBACH (1979) Economic Development: The Challenge of the 1980s. Washington, DC: Council of State Planning Agencies.
PEÑA, F. (1984a) State of the City Address, July 5.
———(1984b) "Denver's neighborhoods." Washington Park Profile (June): 1, 8.
———(1983) The Peña Neighborhood Program: Neighborhood Planning, Preservation and Development (March 19).
RICE, M. F. and W. JONES, Jr. [eds.] (1984) Contemporary Public Policy Perspectives and Black Americans. Boulder, CO: Greenwood.
Sabre Foundation (1983) Enterprise Zone Activity in the States: Summary of Survey Findings. Washington, DC: Author.
SAMPSON, W. A. (1986). "The politics of adaptation: the first year of the Washington administration." In S. K. Gove and L. H. Masotti (eds.) Chicago Politics in Transition. Urbana: University of Illinois Press.
SCHMENNER, R. W. (1980) "Industrial location and urban public management," pp. 446-468 in A. P. Solomon (ed.) The Prospective City: Economy, Population, Energy, and Environmental Development. Cambridge, MA: MIT Press.
STONE, C. N. (1976) Economic Growth and Neighborhood Discontent: System Bias in the Urban Renewal Program of Atlanta. Chapel Hill: University of North Carolina Press.
SWANSTROM, T. (1985) The Crisis of Growth Politics: Cleveland, Kucinich and the Challenge of Urban Populism. Philadelphia: Temple University Press.
TABB, W. K. and L. SAWERS [eds.] (1978) Marxism and the Metropolis: New Perspectives in Urban Political Economy. New York: Oxford University Press.
U.S. Department of Commerce (1975) Industrial Location Determinants. Washington, DC: Government Printing Office.
U.S. Department of Housing and Urban Development (1982) The President's National Urban Policy Report: 1982 (July). Washington, DC: Government Printing Office.
VAUGHAN, R. J. (1979) State Taxation and Economic Development. Washington, DC: Council of State Planning Agencies.
WALKER, B. (1983) "Old guard joins in praise for victor." The Denver Post (June 22): 12.
WASHINGTON, H. (1984) A Federal/Urban Partnership to Renew Our Cities.
WASYLENKO, M. (1981) "The location of firms: the role of taxes and fiscal incentives," pp. 155-190 in R. Bahl (ed.) Urban Government Finance: Emerging Trends. Beverly Hills, CA: Sage.
WATSON, S. (1984) "The second time around: a profile of black mayoral reelection campaigns." Phylon (Fall): 165-178.
WELCH, S. and M. W. COMBS (1983) "Interracial differences in opinion on public issues in the 1970s." Western Journal of Black Studies 7 (Fall): 136-141.
WILKINSON, R. (1984) "Downtown vacancy rate highest in the U.S." The Denver Post (July 24): 1D.

WOLFE, A. (1981) America's Impasse: The Rise and Fall of the Politics of Growth. Boston: South End Press.

YACK, P. (1983) "Peña has overcome one issue political label." The Denver Post (April 26): 7B.

YOUNG, C. A. (1981) "Detroit: moving forward in the frost belt." USA TODAY (November): 20-22.

Part III

Theoretical Perspectives

□ THE CASE STUDIES above isolate some important themes that stand in contrast to earlier work on the urban crisis. First, the fiscal problems of cities are not related directly to economic mechanisms, especially the cycles of growth and decline tied to crises in capital accumulation. If political economy is relevant to urban analysis, then it must be a new version of that inquiry that also abandons economism and captures, instead, the mutual relations between the economy and the state.

Second, the ability of state managers to control stress stands out as a principal means by which most municipalities have escaped fiscal problems. Thus state managers have been underestimated in their ability to use the framework of political power in the administration of public finance.

Third, the social causes of urban unrest and the extreme crisis of inequality documented in the 1960s are both still with us. In some places politics has changed to allow greater minority representation. Yet a tale of two cities remains, and new urban coalitions must face the old problems of their political predecessors. A need exists to explore why social change remains elusive and why it is that, despite the persisting efforts of minority-led local politics, ideological and structural mechanisms remain in place that present formidable barriers to the search for social justice.

The remaining chapters amplify these themes and introduce others by addressing some of the theoretical issues brought into clearer relief by case studies of the urban crisis. Irene and Herbert Rubin and Alberta Sbragia introduce new perspectives on urban political economy. The Rubins follow the path of restructuring after the crisis or threat of crisis has occurred. They assess the relative abilities of neo-Marxism and public choice theory to predict the course of crisis adjustment. According to the Rubins, both theories overemphasize the severity of crisis and underestimate the ability of cities to respond to stress. Results from several case studies indicate that cities have found new ways of running themselves fiscally. They have taken advantage of linkages to other levels of government, changed revenue supports of services through the adoption of such measures as user fees, and renegotiated their relation to financial sources. Rather than following a particular public policy philosophy, city managers have worked in a practical and efficient manner to mix and match several different means of controlling stress, thereby cushioning the impact of urban restructuring from fiscal performance.

The success of fiscal administration is not without its adverse effects. In particular, issues associated with the supply of separable public goods and the ability of local government to manage them remain. Thus both crime fighting and the promotion of growth were responses in many cities to urban crisis. After the ghetto riots, for example, the demand for more police protection was insatiable. Driven by this demand, cities were plunged into fiscal strain to support increases in police expenditures. Similarly, because the benefits of growth do not match its public costs, progrowth policies of depressed cities may serve to exacerbate rather than reduce fiscal stress. Consequently, and in contrast to theories that link political crisis directly with economic decline, government responses to social crisis may touch off a syndrome leading to fiscal crisis that can be repeated no matter how well the crisis itself has been managed. The Rubins conclude that the threat of crisis, rather than the experience of it, has been most effective in altering the nature of public administration. Cities today are more concerned about development and austerity than in running an open government responsive to the larger needs of their residents.

The need for a new perspective on political economy is echoed in the work of Alberta Sbragia, a political scientist whose specialty has been researching the nature of finance capital. According to Sbragia, although political economists often use the term "finance capital" in discussing city growth and financing, its exact nature is little understood. When it comes to analyzing the role of the financial infrastructure, both mainstreamers and Marxists miss the complexity of operation constituting money market links between the state and capital.

According to Sbragia, the bond market is the single greatest source of funds for cities outside of tax revenue. Yet the relation between the two has changed greatly following the fiscal crisis. Three sources of restructuring are examined: those stemming from the market, from federal tax law, and from state laws regulating the local-state governmental system. By examining these sources of change, Sbragia extracts the following observations that can provide the basis for a new understanding of the relation between the city and the economy:

First, due to the fiscal crisis, financial arrangements between local governments and lending sources have been rationalized. In addition to city managers injecting greater technical expertise into administration, as already noted, Sbragia highlights the increasing role and power of financial planners in managing public finances. Second, received knowledge to the contrary, banks and investment corporations are not the principal source of money in the municipal bond market. Due to federal tax laws, individual investors are the major purchasers of bonds. According to Sbragia, federal tax policy rather than the dictates of finance capital constitutes the principal force in the link between sources of money and city coffers.

Third, in response to the threat of crisis, and under the ideological spell of progrowth boosterism, cities have pursued development as a means of hoping to avoid crisis, an observation also made by the Rubins. According to Sbragia, much of municipal borrowing is devoted to the underwriting of these endeavors. Thus cities have become brokers of tax-exempt capital to the private sector in addition to subsidizing development through the relaxation of regulations. Sbragia notes that by 1985 between 60% and 80% of all municipal borrowing went to subsidize private sector development.

Finally, as in the chapter by Monkkonen, Sbragia documents the retreat of government from the direct rule by the polity under pressure of fiscal restructuring. With regard to finances, the need to circumvent state-level restrictions on local borrowing by cities desperate for development has generated a proliferation of quasi-public authorities and special districts that borrow and broker money for growth. Because these agencies no longer answer to the people, grave implications are raised regarding the changed nature of local government itself; these remain unaddressed in the present period of fiscal fright.

Austerity-inspired restructuring has proceeded with little opposition from city residents. At least, whatever opposition has existed has not provided an obstacle to city managers and business interests in their remodeling of the relation between local government and the economy. Jeff Henig, a political scientist interested in neighborhood mobilization, examines this apparent paradox. At the outset of his chapter, however, he suggests that alleged political quiescence is largely a myth. Throughout the country, grass-roots responses to austerity have occurred. What has been missing, rather, is the aggregation of ad hoc, localized responses to a level that could act as a political force in the arena of city politics. Henig takes on the task of examining the factors that have prevented effective political protests against austerity. Among those that stand out are the decline in leadership resources for the urban poor, the failure to implement activist interests after mobilization has occurred, and the ideological control of decision making and alternative choice searches by the hegemony of capital. Each area is discussed in detail.

In a final section Henig examines the direct effect that austerity itself has played as a formidable ideological mechanism in attenuating political activism within beseiged cities. Henig sees a new balance of values and normative judgments pervading the society at a deep level following a decade of fiscal problems. The new public ethos distrusts political activism and eschews the political itself as a remedy for social problems in favor of more privatized solutions. This new form of ideological control concordant with fiscal austerity restructuring involves a shrinking of both "the realm of the possible and the realm of the public." The final chapter, by C. G. Pickvance, manages to touch on all these themes while sticking closely to a case study. Pickvance supplies a much-needed contrast to the United States by assessing the record of urban crisis in the United Kingdom. Several structural features of governance distinguish the British case from our own. First, Britain possesses a unitary political system with close linkages between local levels and the nation-state. Among other things, this structure is characterized by the presence of national political parties in the fight for local office. In contrast, the United Sates is a federated system with power administered principally by the state level to local areas. Local politics is insulated from national politics by several structural mechanisms, including, for some areas, "nonpartisan" elections.

Second, the urban crisis in the United Kingdom is a crisis initiated by national government. Under Thatcherism the spending autonomy of local areas was targeted for control and austerity restrictions. Consequently, the urban crisis there involves a "permanent confrontation" between the national government and the town councils. In the United States, in contrast, the urban crisis was initiated by dramatic social events and by the private sector

Finally, resistance to restructuring in the United Kingdom involves a three-way struggle among parties in control of town councils, professional city administrators, and the bureaucrats of the nation-state. In the United States both city administrators and public officials in Washington, D.C., have often acted in concert to effect change and at the expense of local government autonomy. National parties, in contrast, are virtually absent in local contests. More important, the social issues of austerity and the differential impact of cutbacks on the poor have not played well to disinterested politicians at other levels of government.

Pickvance is able to isolate some significant implications of the British case. On the whole he argues that fiscal concerns of local government do not reflect economic cycles and they are not symptoms of some general fiscal crisis of the state. Instead, the relation between economic processes and fiscal well-being is mediated by three independent factors: the strength of local government, political institutions that buffer the local area from systemic shocks, and the ideology surrounding the issue of public spending. Pickvance illustrates how these elements mediate the relation between the public and private realms and indicates how his results can be applied to the U.S. case. Finally, he raises some central theoretical issues that are addressed in my concluding editorial remarks.

7

Structural Theories and
Urban Fiscal Stress

IRENE S. RUBIN
HERBERT J. RUBIN

☐ SINCE THE MIDDLE 1970s, at both the national and local levels, there has been increasing fiscal stress, occasionally reaching crisis proportions. In spite of their radically different perspectives, both neo-Marxist and public choice theorists separately predicted that fiscal stress would confront the public sector. They each argued that there were structural problems with government that would lead to fiscal crisis, and suggested that only a radical restructuring of government could solve the problems.

The purpose of this chapter is to examine the extent to which the origins of urban fiscal stress and cities' responses to that stress support public choice or neo-Marxist theories. The aim is not just to weigh which theory has more explanatory or predictive power, but to sort out and combine those elements of each theory that seem the most descriptive, extending the combined theory to create a better fit with observed reality.

We will first summarize neo-Marxist and public choice theories as they describe urban fiscal stress. Then we will compare theoretically predicted causes of fiscal stress with evidence from studies of cities that experienced fiscal stress. In the third part of the chapter, we will compare theoretically predicted responses to fiscal stress with data on actual cities' responses in the areas of revenue sources, allocation patterns, business dominance, and scope of services. Particular attention will be paid to the theoretical importance of attempts by cities to attract new and expanded businesses as a way of reducing fiscal pressures.

PUBLIC CHOICE AND NEO-MARXIST PERSPECTIVES ON LOCAL FISCAL CRISIS

PUBLIC CHOICE PERSPECTIVES

Public choice theorists view government as a market that follows rules of supply and demand. Governmental failures are interpreted as the inability of government to allocate goods and services in accordance with individuals' market preferences. In addition, some public choice theorists argue that collective provision of goods and services often leads to an oversupply of public goods in comparison to what individuals would purchase on their own (Savas, 1982; Buchanon, 1977, 1968, 1967; Tullock, 1970; Niskanen, 1971).

Goods and services are categorized as either collective and public, or separable and private. Pure collective goods are both unlimited in supply and open to all—there is no way to prevent people from using them. Pure private goods are both limited in supply and have the quality of "excludability"; that is, people can be prevented from using or consuming them. Most publicly provided goods fall on a continuum between the extremes.

According to this approach, government is seen as growing too large because it provides the wrong type of goods and services. Many goods and services that could be provided by the private sector have become the responsibility of the public sector, where they are provided inefficiently, with low productivity, and at high cost. Public choice theorists claim that publicly provided goods benefit only specific groups of citizens rather than the collectivity. These groups of citizens who benefit demand ever-increasing amounts of goods and services because they can share the costs of these goods and services with the rest of the citizens who do not benefit.

These groups of individuals who want specific public benefits impose their will on the rest of the public both through elections and through dominance of political agenda setting. Politicians respond to these demands because they want to be reelected. Some public choice theorists claim that the organized poor act in this fashion. According to these theories, the poor, who receive transfer payments, will dominate the political process and vote for more and more benefits, boosting the size of the public sector.[1]

Public choice theorists relate the excessive demands of the public for more service not only to self-interest but also to poor information that obscures the relationship between costs and the level of service provision. People are fooled by "fiscal illusions" about the real cost of goods and services and, thinking them cheaper than they really are, demand too much. Examples of fiscal illusions include federal grants, which look free to local governments, and hidden or low visibility taxes.

Public choice theorists focus on the nature and effectiveness of public demands, but they also focus on the motivations of bureaucrats to expand their bureaus and the mechanisms linking bureaucrats' preferences to the public agenda. They tend to deemphasize differences in community wealth as an independent variable affecting the supply of public goods, preferring to use community wealth or poverty as a dependent variable, the result of overtaxing the middle class.

Public choice theorists believe that overexpansion of goods and services is inherent in the public provision of private goods and that the public sector is intrinsically inefficient and unproductive. Their solution therefore is to reduce the scope of government by returning to the private sector those functions that benefit individuals rather than the collectivity. They also advocate reducing the degree of fiscal illusion by linking the costs of publicly provided goods more closely with the amount provided, for example, by emphasizing user fees rather than general taxation.

The public choice mechanisms apply at the local level as well as they do at the national level. According to theory, local governments supply the wrong services, individuals and interest groups benefit from them, and then push up the demand for them. The result is an increase in taxes. Those who pay higher taxes but do not benefit proportionately from higher service levels either protest their taxes or leave the city for lower tax burdens in the suburbs. When they leave, the city becomes burdened with a reduced tax base in addition to high demand levels. The result is fiscal stress.

THE NEO-MARXIST PERSPECTIVE

Public choice theorists tend to view the political world as satisfying individual preferences for goods and services. In contrast, neo-Marxists view the world in terms of the exploitation of labor by capital and the dominance of politics by interest groups (see Smith, 1984; Whitt, 1982). Although a number of neo-Marxists have written on fiscal crisis, we concentrate here on one of the most thorough and interesting arguments—that of James O'Connor (1973) in his book *Fiscal Crisis of the State*.

To simplify O'Connor's argument somewhat, he interprets the spending patterns of the national government as a result of the capitalist class, acting as an interest group, pressuring the government for greater support of the private sector. In response to this pressure, the government has taken on two functions: (1) encouraging capital accumulation while enhancing the profitability of the private sector and (2) maintaining social order that might otherwise be disturbed by the vagaries of the marketplace.

Tax and fiscal policy are the tools used to provide support to the private sector. Military activities are also efforts to help business be more profitable. Social expenditures—such as welfare, unemployment insurance, and social security—fall under the category of costs necessary to prevent rebellion. The costs of maintaining both types of expenditures are not only heavy but increasing. According to theory, these costs result in constantly rising levels of taxation and taxpayers' revolts. In the long term, the only solution is a socialist state, but in the short term increased social expenditures will maintain domestic peace.

There is some (acknowledged) difficulty in applying this theory to the local level because local governments do not use fiscal policy to affect the national economy, and are not involved in foreign policy. And, local governments are only indirectly concerned with capital accumulation when providing local infrastructure. Many of the social programs provided at the local level are programs designed and paid for by the federal government and the states. As a result, when the theory is applied to the local level, it is modified to fit local circumstances.

O'Connor argues that state and local governments are more dominated by interest groups than the federal government is, and that these local interest groups are primarily progrowth and probusiness. At the local level, this business group dominance is manifested in redevelopment projects that serve businesses, in police and fire expenditures that serve property owners, and in expenditures for schools that train for jobs—and thereby serve business. Any expenditure that enhances the profitability of business, such as expenditures on infrastructure, also falls into this category.

According to O'Connor's model, business dominance over local expenditures by itself does not create fiscal stress. For fiscal stress to occur, both increased expenditures and constrained revenues are required. As a cause for the constraint on local revenues, O'Connor describes the reduction of the tax base through the exodus of middle-class taxpayers to the suburbs.

The process of suburbanization is not inherently a neo-Marxist argument. However, O'Connor provides a neo-Marxist interpretation of suburbanization by describing how the suburbs economically exploit the central city and how the process of suburbanization has been supported by the federal government as a benefit to capitalist investments. Making the model a bit more trenchant, O'Connor compares the role of the suburbs to that of colonial powers, bleeding off revenues and slowing the rate of growth of the central city, which is treated as an exploited colony.

In localities, fiscal stress occurs because of shrinking local resources and a business-dominated polity making expenditures for itself. In addition, O'Connor describes how state and federal grants temporarily hide or delay the signs of local fiscal stress. However, the surplus at the federal and state level that financed these intergovernmental transfer payments is bound to disappear, leaving the local governments both more dependent and more desperate for revenues. When local governments increase their own taxes to replace vanishing grants, they will provoke tax protests. Ultimately these protests will provoke a fiscal crisis.

OBSERVATIONS ON THE CAUSES
OF URBAN FISCAL STRESS

Both neo-Marxist and public choice perspectives describe mechanisms that cause cities to experience fiscal stress. We will compare their proposed mechanisms with observations of how fiscal stress was generated at the local level (Rubin, 1982; Levine et al., 1981).[2]

COMPARISON OF PUBLIC CHOICE ARGUMENTS
WITH OBSERVATIONAL DATA

Included in the major arguments of the public choice theorists is the idea that the public sector has grown by adding the wrong functions, especially those that serve a limited clientele rather than the whole population of a city. The demand for these services results in an over-supply with respect to what people are willing to pay.

In order to apply this argument at the local level, some clear distinction must be made between services that benefit the whole population and those that benefit only some citizens. Unfortunately, as has often been noted, there is no clear distinction. Even police—who provide such goods as public safety and a sense of security, from which everyone benefits—also provide other services to individuals and groups, such as escorting money from banks to armored trucks and unlocking cars for people who have locked their keys inside. Similarly, economic development activities can be said to benefit the whole community, but clearly some portion of economic development funds benefits particular businesses.

Because budgets are allocated by city departments rather than by specific activities, the analyst trying to apply public choice arguments to cities is forced to characterize particular departments as either providing public goods or separable goods. The dividing line is arbitrary, but police, fire, water, streets, and sanitation are considered to provide the more public goods, whereas social service departments, especially those that serve the poor, tend to focus on separable goods. Governmental services that cater to the rich also tend to be separable.

Empirical data can answer questions posed by public choice theorists. For example, did local governments expand prior to the period of fiscal stress by adding functions that were primarily separable, and did these functions expand city expenditures due to high demand? New York City, for example, markedly expanded its social services, whether these services were new to the city or not, before its fiscal crisis (Horton, 1977; Morris, 1980). But New York City tends not to be typical of cities elsewhere.

In a cross-sectional study on a sample of U.S. cities over 50,000 population, the scope of city services predicted the level of taxation, but was only slightly related to the level of fiscal stress. That is, whether or not cities provided many well-funded services to particular segments of their population did not have much effect on the amount of fiscal stress (Clark et al., 1976).[3]

Case studies of local governments facing fiscal difficulties show that they did not add functions prior to the onset of fiscal stress. Some of them in fact had a history of divesting themselves of functions before the fiscal stress hit. Southside (Rubin, 1982) provided only a narrow scope of functions, with almost no social service functions provided by the city, yet it both increased expenditures and got into severe financial trouble.

For Southside, it was police expenditures that increased very rapidly. To some extent, police were treated by the city council as allocatable goods, to be given to different groups. In the wake of racial rioting, the demand for such police services was almost unlimited and politically irresistible. Given this interpretation of events, the public choice argument that the provision of separable goods may lead to uncontrollable demand was supported, but the argument that local governments grew by adding the wrong functions and making themselves vulnerable to demands was not supported. This case study underscores the idea that almost any good or service can be treated as separable, and demand for almost any service can become extreme.

In Southside, the city council yielded not only to demands for more police but also, and simultaneously, to the implied demand not to raise taxes to pay for increased services. The result was to make the service expansion look cheap and perhaps overstimulate or fail to curb demand. The more immediate result was to create operating deficits.

NEO-MARXIST ARGUMENTS COMPARED
WITH OBSERVATIONAL DATA

O'Connor's argument that local-level expenditures are controlled by and favor business, and that such expenditures grow beyond the capacity of a shrinking fisc, was only marginally descriptive of the causes of local fiscal stress. Several parts of the argument have been well-documented, but the argument as a whole does not describe the occurrence of local fiscal stress.

For example, it is now well accepted that interest groups play a major role in state-level politics. It is also generally accepted that urban renewal benefited businesses more than it benefited the poor, especially in the short term (Anderson, 1964; Sanders, 1980; Hill, 1983). But it is not clear that interest groups are as prominent at the local level as O'Connor would have one believe.

Business groups are not always organized or effective. Businesses located in cities are often the branches of larger corporations, which have little interest in local politics and little need for benefits from local government. Business may be fragmented into a number of groups, with competing interests; some may prefer mall development, others may want to protect the downtown; and banks may prefer reinvestment in housing. When business does not speak with one voice, its impact on the polity may be muffled (see Whitt, 1982; Molotch and Logan, 1984).

Even if interest groups were prominent at the local level, and business groups controlled city hall completely, it does not follow that the result would be higher spending levels. Business-controlled cities are often cities that provide few basic services and few social services (Lineberry and Fowler, 1967). They tend to have low levels of taxation. Business-dominated cities are thus likely to have both constrained expenditures and constrained revenues, but not necessarily fiscal stress.

Even more to the point, some business-dominated cities take the nonspending model to the extreme. Whereas the O'Connor model of business domination assumes that businesses (and unions) support construction projects, some extremely conservative cities do not spend money for needed infrastructure. These cities are severely undercapitalized. Ironically, the unwillingness to spend public money contributes to fiscal stress because the cities lack amenities that attract new residents and businesses and lack the facilities to keep teenagers off the streets and out of trouble.[4]

Fiscal problems created by the urban renewal process, which affected the thinking of O'Connor, were less apparent in the case study cities with which we are comparing the neo-Marxist theories. These localities that were worse off financially and that had the largest accumulation of poor and the oldest and most dilapidated housing qualified for more federal grants, some of which were leveraged with municipal and private funding.[5] Usually, there was not much municipal money involved, especially in relation to the size of the projects. The fact that these projects benefited business more than the poor had implications for class analysis and redistribution, but it had little negative impact on the local fiscal health.

Business domination of expenditures does not provide a very satisfactory explanation of the origin of fiscal stress. Case study and comparative data suggest that heavy expenditures on infrastructure were simply not a major cause of fiscal stress in the 1970s and 1980s, across cities, not just in the case study cities. As "stagflation" began to characterize the economy of the 1970s, interest rates rose, curtailing the municipal borrowing that is used to develop infrastructure (Petersen and Hough, 1983).[6]

O'Connor was more successful in calling attention to suburbanization as a cause of local fiscal stress. However, at least for one of the case study cities, Southside, he missed the mechanism by which suburbanization generated fiscal stress.

Southside experienced a considerable outflow of middle-class whites to surrounding suburbs through the 1960s and 1970s, at the same time that there was an inflow of poor blacks and Hispanics to the central city. The inmigration gradually slowed down, revealing a net reduction in population. To recapture the fleeing tax base, the city annexed its suburbs, greatly expanding its area and hence increasing the demands for service delivery. The increased area disproportionately boosted the costs of fire services to the outlying areas. Thus in Southside, it was not decreased revenues from a declining tax base due to suburbanization that caused the fiscal stress so much as it was increased services costs on a stable (not growing) revenue base. This version of events was probably typical of a number of other communities that annexed their new suburbs.

The events in Southside do not invalidate O'Connor's model; they only suggest that the model is not complete. In Southside, it was not suburbanization that caused fiscal stress but rather the city's reaction to that suburbanization.

Examined in the light of the case study cities, O'Connor's argument was more completely on target in his discussion of the effects of grants on local fiscal stress. As O'Connor predicted, the federal and state governments were unable to sustain the level of grants, gradually causing problems for cities that had become dependent on them. Many of the state grants did not increase with inflation, causing cities to absorb gradually more of the costs or cut back on services. In short, O'Connor's prediction that fiscal stress at one level of government would contribute to fiscal stress at other levels of government matches the observational data.

O'Connor did not emphasize the importance of increasing police expenditures in creating fiscal stress, although other neo-Marxists do emphasize this variable. There was major social unrest in the 1960s with rioting in many urban centers. The response to riots was first, on the federal level, to throw program funds at the social problems that generated riots (an action entirely consonant with O'Connor's views). However, that social impulse was followed by increased expenses to improve police (Button, 1979). There were federal grants for arming police and improving equipment as well as attempts to reform police and make them less prone to initiate riots. At the local level the response to riots was in the form of political demands for a huge increase in funding for the police.

There is considerable evidence that the expansion of police forces was a major trend across the country as a response both to increases in the percentage black and to riots (Welch, 1975). In Southside, in particular, after the riots following the assassination of Martin Luther King, there was increased fear of blacks in a city already tense over racial differences. There was increased demand for police to protect the downtown merchants, who were surrounded by the poor. This demand was funneled through the political system and resulted in an expanded police department and greater police expenditures.

A THEORETICAL SYNTHESIS AND EXPANSION

When examined in the light of case study data, both public choice theories and neo-Marxist approaches missed important aspects of how fiscal stress is created. A more satisfactory model combines portions of both theories and extends the combined model to include other causes. What was missing from both models was some explanation of how the political system operated to magnify or modify fiscal strains.

The public choice theorists did deal with bureaucracy as a force pushing for increased expenses, but they did not treat the political and managerial system as a variable that can potentially exacerbate or damp down fiscal stress. Yet the political system is not a constant.

What happened in Southside and many other cities is that a substantial portion of the population—white middle classes and business—was shaken by the riots, and racial unrest more generally, and thus demanded not just more but an unlimited amount of police protection. However, the demand alone was not enough to precipitate a fiscal crisis. It had to be processed by a political and administrative system that would try to satisfy the demands without increasing taxes to pay for them.

It turns out that in Southside (and elsewhere) there were some changes in the political system that made city hall particularly vulnerable to demands. The decline of an old political machine and a changing ethnic mix broke up old coalitions of voters and led politicians to seek votes through broad appeals such as lowering taxes—at precisely the time when police were expanding. The administrative structure was not strong enough to resist demands for deficits. These factors helped translate fiscal stress into fiscal crisis.

We suggest taking from each theory the parts that work and adding to the combined version the concept of political vulnerability. The resulting model for how fiscal stress occurs then has the following elements. There is political support for repressing civic unrest such as occurred with the riots (consistent with neo-Marxian views). This political pressure is combined with an increased demand for protective services (consistent with public choice views). Although they are demanding increased services, citizens are unwilling to pay for them (consistent with both views, after modification). The political system yields to demands to provide more services without raising more revenues because it has become overly sensitive to citizen demands. (That politicians should simply reflect citizen demands in order to be reelected is consistent with public choice theory, but varying sensitivity to citizen demands is not part of the theory.) And, as state and federal transfers decrease, fiscal pressure becomes more acute (consistent with O'Connor).

This combined and extended view of the causes of local fiscal stress is considerably less structural and more contingent than either of its progenitors, while maintaining the idea of some structural antecedents of fiscal crisis. As presented, this more comprehensive approach is largely compatible with the neo-Marxian thesis. The substitution of repression expenses for social service expenditures not only does not weaken the model, it probably strengthens it. Police cost money, just as social services do, and repression is a substitute for buying off conflict with social programs.

The extended model poses more of a challenge to public choice theory. Demand for police rather than for social services caused the increase in expenditures. The structural assumption that the cities were performing the wrong functions underlay the public choice solution—reduce the number of nonbasic functions performed by local government. That diagnosis and that solution were called into question.

IMPLICATIONS FOR THEORY OF CITIES'
RESPONSES TO FISCAL STRESS

So far we have discussed how two contrasting theories explain why fiscal stress occurs. Both theories also have implications for how cities will respond to fiscal problems. The theories predict crises and widespread restructuring. Yet widespread fiscal crises on the pattern of New York or Cleveland have not developed. Cities are still experiencing fiscal problems, but they are handling them. Such outcomes create questions about the structural views of urban fiscal problems.

The neo-Marxist argument states that the expected crisis can be delayed by continuing and increasing social expenditures, but expenditures for social services have been reduced. According to this argument, financial crisis should be succeeded by social crisis. This may happen, but it has not happened yet.

Public choice theorists argue that the scope and overall expense of the public sector will provoke voter resistance that will precipitate a crisis. There is clearly some taxpayer resistance, but Proposition 13 has not led to a larger successful movement to cut back local services. People want to cut back their tax burden but maintain their service levels (they want something for nothing). To the extent that they succeed, the fiscal crisis ought to be exacerbated, not quietly handled.

Both theories assume that fiscal problems will take crisis proportions, and the crisis will precipitate some radical change. Both neo-Marxist and public choice models do not take the quality of management into consideration and so do not assume that the problems can be resolved managerially. But the possibility should be considered that the problems are being resolved because they are not structural but rather political and managerial.

There is, however, another alternative, namely, that the problems are at least in part structural, but that the quality of public management helps cities avoid reaching the crisis stage by making fundamental changes earlier in the process. This alternative suggests that cities' responses to fiscal stress are as important for developing theories of urban processes as are the causes of that stress.

Managers and politicians confronting and resolving fiscal problems have altered the way cities operate. Cities' responses to fiscal stress have resulted in substantial changes in (1) revenue sources, (2) the allocation of urban services, (3) the degree of emphasis on economic development, and (4) the range of services provided. These changes have implications for the equity, openness, autonomy, and responsiveness of local governments.

CHANGES IN REVENUE SOURCES

The first issue in considering how cities are responding to stress is to consider what changes they are making in their revenue sources. Because local officials prefer not to cut employees or programs, they often wish to increase revenues as a solution to fiscal stress, but the acceptable and legally possible alternatives are not numerous. The property tax is unpopular and in some cases has been curtailed, either by referenda or by the state legislature. Intergovernmental revenue has been declining for several years. As a result, cities have moved toward increased reliance on user fees (Criz, 1982; Smith and Keller, 1983). The increased use of such fees is consistent with the public choice perspective because it links costs and demands, and thereby reduces demands. However, it would be overstating the case to argue that administrators adopted user fees because they had accepted a public choice perspective. Rather, these fees were less objectionable politically than many other forms of taxation.

The implications of this increase of user charges depend somewhat on how the fees are set. If the fees are not graduated based on the ability to pay, and if money or entitlements of some sort are not distributed to the needy to pay the fees, city services will be allocated in such a way as to be more of a burden on the poor.

The effect of increased use of user charges also depends on the type of service for which fees are charged. For some services user charges may defeat the purpose of public provision of that service. For example (and all the following examples have been observed in cities in the last two years), setting ambulance fees at a level to discourage their use may save the city money, but may prevent those who need the service from using it. Setting swimming pool fees above the level that poorer families can afford may defeat the purpose of the pools, which is to provide recreation for teenagers and keep them off the streets. If user fees are used to pay a higher proportion of public transportation costs, riders may become discouraged and drive to work. The collective result may be traffic jams, wasted time, depletion of gasoline supplies, and costly road repairs. The problems that occur when these functions are provided in a more marketlike fashion call attention to the collective aspects of those services and the very reasons why they were provided as public goods.

CHANGES IN ALLOCATION PATTERNS

A second way cities respond to fiscal stress is to change the allocation of governmental services. Despite the increased use of user fees, real and imagined limits on revenue sources often make it difficult to replace declining revenue. In a situation of declining revenue, local officials often try to stretch resources to maintain existing services. When they cannot stretch resources, they have to reduce service levels. Generally speaking, social services have had lower priority compared to police, fire, streets, water, and sanitation. However, these basic services often have been cut back before federally funded social services, either because social services have been mandated or because federal subsidies earmarked for particular services made them so cheap from the perspective of the local budget that it did not make sense to cut them (Wolman, 1980).

Nonearmarked federal funds clearly posed a different problem because they could be spent on social or basic services. When fiscal stress occurred, it became extremely tempting to take money that had been spent on social services and spend it on basic services. For example, in Southside, at the height of that city's fiscal problems, revenue-sharing funds were reallocated from support of community social service agencies to the fire department to cover deficits in that department.

Spending for programs sponsored by the federal government was sustained as long as the flow of federal money was maintained, but when major cuts in federal programs reduced the flow of funds, local governments tended on the whole to ratify the cuts. Cities were not willing or able to replace many of the cuts imposed by the federal government (Nathan et al., 1983: 143). Because many of the programs cut were social services, the effect has been a reduction in spending on programs for the poor.

EMPHASIS ON ECONOMIC DEVELOPMENT

A third way that cities are changing as they cope with fiscal stress is through increasing their emphasis on economic development, in the hope of maintaining or expanding a revenue-producing tax base. The neo-Marxists see emphasis on economic development and growth as a constant, caused by the dominance of business groups over local government. In fact, however, the emphasis on growth and development was highly variable between cities. Cities that were economically and fiscally stressed tended to have the most aggressive economic development programs.

In a study of municipalities in Illinois (Rubin, 1984), cities that had a higher property tax rate in 1982, a lower median family income in 1980, a larger number of families below poverty in 1980, and a higher unemployment rate in 1980—all signs of fiscal stress—tended to engage in more economic development activities. The relationships are reported in Table 7.1.

Table 7.1 was formed by creating an index that measures economic development activities and then dividing cities into three categories—

TABLE 7.1   Associations of Economic Development Activity
with Fiscal and Economic Hardship Measures (N = 156)

Hardship Measures	Chi Square (d.f.; sig.)	Kendall's TauB (sig.)
Property tax rate, 1982	17.54 (4; .015)	.225 (.010)
Median family income, 1980	11.05 (4; .026)	.214 (.002)
Families in poverty, 1980	17.51 (4; .002)	.269 (.001)
Number unemployed, 1980	11.57 (4; .021)	.204 (.003)

SOURCE: Rubin (1984: Table 7).

high, medium, and low—in terms of how many activities were attempted. For measures of stress and poverty, cities were also placed in three categories, of high, medium, and low. Then the index of economic development activities was cross-tabulated with different measures of fiscal stress and urban poverty. Table 7.1 summarizes the analysis of 4 of these 3 X 3 tables, giving the strength of the correlations and significance of each relationship.

Although only moderate in their strength, the relationships are statistically significant and theoretically suggestive. Measures of local poverty also correlate with the individual actions taken by cities to develop the local economy. For example, whether or not the city owned and managed its own development site correlated with several poverty measures. The correlations are shown in Table 7.2.

Table 7.2 summarizes three 2 X 3 tables. The dependent variable—whether or not the city owns or operates its own economic development site—is dichotomous. Cities were divided into high, medium, and low on the poverty measures. The table reports on the strength and significance of the relationship of each of three poverty measures with the dependent variable.

The tendency of fiscally stressed cities to engage in economic development is significant in part because public officials showed a tendency to ignore the potential negative financial effects of development. This tendency could actually lead stressed cities to make their situations worse. Only about 20% of the mayors and economic development people surveyed in Illinois (Rubin, 1984) expressed a concern that tax concessions to attract business might be a waste of money; only about 32% agreed that mall development could harm the local economy by hurting business elsewhere in the city; and only 20% of the mayors and 16% of the economic development officials agreed that the cost to a municipality of new business could exceed the benefits.

TABLE 7.2   Associations Between a City Owning or Operating
            Its Own Economic Development Site and Measures
            of Poverty (N = 148)

Poverty Measures	Chi Square (d.f.; sig.)	Kendall's TauB (sig.)
Median family income, 1980	19.01 (2; .0001)	.337 (.0000)
Number in poverty, 1980	17.44 (2; .0088)	.323 (.0000)
Number unemployed, 1980	9.42 (2; .008)	−.231 (.0015)

SOURCE: Calculated from Rubin (1984).

Not only are fiscally stressed cities more likely to undertake economic development activities, there appears to be a pattern in which fiscal and economic stress leads cities to take a more probusiness attitude that results in tax breaks and user fee subsidies to businesses (Rubin, 1985).[7] The effectiveness of these subsidies to attract and retain businesses is highly questionable (Ambrosius, 1985; Kale, 1984). Such incentives may be transfers to business that produce little public good (Fainstein et al., 1983; Reich, 1983; Bluestone and Harrison, 1982; Smith, 1984; Pascarella and Raymond, 1982; U.S. Department of Housing and Urban Development, 1982).

It has been difficult to measure tax expenditures and business subsidies at the local level, and hence difficult to demonstrate any relationship among fiscal stress, probusiness attitudes, and subsidies to business. However, our research suggests some evidence for such a linkage. The degree of stress—as measured by changing sales tax revenues, changing assessed values, the number of families below the poverty level, and the changing number of jobs influence the likelihood of doing a business retention study, that is, a study to see what businesses need or want to stay in the city and expand. Cities that did a business retention study were more likely to subsidize commercial and business users with lower water rates.[8] The associations between fiscal and economic stress measures and doing a retention study are reported in Table 7.3. The association (Kendall's TauB) between doing a retention study and subsidizing businesses in the water rate was .33, with a significance level of .004.

Tables 7.1, 7.2, and 7.3 are not intended as explanatory models. Rather, as presented, they are meant to add credence to our arguments that the more economically deprived cities are more willing to make concessions to promote business growth. As such, they provide an indication for future research on the costs of such concessions to cities in the greatest economic need.[9]

This analysis suggests a different kind of neo-Marxian analysis in which progrowth attitudes are a result of fiscal stress rather than a cause of it. In the communities with severe economic problems, officials were acting less at the direction of their business community than on behalf of the whole community and on behalf of city hall. The need for jobs was so desperate that almost any business that brought in jobs seemed to be a plus; the need to prevent further erosion of city revenue, and the impossibility of raising additional revenue in a city marked by high unemployment, made expansion of businesses a highly desired policy. The outcome of the policy might be to give additional influence to the

TABLE 7.3   Association Between Fiscal and Economic Stress Measures
and Doing a Business Retention Study (N = 146)

Stress Measures	Chi Square (d.f.; sig.)	Kendall's TauB (sig.)
Sales tax Receipts, 1982	9.81 (2; .007)	−.243 (.0009)
Sales tax receipts, 1977	15.64 (2; .0004)	−.306 (.0000)
Percentage change in assessed valuation, 1977-1982	8.11 (2; .0173)	.173 (.0132)
Percentage change in sales tax, 1977-1982	7.55 (2; .0228)	.208 (.0038)
Number of families in poverty, 1980	7.38 (2; .0249)	−.203 (.0047)
Percentage change in number of jobs	10.16 (2; .0062)	.248 (.0008)

SOURCE: Analysis taken from Rubin (1984).

business sector, but it was not necessarily business influence that created the policy.

THE SCOPE OF SERVICES

The fourth impact of managing fiscal stress on changes in city government has to do with the changing scope of city services. Cities tried to avoid where possible cutting back or eliminating services. One response when cities could not afford to pay for the full scope of their services was to shift some functions to other levels of government rather than cut them back or eliminate them entirely. Some cities that supported colleges tried to give them to the state; some cities tried to give more social service functions to the county and state governments; others tried to divest themselves of their jails, courts, and museums. In many cases they were successful (Levine et al., 1981; ACIR, 1976).

The interpretation of such a reduction in scope of the local government depends somewhat on whether one perceives local government as responsive to citizens or controlled by an elite. If local government is generally responsive, then the shifting of services elsewhere may reduce the control citizens have over their services. At the very least, divestment of functions makes it more difficult for citizens to know to whom to complain in case of poor service. However, if one begins with the view that local government is controlled by an elite, the shift to other levels of government may have little impact on citizen access to service delivery.

Sometimes cities do not shift the service burden to other levels of government, but contract out to the private sector for services. The idea is that the private sector can produce the services more cheaply. City hall eliminates its capacity to produce the services directly. The effect is often a reduced capacity of city hall to respond to citizen complaints. City services are, and yet are not, produced by city hall.

In a related effort, a number of communities are trying to save money and increase efficiency by contracting for services with neighboring local governments. Cities that enter such interlocal agreements often have little say over how the service will be delivered. Such arrangements tend to reduce the ability of a city to respond to citizen complaints.

In summary, in response to fiscal stress, cities have changed in an incremental fashion rather than in a radical restructuring. There seems to have been some changes in allocation patterns to the disadvantage of the poor; there seems to have been a tilt toward a more probusiness and prodevelopment stance, especially in cities with a large number of poor people. These changes are consistent with a neo-Marxian view. Some cities have shifted functions to other levels of government and to the private sector, and many have had increasing resort to user fees to generate additional revenue. These responses are consistent with a public choice perspective. But at the moment, none of these changes is enhancing the responsiveness of local governments to citizens, which was the goal of both neo-Marxians and public choice theorists.

CONCLUSIONS

Both neo-Marxian views (especially those of O'Connor) and public choice views of the local fiscal crisis served to call attention to important parts of the process of generating fiscal stress. But to model observed events effectively requires piecing together parts of each theoretical approach (an outcome that would horrify both the neo-Marxists and the public choice economists.) In addition, an expanded theory would have to add contingency factors to the more structural approaches, and in particular would have to pay more attention to the structure of politics and the quality of management.

The revised approach allows for the possibility that good managers can anticipate fiscal stress and respond to it short of crisis. There is considerable evidence that this is what cities have been doing. And in responding to fiscal stress, cities are making important changes in an incremental manner.

It is still too early to state definitively what the directions of the changes are, but we suggest some tentative outlines. Cities are depending more on user fees, are allocating somewhat less to social services, are becoming more probusiness, and are reducing the scope of services that they provide directly to citizens. These changes may diminish the openness and responsiveness of local government. The obliviousness of city officials to the costs of development suggests that many communities may put themselves in a worse situation—by capitulating to business demands—than they were in at the start. And the increased use of user fees may reflect a change in the patterns of equity that underlie urban service delivery.

NOTES

1. This logic describes the Tiebout model, and much of the literature that this famous economic model spawned. The model assumes that people of differing incomes have specific patterns of demands from city hall, leading to specific packages of taxes and services. Individuals are said to shop for communities to live in that reflect their own most desired package of taxes and services. Suburbanization reflects the economic segregation of citizens into relatively homogeneous income groups because of their desire to escape the distributional patterns generated by inner city poor in the larger central cities. See for example Julius Margolis's summary of this argument in Aronson and Schwartz (1981: 221-222).

2. The Rubin (1982) study is from *Running in the Red*, a case study of a midwestern city manager city that ran deficits. The city was given the pseudonym "Southside" to protect informants. The Levine et al. (1981) book, *The Politics of Retrenchment* is about the responses of four local governments to fiscal stress: Baltimore, Maryland; Prince George's County, Maryland; Cincinnati, Ohio; and Oakland, California.

3. In the paper, "How Many New Yorks?" fiscal stress was measured primarily by the size of the short-term debt outstanding at the end of the fiscal year. This is not a perfect measure because some cities have legitimate reasons to have short-term debt outstanding at the end of the year, but most such debt implies borrowing to cover operating costs, a good indicator of fiscal stress. The scope of services was measured by a ratio of expenditures on the common functions divided by all revenues. The higher this ratio, the lower the expenses on noncommon functions, such as social services.

4. Southside in *Running in the Red* is a good example of the extreme of the conservative model, resulting in undercapitalization.

5. See especially the Baltimore case in Levine et al. (1981), *The Politics of Retrenchment*.

6. "Since 1968 state and local capital investment in constant 1972 dollars has fallen by one-third, from a high of $35.9 billion to $23.6 billion in 1981. . . . Capital expenditures make up a diminishing share of total outlays of states and local governments: in 1960 state and local governments spent 27.1% of their budgets on infrastructures; by 1980, they were spending 15.4% on capital items" (Petersen and Hough, 1983: 11).

7. For this analysis, the two coauthors merged two data sets on Illinois municipalities, and used the cities that were in both sets of data. There were about 100 cities in both sets,

but due to missing data, most of the analysis is based on about 70 cities. The economic development data set contained information on 156 cities in Illinois, and included questions to mayors and economic development officials as well as descriptive data about finance and the economy. The second data set was based on a survey of finance officers in 188 Illinois cities about local revenue sources. The data on water rate structures come from this second data set. Both surveys were done in 1984. Results of both surveys are available from the Center for Governmental Studies, Northern Illinois University, Dekalb, Illinois.

8. The degree of subsidy to business users was measured as the percentage difference in the cost per thousand gallons for the smallest users and the largest users. Because the costs of water production and delivery overall do not markedly decline with greater usage, a reduced rate for large volume users represents a subsidy to commercial and industrial users. Other studies have confirmed that businesses often do not pay their share of costs for water production, and that residential consumers tend to pay more to cover the subsidy (Williams, 1985).

9. Elsewhere, we have developed path models suggestive of causal explanations for the different number of economic development activities attempted by cities (Rubin, 1985). The models combined indicators of fiscal stress and poverty, the presence of an economic development organization and attitudes of local mayors and economic development officials concerning the urgency of the need for development, the degree of business-government cooperation, and the sense of public officials that they can control future developments. Because of the high multicollinearity between separate indicators of city fiscal stress and the poverty of its inhabitants, only one indicator of each was used in the resulting models. Overall, the models explained about a third of the variance in the number of economic development actions taken. The most important explanatory variable was the presence of an economic development organization. Perceptions of government-business involvement and the median family income provided the second best set of predictors, though much of the effect of median family income was an indirect one acting through the sense of urgency felt by officials and leading to the creation of an economic development organization. At least in our sample, the effect of the fiscal stress experienced by city government (as opposed to the poverty of residents) was weaker than that of other variables.

REFERENCES

ACIR (1976) Pragmatic Federalism: the Reassignment of Functional Responsibility. Report M-105, July. Page 4. Washington, DC: Government Printing Office.

AMBROSIUS, M. (1985) "Olson's thesis and economic growth in the states: the role of interest group strength in state economic development policymaking, 1969-1980." Presented at the Midwest Political Science Association, Chicago, April.

ANDERSON, M. (1964) The Federal Bulldozer: A Critical Analysis of Urban Renewal. Cambridge, MA: MIT.

ARONSON, J. R. and E. SCHWARTZ (1981) Management Policies in Local Government Finance. Washington, DC: International City Management Association.

BLUESTONE, B. and B. HARRISON (1982) The Deindustrialization of America: Plant Closings, Community Abandonment and the Dismantling of Basic Industry. New York: Basic Books.

BUCHANON, J. (1977) "Why does government grow?" pp. 3-18 in T. Borcherding (ed.) Budgets and Bureaucrats. Durham, NC: Duke University Press.

———(1968) Demand and Supply of Public Goods. Chicago: Rand McNally.

———(1967) Public Finance in Democratic Process. Chapel Hill: University of North Carolina Press.

BUTTON, J. (1979) Black Violence: The Political Impact of the 1960's Riots. Princeton, NJ: Princeton University Press.

CLARK, T. N., I. RUBIN, E. ZIMMERMAN, and L. PETTLER (1976) "How many New Yorks?" (Mimeo, University of Chicago)

CRIZ, M. (1982) "The role of user charges and fees in city finance." Urban Data Service Reports 14 (June). Washington, DC: International City Management Association.

FAINSTEIN, S., N. FAINSTEIN, R. HILL, D. JUDD, and M. SMITH (1983) Restructuring the City: The Political Economy of Urban Redevelopment. New York: Longman.

HARRINGTON, M. (1984) The New American Poverty. New York: Holt, Rinehart & Winston.

HILL, R. (1983) "Crisis in the motor city: the politics of economic development in Detroit," pp. 80-125 in S. N. Fainstein et al., Restructuring the City: The Political Economy of Urban Redevelopment. New York: Longman.

HORTON, R. (1977) The City in Transition: Prospects and Policies for New York. New York: City of New York Temporary Commission on City Finances.

KALE, S. (1984) "U.S. industrial development incentives and manufacturing growth during the 1970's." Growth and Change 15: 26-34.

KENNEDY, M. (1984) "The fiscal crisis of the city," pp. 91-110 in M. Smith (ed.) Cities in Transformation: Class, Capital and the State. Beverly Hills, CA: Sage.

LEVINE, C., I. RUBIN, and G. WOLOHOJIAN (1981) The Politics of Retrenchment. Beverly Hills, CA: Sage.

LINEBERRY, R. and E. FOWLER (1967) "Reformism and public policies in American cities." American Political Science Review LXI (September).

MOLOTCH, H. and J. LOGAN (1984) "Tensions in the growth machine: overcoming resistance to value-free development." Social Problems 31 (5): 483-499.

MORRIS, C. R. (1980) The Cost of Good Intentions. New York: W. W. Norton.

NATHAN, R., F. DOOLITTLE, and associates (1983) The Consequences of Cuts: The Effects of the Reagan Domestic Program on State and Local Governments. Princeton, NJ: Princeton Urban and Regional Research Center.

NISKANEN, W. (1971) Bureaucracy and Representative Government. Chicago: Aldine Atherton.

O'CONNOR, J. (1973) The Fiscal Crisis of the State. New York: St. Martin's.

PASCARELLA, T. and R. RAYMOND (1982) "Buying bonds for business: an evaluation of the industrial revenue bond program." Urban Affairs Quarterly 18, 1: 73-90.

PETERSEN, J. and W. HOUGH (1983) Creative Capital Financing. Chicago: Municipal Finance Officers Association.

REICH, R. (1983) The New American Frontier. New York: Times Books.

RUBIN, H. (1985) "The political context of local economic development." Unpublished manuscript, Center for Governmental Studies, Northern Illinois University, DeKalb.

———(1984) "Getting moving again: attitudes and actions taken by local officials toward economic development." Presented at the Region VI meetings of the American Society for Public Administration, October 4.

RUBIN, I. (1982) Running in the Red: The Political Dynamics of Urban Fiscal Stress. Albany: State University of New York Press.

SANDERS, H. (1980) "Urban renewal and the revitalized city," pp. 103-126 in D. Rosenthal (ed.) Urban Revitalization. Beverly Hills, CA: Sage.

SAVAS, E. S. (1982) Privatizing the Public Sector: How to Shrink Government. Chatham, NJ: Chatham House.

SMITH, M. [ed.] (1984) Cities in Transformation: Class, Capital and the State. Beverly Hills, CA: Sage.

———and M. KELLER (1983) " 'Managed growth' and the politics of uneven development in New Orleans," pp. 126-166 in S. Fainstein et al., Restructuring the City: The Political Economy of Urban Redevelopment. New York: Longman.

TULLOCK, G. (1970) Private Wants, Public Means. New York: Basic Books.

United States Department of Housing and Urban Development (1982) An Impact Evaluation of the Urban Development Action Grant Program. Washington, DC: HUD.

WELCH, S. (1975) "The impact of urban riots on urban expenditures." American Journal of Political Science 19 (November): 741-760.

WHITT, J. (1982) Urban Elites and Mass Transportation: The Dialectics of Power. Princeton, NJ: Princeton University Press.

WILLIAMS, M. (1985) "Interclass water rate differentials and the capture theory of regulation." Unpublished paper, Economics Department, Northern Illiois University.

WOLMAN, H. (1980) "Local government strategies to cope with fiscal stress," pp. 231-248 in C. Levine and I. Rubin (eds.) Fiscal Stress and Public Policy. Beverly Hills, CA: Sage.

8

Finance Capital
and the City

ALBERTA M. SBRAGIA

☐ IN URBAN POLITICS and sociology, analysis of the role of "finance capital," as of capital in general, is usually associated with neo-Marxist scholarship. Because of the impact of investment decisions on class relations within the city, neo-Marxists have given more attention to investment patterns and investors than have conventional analysts. Yet neo-Marxists have not shown much detailed interest in the complex mechanisms by which financial capital actually works and the many specialized markets in which it functions. The very term "finance capital" in fact obscures more than it clarifies, for it groups together a complex set of financial institutions and capital markets that differ considerably from each other. The lack of detailed understanding of the internal operations of institutions and markets causes particular problems if we are trying to explore such issues as how American cities may "restructure" themselves (Fainstein and Fainstein, 1982).

Such restructuring has already produced surprises for neo-Marxist and conventional analysts of urban phenomena alike. Despite years of writing about the political and social effects of "disinvestment" in older inner cities, neither group anticipated the "reinvestment" that has recently taken place in such cities and the effects it has had. Analysts of both camps really need to be more respectful of the sheer complexity of the market forces affecting the social structure and political life of American cities. Neo-Marxists may retort that this admonition does not apply to them. After all, "capitalism" is the very hub around which Marxist thinking revolves. Yet, for a body of work so preoccupied with the power of market forces, neo-Marxist scholarship has performed little detailed analysis of market mechanisms and their varying operation in different types of markets. Whereas the conventional analysis of urban sociology or urban politics is overly narrow, neo-Marxist analysis is overly generalized. Neo-Marxist scholars need to look much more closely at how particular markets actually work.

Conventional and neo-Marxist scholars should also look more closely at the different ways in which government policy influences and shapes markets. In particular, both should pay more attention to federal tax policy; the Internal Revenue Service Code is a much neglected force in urban political economy. For example, to understand the dynamics of "reinvestment," scholars should scrutinize the generous historic preservation tax credits provided by the Economic Recovery Tax Act of 1981. Markets and tax policy are inseparable.

This chapter examines changes in the relationship between cities and the financial market that lends funds for *public* investment. It examines city-market restructuring by analyzing the impact of the market and of the tax policy within which the market is enmeshed; it also explores the role played by local borrowers themselves in shaping city-market relations. I shall argue that to understand the restructuring that has gone on in the past ten years in the world of city borrowing, we need to examine the triangular relationship that exists among local governments, lenders, and the federal government.

This chapter does not examine the operations of all financial markets and all financial institutions as they affect the city. The financial market it analyzes is only one part of that incredibly diverse and complex set of financial institutions and capital markets neo-Marxists refer to as "finance capital." Consequently, this chapter does not examine many of the facets of the financial world that influence both public and private investment decisions. This chapter does not discuss monetary policy; differences in the government regulations and taxes to which commercial banks and savings and loans institutions are subject and how they affect investment decisions; the powerful role of pension funds and the regulations governing their investments; or detailed differences between investments financed by banks and those financed through the capital market.

CITY BORROWING

Traditionally, subnational governments have borrowed to build public facilities. In fact, such governments in the United States are responsible for the bulk of civilian public investment. Between 1946 and 1982, 90% of all U.S. public sector investment in fixed, government-owned domestic capital facilities was financed by state/local government whereas only 10% was financed by the federal government (Government Finance Research Center, 1984: 2). Such public investment provides roads, bridges, sewers, mass transit systems, water systems, airports, harbors, and the like. Capital spending in the 1970s at least checked the deterioration in the physical infrastructure of cities; after 1980, capital spending did not even do that. John Petersen (1985: 1.2) concludes that "the nation's physical plant of public works is beginning to contract in per capita terms." Many analysts, reports, and congressional hearings have emphasized the need for increased public investment in capital infrastructure, and the financing of public investment is receiving more attention than it has for a long while.

State and local governments do not, however, borrow just to build infrastructure. They have also borrowed in order to lend to private bodies that, they hope, will generate economic growth and contribute to the tax base by creating jobs. During the 1970s, federal grants became more important in paying for physical infrastructure. But state and local borrowing also climbed as subnational governments used borrowed money to stimulate local economic development and to help middle-income residents become homeowners. State and local borrowing, therefore, has now become a major factor in American financial markets. In 1984, state and local governments borrowed roughly 125 billion dollars, up from 65 billion in 1979 (Petersen, 1985: Figure 2.1).

State general-purpose governments have borrowed less and less compared to other subnational governments. Whereas in 1966-1970 states accounted for 23% of the dollar volume in borrowing, by 1983 they accounted for only 8.2% (Petersen, 1985: Figure 2.4). Statutory authorities, by contrast, accounted for 54% of the dollar volume in borrowing, whereas municipalities accounted for 20%. The increase in the importance of statutory authority borrowing is one sign of the growing importance of borrowing for "nontraditional" purposes, for such authorities are usually the governmental units that borrow in order to lend.

BORROWING IN THE MARKET

If an individual wants a mortgage for a home, he or she will probably go to a savings and loan institution. If he or she desires a mortgage for a commercial building, the individual will probably approach either a commercial bank or a life insurance company. However, a city government is unlikely to borrow long-term funds for any type of public investment from such lenders.

State and local governments (along with the federal government and corporations) borrow long-term funds in the bond market—one market within the American system of capital markets. They do not borrow long-term funds from banks. Instead, they issue a debt instrument known as a "bond." Investors buy such bonds from the issuer, in effect lending the money to him or her. The issuer, in turn, promises to pay a specified rate of interest and repay the principal (the amount for which the bond has been issued) at an agreed-upon date. The date of maturity can range anywhere from, say, five to thirty years after the bond's issue date. To put it simply, if an investor buys a bond maturing in the year 2000 for $100,000 at 10% interest, he or she will receive $10,000 interest every year until the year 2000, when the investor receives his or her $100,000 and the bond is redeemed.

Bonds are traded in specialized markets because bonds issued by, for example, the federal government have different characteristics from corporate bonds and therefore attract investors for different reasons. Bonds are bought and sold, and then often resold, in these specialized markets. Corporate bonds, therefore, are traded in what is known as the "corporate bond market," federal government bonds in the Treasury market, and state and local bonds in the municipal bond market. Municipal bonds are bought and sold through networks of dealers and investment bankers rather than in a centralized forum such as the New York Stock Exchange. Thus the municipal bond market can be defined as "a nation-wide network of investors, investment institutions, securities dealers, and governmental borrowers. In this setting, hundreds of new and outstanding municipal securities are traded each business day" (Twentieth Century Fund Task Force on Municipal Bond Credit Ratings, 1974: 1).

Before considering how the municipal bond market differs from other bond markets, we should note that participating in the bond market is very different from dealing with the banking system. The market works differently. In bank lending, bankers meet their borrowers personally and must make discretionary decisions about how much to lend and at what interest rate. Lending is usually for short to medium periods, and bankers and borrowers can negotiate various terms.

By contrast, the operation of bond markets is much more impersonal than bank lending and involves much wider time horizons. Where banks provide short-term loans, bond markets can sometimes provide funds that will not need to be repaid for as long as 30 years. So many participants are involved in a bond market that no one institution or individual can control or even shape it, much less set interest rates (Zysman, 1983: 70). Further, if a bank makes a loan for $100,000, it can be sure that, barring default, it will be repaid $100,000 plus interest. However, the bank usually cannot sell that loan; it is a relatively illiquid investment. A buyer of $100,000 bond can, by contrast, sell his or her bond before the date of maturity, but may lose money in the process. Depending on market conditions, the buyer may only be able to sell his or her bond for, say, $95,000.

An example may clarify the difference between the organization of a bond market and that of a banking system. If a borrower is near default and has borrowed from a group of banks, it is possible to call a meeting of all the lenders and the borrower. When the government of Poland or Brazil is experiencing difficulty in servicing the debt, that is what happens. A meeting is called, and negotiations begin. Bank loans can be structured in many different ways, and the negotiations will deal with possible changes in the structure of the bank loan. As Cochran (1975: 148) puts it, a significant advantage of bank loans is that a "bank term loan can be tailored to the specific needs of the individual borrower through direct negotiations with the lending bank, so that the borrower can have more freedom in determining the repayment schedule." However, if the borrower had borrowed in the bond market, it would be nearly impossible to hold such a meeting. The number of lenders would be far too great; further, in some bond markets, it would be impossible to identify many of the current holders of the bonds. Finally, it would be much more difficult to restructure the repayment schedule, for bond issues publicly sold to the investment community cannot be as easily tailored as bank loans.

When borrowing, state and local governments are thus generally involved with the bond market rather than directly with a bank. Some small, relatively unknown local governments do issue bonds that are not publicly offered and that are privately placed with lenders, usually commercial banks. Although these types of bond issues are numerous, they account for only a small percentage of state and local borrowing. The more important state and local governments typically issue bonds publicly in the municipal bond market.

There have been highly newsworthy cases, however, in which observers depicted city governments as hostages to banks. The financing crises of Cleveland and New York City left the impression that local governments do go to local banks and take out loans. In reality, both cases involved short-term rather than long-term borrowing and had some unusual features. Local banks, for a variety of reasons, held municipal notes (repayable in less than a year). Because of their short-term nature, these notes had to be "refinanced"—that is, new capital had to be borrowed in order to repay the notes as they fell due. The need to refinance in the face of extraordinary financial and political difficulties exposed both the banks and the cities to unusually severe stress (Leeds, 1983; Sbragia, 1983: 82-83). The cases were atypical in the 1970s and would be even more so in the 1980s, for in the mid-1980s banks are not as likely to hold municipal notes. Of the roughly 30 billion dollars borrowed in the municipal note market in 1984, only 10% was lent by commercial banks (Petersen, 1985: Figure 4.7).

MUNICIPAL BOND MARKET

State and local governments borrow in a bond market that is different from all others in that lenders are exempt from federal income tax on their interest incomes. For that reason, it is often referred to as the "tax-exempt" market. Because of the tax exemption, state and local borrowers are able to borrow at lower interest rates than either the treasury or corporations pay. They can, in effect, borrow "cheap money"—that is, at below market rates. The ratio between tax-exempt and taxable interest rates varies, but the local borrowers usually pay several percentage points less than if the bond carried a taxable rate. By foregoing tax revenue, the federal government gives local borrowers an "invisible subsidy."

Tax exemption makes the buying of municipals attractive only to lenders in high tax brackets. For them, the comparatively lower interest income received from a municipal bond is higher than the after-tax interest income they would receive from a taxable bond. Therefore, lightly taxed lenders, such as pension funds, which are extremely important in the Treasury and corporate markets, are absent from the municipal bond market. By contrast, lenders such as commercial banks, casualty insurance companies, and upper-income individuals are interested in sheltering income from taxes. These are the investors who, under certain conditions, are interested in buying municipal bonds. Municipals, consequently, compete for investors with other tax shelters as well as with taxable bonds. The narrowness of the market and its sensitivity to changes in tax law have affected, as we shall see, the restructuring that has occurred between cities and their creditors.

Although banks buy and sell municipal bonds in the market, their relationship to the issuing city is rather different than if a specific loan had been granted. A loan is not sold to anyone else; it is simply repaid by the borrower. However, a bond can be bought by a commercial bank and resold five minutes later in what is known as the "secondary market." It involves a strictly impersonal transaction, and no one from the bank ever needs to meet any official from the city whose bond it buys. Generally, a bank (like every other investor) trades a bond but does not interfere in the internal operations of the issuer.

Lenders can invest in a wide variety of municipal bonds. Bonds vary in maturity dates, the type of special features they include, and the interest rates they offer. The specific rate of any bond at any one time is determined by the general level of rates (which is strongly influenced by the Federal Reserve Board), the relationship between supply and demand in the tax-exempt market, and the specific credit rating of the borrowing locality. Such a credit rating indicates to lenders the likelihood that the borrower will be able to meet principal repayment and interest costs at the times specified in the bond issue. The lower the credit rating, the higher the interest rate a borrower must pay in order to attract investors, all other things being equal. Thus any local borrower's costs are affected by general market conditions and by a credit rating that gives investors an idea of the risk involved in lending to that specific borrower.

Two private ratings agencies perform the task of assigning ratings to bond issues. Standard and Poor's Corporation and Moody's Investors Service are paid by the issuing locality to rate its bond issue before it goes to market; although some bonds are sold without a rating, they usually pay a higher interest rate and are more difficult to resell in the secondary market. Although the two agencies differ somewhat in the data they consider when deciding upon a rating, both, broadly speaking, examine the health of the borrower's economic base, the amount of debt it is already financing, and the general soundness of the locality's budget.

City officials tend to view the rating their city receives as a barometer of economic health. Not only does a lowered rating cost the city money in the form of additional interest costs, but it is also a sign that the city's economic and budgetary health may be declining. Conversely, a rating that is raised is seen as good news for the city's future viability. Usually a change in credit rating is front-page news in a local newspaper and may even attract national media attention. For example, when Houston's credit was lowered by Standard and Poor's in June 1985, the *New York Times* carried the story (King, 1985: 15).

Lenders also can choose between two types of municipal bonds—"general obligation" bonds backed by the "full faith and credit" of the issuer or "revenue" bonds backed by a specified revenue stream, usually from a revenue-producing facility. General-obligation bonds are issued by general-purpose governments that can use their taxing power to repay the bond; such bonds are used to build non-revenue-producing facilities such as roads, schools, and libraries. Revenue bonds are issued by both general-purpose governments and by special-purpose governments such as public authorities to finance revenue-producing services. Whereas in the 1960s general obligation bonds dominated the market, by the mid-1980s they represented, at most, 25% of the market's dollar volume (Petersen 1985: 2.6). Such a rise in the use of revenue bonds is linked to the increasing use of borrowed funds for purposes not thought of as "traditional" public investment, a subject to which I shall return in the next section.

After the New York City crisis, the relationship between local borrowers and various participants within the municipal bond market changed dramatically. Some of those changes were due to the crisis itself, whereas others were due to tax laws and changes in the purposes for which localities borrowed. In tracing these changes, it becomes clear that the relationship between the city and the municipal bond market is mediated by state and federal laws. Not only is the tax-exempt market itself a creation of federal law, but governmental policies are crucial in discussing "finance capital and the city."

This chapter examines three types of changes in the relationship between local governments and the municipal bond market: (1) those demanded by market participants in the wake of the New York City crisis; (2) those caused by changes in federal tax law; and (3) those caused by the assumption of new local responsibilities within the framework of state laws designed for an earlier era. We thus examine changes driven by the market, the national government, and the state-local government system.

RESTRUCTURING THE CITY-MARKET RELATIONSHIP

MARKET-DRIVEN RESTRUCTURING

New York City's "financing crisis" was traumatic for lenders in that an investment once assumed to be absolutely safe became perceived as potentially risky. As Patricia Leeds (1983) points out, New York City's fiscal "crisis" was in reality a fairly stable and continuous pattern of spending more than the city was taking in as revenue; it was dependent, for its maintenance, on heavy local borrowing. In one sense, it was not a "crisis" at all. But, on March 11, 1975, when the mayor was informed by officials from local banks that the market was closed to New York City, the city's "fiscal crisis" became transformed into a "financing crisis." Once the financing crisis—defined as "the inability of a city to continue to market its debt"—begins, "the ability to cover up the fiscal crisis with borrowing is eliminated" (Leeds, 1983: 115). All participants in the national market, not simply those holding New York City securities, became suddenly aware that all cities faced with a fiscal crisis could potentially also face a financing crisis.

The inability of New York City to service its short-term debt made it clear to investors that the management of cities' financial affairs was appallingly bad and lagged far behind contemporary management techniques for financial control. As one analyst put it, the crisis had demonstrated that "in city after city and county after county, budgeting, accounting, payroll, purchasing and program evaluation systems and procedures have become antiquated and wholly inadequate to meet the needs of modern management" (Lodal, 1976: 1133-1134). Essentially, "standard accounting, auditing, and reporting procedures" did not exist (Shalala, 1979: 19).

Lenders began demanding that borrowers disclose much greater information about their finances than had been customary. Because of the assumed safety of municipal bonds, lenders had been far less stringent with state and local borrowers than with corporate borrowers. Now they began to push for modern accounting systems and for much greater internal financial organization than most cities possessed.

The rating agencies, for their part, began penalizing cities that did not disclose financial information as requested, and gradually quite comprehensive financial disclosure statements at the time of bond issuance became commonplace. The agencies also began to include the quality of a locality's financial management system in their assessments; cities that did not modernize their systems of control were penalized. Local government, in turn, slowly began using modern accounting techniques and upgrading their systems of financial management.

The role of rating agencies also declined as the role of credit analysis grew. Because the agencies had not recognized New York City's problem until after many investors had, their credibility was damaged by the New York City crisis. Financial institutions, including commercial banks, began to develop their own credit ratings instead of relying solely on the rating agencies. Local officials, therefore, had to learn to deal much more extensively with the investment community than before. They had to "sell" their cities to a variety of analysts, and officials from large- and medium-size cities began to learn how to talk to a wide variety of credit analysts at numerous Wall Street breakfasts, lunches, and dinners. Investors' nervousness about potential defaults, therefore, led to pressure for better internal management of city finances and for better communication between city officials and the investment community.

The pressure for better financial management within city government—which originated with lenders—was soon reinforced from other sources. The federal government, in particular, began to demand more extensive audits: The State and Local Fiscal Assistance Amendments of 1976, for example, required an audit of all city monies, not just of federal monies related to a specific program (Funkhouser, 1979: 13). Thus in response both to the market and to Washington, city governments changed their operational procedures and improved the management of the resources at their disposal. Certainly, the municipal bond market helped impose a more clearly "managerial" style of operation on city governments, and in this the federal government was an influential ally.

Bitter debates continued about which financial standards should be adopted (whether, for example, public pension funds should use private sector or traditional public sector accounting principles; Findlay, 1981). Nonetheless, by 1985 the finance officer was being urged to view him- or herself as a "public strategist" who should engage in "strategic planning." The following quote gives the flavor of the new role that finance officers are increasingly expected to play:

> It is clear that in the future finance directors must be concerned with much more than care of and control over the public purse. The future of

municipal governments depends on the finance director's ability to invest the office with analytical and planning values. Simply because governments provide public services that generate *political* dividends, rather than monetary profits, this must not obscure their importance as representatives of very large financial enterprises. . . . Strategic planning is now beginning to make a name for itself among government managers as public officials more and more frequently consider themselves business persons [Wetzler and Petersen, 1985: 7-8].

The notion of "the finance officer as public strategist" had its birth in the aftermath of New York City's problems. Those problems forced investors and, subsequently, Congress to begin thinking of cities as "financial enterprises" rather than simply as service providers. Macroeconomists had long thought of cities as analogous to private firms, but neither lenders (seduced by the seemingly ironclad guarantee of a city's "full faith and credit") nor Congress (worried about the "urban crisis" with its overlay of social and racial problems) had been attracted to the analogy. New York City's financial trauma highlighted the importance of financial management and thrust it into the limelight during the next decade.

STATE-DRIVEN RESTRUCTURING

The United States does not have a "state" in the classic European continental sense. Whatever the American "state" may be, however, one of its main instruments is tax policy (Hansen, 1983). The Internal Revenue Service Code is a vivid illustration of Schumpeter's (1954: 17) point that "tax bill in hand, the state [has] penetrated the private economies and won increasing dominion over them." Federal tax policy penetrates every aspect of private sector operations—and, as we shall see in the next section, some local government operations as well. It makes no sense to discuss investment decisions—whether public or private—without considering the objectives and impact of federal tax policy. In fact, it is probably dangerous to analyze any aspect of urban political economy without discussing taxes.

Federal tax policy has clearly affected the relations between cities and their creditors. As already mentioned, the municipal bond market, because of its tax status, attracts a narrow band of investors—most institutional investors are not interested in the yields offered by tax-exempt bonds. Further, foreign lenders, not being subject to American tax laws, do not invest in the municipal bond market. Unlike British local governments, American local governments are therefore insulated from the volatility of international capital flows (Sbragia, 1985). Because of the narrowness of the market, however, the municipal bond market does feel acutely any changes in the investment behavior of its participants. If commercial banks, property casualty insurance companies, or individual investors change their behavior, local borrowers may have to pay higher interest rates, may find that capital is less available, or may be faced with shorter maturities in debt instruments.

A change of investor's behavior did in fact occur in the 1970s, and it was caused by the provisions of tax law. Simply put, commercial banks began to buy fewer municipals. Commercial bank buying had always fluctuated (partially because commercial banks tended to use only residual funds to buy municipals), but in the 1970s commercial bank buying began a secular decline. Banks began to find an increasing number of attractive tax shelters and they preferred such shelters to municipals (Kimball, 1977).[1] Banks began using "leases in order to take advantage of the investment tax credit and deductions for depreciation" (Campbell, 1982: 355). Furthermore, as income from foreign operations grew, banks were able to claim higher deductions for taxes paid to foreign governments. By the early 1980s, banks were buying only enough municipals to maintain their holdings: otherwise they had "practically abandoned the long-term municipal securities market" (Petersen, 1985: 2.12).

Casualty insurance companies stepped in to replace commercial banks during the mid-1970s. In 1977 and 1978, they became very important investors. In 1979, however, they began to suffer severe losses and thus had little need for tax shelters. By 1981, they too had largely abandoned the municipal bond market.

As cities have continued to borrow, the third category of investor has obviously picked up the slack. In fact, the rise of individual investors as a force in the tax-exempt market has been quite dramatic. Between 1981 and 1983, "The household sector's share of outstanding bonds rose from 30% to over 40%" (Petersen, 1985: 2.15). Many of these investors operate through money market mutual funds that collect small amounts of money and invest the aggregated—very large—sums in municipal securities.

The reasons that individuals are now so interested in buying tax-exempts have to do with the sociology of income tax. As more women have joined the labor force, two-earner families have seen their taxable incomes climb. Further, as inflation drove nominal incomes up while tax brackets remained unindexed for inflation, taxpayers moved into higher tax brackets. More households—and more money—therefore went seeking tax shelters during the late 1970s and early 1980s. Middle-class families began to see municipals as an appropriate investment for them—municipals were no longer just for the rich. Lowering marginal tax rates after 1981 did not blunt taxpayers' appetite for municipals: In 1985, 85% of all new issues were being bought by the household sector.

Interest rates rose significantly as households replaced institutional investors; borrowers had to pay higher interest costs to attract individual investors than to attract institutional ones. However, the sheer quantity of money pouring into tax shelters prevented a skyrocketing of tax-exempt interest rates. In previous periods (in 1966, 1969, 1974, and 1975), individual investors had moved in on the market, pushing up interest rates to the detriment of local borrowers. Local governments thus watched the decline of bank and insurance company investment with alarm. However, tax-exempt rates in the 1980s, although higher than they would have been in a market dominated by institutions (Braverman, 1982: 42), did not climb as much as he had feared, even though the volume of borrowing was extremely heavy. The number of individuals seeking tax shelters increased so much that yields (compared to those on taxable bonds) did not, as one analyst put it, "go through the roof" (Petersen, 1985: 2.17). Nonetheless, interest rates have risen so dramatically in the market that whereas earlier 75% of debt service payment had been allotted to repayment of principal, the same proportion now goes for interest costs (monetary policy was also responsible for this reversal; Hamilton, 1983: 22).

The increasing importance of the individual investor affected not only the interest rates that local borrowers had to pay but also their way of operating in the markets. Local governments became much more active as short-term borrowers. Tax-exempt money market funds have to lend monies for very short periods of time because they badly need liquidity. Local borrowers in the 1980s thus began issuing tax-exempt commercial paper (TECP), a borrowing instrument that can mature in as little as a single day, though the usual maturity is between thirty and sixty days. Investor demand has been so strong that TECP interest rates have stayed extremely low. Nevertheless, local governments are exposing themselves to all the uncertainties associated with short-term borrowing and specifically are facing the risk that adverse conditions in the market or a drop in their future credit rating will make it more difficult to "refinance" their debt. Short-term borrowing also makes it much harder to forecast future interest costs, especially when interest rates are volatile.

Local borrowers in 1985 thus depend mainly, if unwillingly, on individuals rather than on institutions for their borrowed capital. They have paid for this change through higher interest costs, increased uncertainty about future interest costs, and greater vulnerability to changes in future market conditions. They are now very sensitive to tax changes that might drop the marginal tax rate for individuals, thus making existing tax shelters less attractive. Further, any change in tax law that made tax-exempts even less appealing to commercial banks and ensured that they would never reenter the municipal bond market as significant investors would be very threatening to local governments. The kind of anxiety that proposals to alter income tax rates stir in local officials was evidenced in the special message that they sent to all members of the Government Finance Officers Association in mid-June 1985. Referring to President Reagan's announced plans to reform the income tax system, they declared:

> State and local officials need to be concerned about the demand for tax-exempt bonds by individuals who are purchasing more than 85 percent of newly issued bonds if tax rates fall.... The President is proposing a modification in the corporate minimum tax that will reduce the demand for bonds from another segment of the market that historically was a major purchaser of tax-exempt obligations—banks and financial institutions. The tax reform plan denies the deduction for costs incurred in buying and carrying tax-exempt obligations taken by these institutional buyers. Until 1982 a 100 percent deduction was allowed and it has been reduced twice in tax legislation. The bottom line on this provision is to drive away a potentially significant segment of our market for municipal bonds [Government Finance Officers Association, 1985].

Much of the writing on the "political economy of cities" views banks as key actors in the urban arena, but the complexities both of tax policy and financial markets should force us to view banks in a more nuanced fashion. In the arena of public investment, they have been largely replaced by individuals using the tax-exempt market to shelter income from a tax system that, until very recently, systematically refused to recognize the impact of inflation on real living standards. Financial markets, by their nature, allow different kinds of investors to fluctuate in importance over time, and tax policy is a major cause of such fluctuation.

Cities, by becoming so dependent on the household sector, have also become vulnerable to the ways in which the tax system treats households. After New York City, critics often complained that "banks held cities hostage." Now, however, it may be truer to say that federal tax policy holds cities hostage.

CITY-DRIVEN RESTRUCTURING

During the last fifteen years, local governments have begun using the municipal bond market for new purposes. They have used it to redefine the role of local government, to change both the relationship between local governments and that between local government and state government, and—not least—to refashion the federal-local relationship. In all these changes, local governments have taken the lead. They have created new governmental units and put together complex financing arrangements in which tax-exempt capital, private firms or households, local government, and federal tax policy are all intimately involved (Benjamin, 1984: 40). In essence, local governments have tried to enlarge the concept of a "public purpose"; in this endeavor, the municipal bond market has served as their instrument.

In the 1970s, local governments began using the municipal bond market to promote various forms of private sector activity not traditionally considered as fulfilling the business of government. Funds borrowed in the tax-exempt market have increasingly been used to finance projects for private firms or households (or projects in which private firms and public entities serve as partners). Local governments have borrowed in order to lend to third parties rather than to build public facilities. A local government borrows in the tax-exempt market, lends the borrowed funds to a private or not-for-profit firm, and receives a mortgage or a lease agreement in return. The third party repays the loan with interest, and the local borrower uses that money to repay its own debt service.

Thus, whereas local borrowing for "traditional" facilities such as schools and water and sewer systems declined throughout the 1970s, borrowing for housing, hospitals, recreation facilities, utilities, private firms, pollution control equipment, and industrial development exploded. In 1966-1970 on average only 7.2% of all new issues financed housing, hospitals, and recreation facilities; by 1979, the figure had risen to around 25%. Housing revenue bonds in particular grew sharply; in 1979, $12 billion of such bonds were sold, accounting for nearly 30% of all funds raised in the bond market (Kaufman, 1981: xii). In 1978, only $5.5 billion had been sold, and between 1973-1977 only $5 billion in the aggregate had been sold. The astonishing popularity of such bonds in 1979 was due to the entry of local governments into the tax-exempt market for the purpose of funding middle-income home buyers; before July 1978, only state governments had sold housing bonds. In July 1978, however, Chicago sold the first city housing bond. Denver quickly followed suit, and in 1979, 350 new issues were sold in the market (Kaufman, 1981: xii).

Although Congress restricted the issue of mortgage revenue bonds by passing the Mortgage Subsidy Act of 1980, the tax-exempt market continued to be used for numerous "private" purposes. By 1983, bonds for hospitals, housing, pollution control, and industrial developments accounted for over half of all tax-exempt long-term borrowing (Petersen, 1985: 2.4). By 1985, between 60% and 80% of all borrowing was used for projects that could be classified as fulfilling a "private purpose."

Local governments began using the municipal bond market for new purposes at least partly because of their concern with low rates of economic growth during the 1970s and, in the Northeast, because of worries about the "job flight" to the Sunbelt. In the United States, unlike Britain and France, the creditworthiness of local borrowers is based at least partially on the economic health of the private sector firms located within their jurisdiction (Sbragia, 1981).[2] Through their credit ratings, therefore, American local governments are affected directly by a declining economic base. (Their budgets are, of course, affected as well.) Local officials also began to worry about the impact of inflation on home-ownership among middle-income groups. As housing prices skyrocketed, residents who in 1965 would have been able to buy a home were unable by 1977 to do so. Local officials saw homeownership by middle-income earners as crucial for stabilizing city and school populations, and for retaining the property-tax-paying middle class.

Local officials in the 1970s consequently began to lend the "cheap money" they were borrowing in the tax-exempt markets to finance a variety of projects intended to generate jobs and increase homeownership. However, they helped finance not only factories but also K-Marts, McDonalds, liquor stores, and luxury housing units. In 1982, Congress acted to prohibit the use of private-purpose bonds for financing facilities that it felt did not fulfill a "public purpose." The Tax Equity and Fiscal

Responsibility Act of 1982 also forced issuers of most types of private purpose bonds to report the interest they paid to the Internal Revenue Service. Before this requirement was enacted, there had not even been a centralized collection of data on the use of such bonds. The Tax Reform Act of 1984 imposed further congressional restrictions on private-purpose bonds, and President Reagan's tax proposals in 1985 sought to remove the tax exemption from "private purpose" bonds altogether.

Redefining the intergovernmental relationship. The use of bonds for purposes other than those traditionally associated with local government service delivery affected both the structure of the local government system and the relationship between that system and the federal government. Localities, in essence, used the municipal bond market to change relations between themselves, between themselves and state governments, and between themselves and Washington.

In order to borrow the amounts involved in financing "private purposes," local government had to circumvent state constitutional requirements and laws designed to keep municipal debt at "reasonable" levels. Some of these legal restrictions went back to the nineteenth century, and others to the period after the Great Depression when there were numerous bond defaults. They were based on the premise that cities would keep defining "public investment" as they always had (a sewer system, yes, but not a factory) and that most debt would involve the "full faith and credit" of the issuer rather than being directly linked to a specific revenue stream. As city governments began to conceive a larger role for themselves in economic development, they found state laws a real hindrance. Not only did they fix debt levels, but they often called for referenda in which significant majorities of the electorate would have to approve specific bond issues.

General-purpose governments (municipalities and counties), therefore, began to establish public authorities. Each authority could borrow up to its own debt limit without contributing to the general-purpose government's limit and, by issuing revenue bonds, could avoid holding a referendum before borrowing. State legislatures, for their part, found it much easier to approve the establishment of authorities than to amend state constitutions or update state statutes. Authorities thus proliferated during the 1970s, and by the end of 1983 authorities were borrowing more than 50% of all funds borrowed in the tax-exempt market. Whereas some authorities now borrow so as to provide revenue-producing services for the public (Walsh, 1978), many others act simply "as a conduit for financing private purpose activities by use of tax-exempt securities" (Petersen, 1985: 2.6).

The local government system is now a complex mosaic made up of general-purpose governments, school districts, "traditional" public authorities that borrow but also manage service delivery (for which users fees are charged), and "conduit" authorities that exist only to borrow tax-exempt funds for the use of a (profit-making or not-for-profit) third party rather than to operate a public enterprise. State laws are now an inconvenience, but do not put an effective "cap" on local per capita debt (nor, for that matter, on state-level debt, as some authorities are statewide).

The use of the tax-exempt market by local governments also helped to redefine the federal-local relationship. Federal grants, whether categorical or block, essentially imposed the federal policy agenda on local governments. The market, by contrast, has allowed local governments to turn the tables.

The federal Treasury foregoes the tax revenue it would receive if municipal bonds were taxable. By borrowing in the tax-exempt market for policy activities they deem important, local governments force the federal government to give an "invisible subsidy" to their own priorities. Further, many of those local priorities have not been federal priorities. Local governments, for example, have used their "cheap money" to help middle-income people become homebuyers rather than using that money to build low-income rental units—the latter being the purpose for which state housing bonds were issued and that which the U.S. Treasury approved. In the area of economic development, local governments have used the market to help nonhousing-related businesses far more than has the federal government through its "credit budget" (Sbragia, 1985: 17-22).

Local governments, therefore, changed their relationships with higher levels of governments by using the market to pursue their own priorities. Clearly, the federal government, through a string of legislation, has tried to halt this trend. Washington can use tax policy to decide just how far local governments can go in using the market for purposes incompatible with its own. Nonetheless, unlike British and French localities, American local governments can use their access to the market to support policies of their own (Sbragia, 1981).

The role of the municipal bond market has thus been transformed. From being a steady provider of funds for traditional public facilities in the 1960s, that market has become a tool by which local governments can achieve some political independence, despite their own "fiscal crisis" and the strongly centralizing direction of both the state-local and the federal-local relationship.

CONCLUSION

The "restructuring" that has gone on between city governments and the lenders of capital has been complex, involving a triangular relationship among local government, the municipal bond market, and higher levels of government (in particular, the federal government).

This triangular relationship raises questions about how to depict the role of "finance capital" in urban development. Marxist-inspired analysts tend to assume that financial institutions, and commercial banks in particular, are the primary sources of capital. In fact, banks are of interest to neo-Marxists precisely because Marxism is interested in the power of concentrated money. Yet, in the arena of public investment, banks are no longer major sources of either long-term or short-term finance. Households are the dominant lenders. Although the withdrawal of banks from the market raised the cost of borrowing for the local governments, new investors were found; banks may be useful to cities, but they are not essential. Lenders are essential, but their identity is not of overriding importance to borrowers. Thus we need to ask: Does it make a difference if households rather than commercial banks are the primary lenders to cities? How should we think about "finance capital" in light of this development?

The second question that is raised has to do with the relationship between tax policy and lenders. It is clear that tax policy is influential in defining what is profitable; "profit" is to some extent a function of tax minimization. Through taxation, the national government can channel lending activity. From this perspective, the financial market seems to respond to government policy rather than shaping it. However, if one were determinedly economistic, one might argue that banks, through the exercise of political power, are able to write tax law to their benefit. If this were completely true, however, it is difficult to see why banks have allowed themselves to be taxed so heavily—much more heavily, it should be said, than other financial institutions. The enormous importance of tax policy does, I believe, raise doubts that lenders have much real independence beyond that allowed by tax policy. One could reply, nonetheless, that tax policy works within a framework that allows lenders to receive a return for the use of their money. Such is certainly the case, but it is not unique to "capitalist" polities: Mao's China required local borrowers to repay state loans with interest (Sbragia, 1979).

The third question that must be considered has to do with whether the municipal bond market only benefits lenders. Local governments, for their part, seem able to maneuver within the market to achieve what they want just as private investors do. Local governments have been able to participate in the market so as to force the federal government to give an "invisible subsidy" to investments undertaken by the locality. Local governments have been able to use the tax-exempt nature of the municipal bond market (a status conferred by tax policy) to act autonomously of Washington.

Many of the investments facilitated by local governments benefit private sector firms at the expense of the federal Treasury. Although such action may seem to support those who see the major function of government as supporting the process of capital accumulation, it is noteworthy that the federal government has opposed such local action. The federal government does not support all efforts at what Tomaskovic-Devey and Miller (1982: 24) term the "recapitalization of capitalism."

The operations of the municipal bond market, therefore, raise a set of questions that cannot be tidily answered by either neo-Marxist or conventional analysis. It may well be that systematic investigation of other markets will also raise uncomfortable questions about the role of capital within cities.

NOTES

1. The inability of the government to conquer inflation was a second factor leading to diminished commercial bank investment in long-term municipal bonds. Not only did inflation diminish the attraction of all bonds (the value of bonds held in bank portfolios declined as inflation rose), but banks had to adapt their investment strategies to respond to the devastation inflation wreaked on all fixed-income long-term investment. Banks began "issuing variable rate loans and using 'spread banking' techniques," and "the old fixed-income tax-exempt debt instrument became too inflexible and illiquid to fit the new money management techniques" (Petersen, 1985: 2.12).

2. In Great Britain, local governments are spared from worrying about their creditworthiness through a national government guarantee of loan repayment but, on the other side of the ledger, do not benefit from below-market rates. In France, local governments do receive subsidized loans and do not worry about creditworthiness but they do not enjoy the financial autonomy enjoyed by British, and especially American, localities (Sbragia, 1981).

REFERENCES

BENJAMIN, R.L.C. (1984) "Public investment for cities, 1815-1980," pp. 23-46 in R. D. Bingham and J. P. Blair (eds.) Urban Economic Development. Beverly Hills, CA: Sage.

BRAVERMAN, P. (1982) "State and local finance: outlook for the '80s." Governmental Finance 11 (September): 41-43.

CAMPBELL, T. S. (1982) Finance Institutions, Markets, and Economic Activity. New York: McGraw-Hill.

COCHRAN, J. A. (1975) Money, Banking, and the Economy. New York: Macmillan.

FAINSTEIN, N. I. and S. S. FAINSTEIN (1982) "Restructuring the American city: a comparative perspective," pp. 161-189 in N. I. Fainstein and S. S. Fainstein (eds.) Urban Policy Under Capitalism. Beverly Hills, CA: Sage.

FINDLAY, G. W. (1981) "The PERS financial reporting dilemma." Governmental Finance 10 (March): 3-6.

FUNKHOUSER, G. E. (1979) "Experiences with the revenue sharing audit requirements." Governmental Finance 8 (September): 13-16.

Government Finance Officers Association (1985) "Why GFOA opposes the president's bond and deductibility proposals." Newsletter, Washington Update (June).

Government Finance Research Center (1984) State and Local Capital Spending and Borrowing: Levels of Need and Costs of Financing. Washington, DC: Municipal Finance Officers Association.

HAMILTON, R. (1983) "The world turned upside down: the contemporary revolution in state and local government financing." Public Administration Review (January/February): 22-31.

HANSEN, S. (1983) The Politics of Taxation: Revenue Without Representation. New York: Praeger.

KAUFMAN, G. G. (1981) "Preface," pp. xi-xvi in G. G. Kaufman (ed.) Efficiency in the Municipal Bond Market: The Use of Tax Exempt Financing for "Private" Purposes. Greenwich, CT: JAI.

KIMBALL, R. C. (1977) "Commercial banks, tax avoidance, and the market for state and local debt since 1970." New England Economic Review (January/February): 3-21.

KING, W. (1985) "Houston's credit rating is cut but remains high." New York Times (June 16).

LEEDS, P. G. (1983) "City politics and the market: the case of New York City's financing crisis," pp. 113-144 in A. Sbragia (ed.) The Municipal Money Chase: The Politics of Local Government Finance. Boulder, CO: Westview.

LODAL, J. M. (1976) "Improving local government financial information systems." Duke Law Journal (January): 1133-1156.

PETERSEN, J. E. (1985) "Recent developments in tax-exempt bond markets." Washington, DC: Government Finance Research Center. (mimeo)

SBRAGIA, A. M. (1985) "The politics of public investment: an Anglo-American comparison." Studies in Public Policy, No. 139, Centre for the Study of Public Policy, University of Strathclyde, Glasgow, Scotland.

———(1983) "Politics, local government, and the municipal bond market," pp. 67-112 in A. Sbragia (ed.) The Municipal Money Chase: The Politics of Local Government Finance. Boulder, CO: Westview.

————(1981) "Cities, capital, and banks: the politics of debt in the United States, United Kingdom, and France," pp. 200-220 in R. Newton (ed.) Urban Political Economy. New York: St. Martin's.

————(1979) "Borrowing to build: private money and public welfare." International Journal of Health Services 9: 207-218.

SCHUMPETER, J. A. (1954) "The crisis of the tax state." International Economic Papers 4: 5-38.

SHALALA, D. E. (1979) "Using financial management to avert financial crisis." Governmental Finance 8 (December) 17-21.

TOMASKOVIC-DEVEY, D. and S. M. MILLER (1982) "Recapitalization: the basic U.S. urban policy of the 1980s," pp. 23-42 in N. I. Fainstein and S. S. Fainstein (eds.) Urban Policy Under Capitalism. Beverly Hills, CA: Sage.

Twentieth Century Fund Task Force on Municipal Bond Credit Ratings (1974) The Rating Game. New York: Author.

WALSH, A. H. (1978) The Public's Business: The Politics and Practices of Government Corporations—A Twentieth Century Fund Study. Cambridge, MA: MIT Press.

WETZLER, J. W. and J. E. PETERSEN (1985) "The finance officer as public strategist." Government Finance Review 1 (April): 7-11.

ZYSMAN, J. (1983) Governments, Markets, and Growth: Financial Systems and the Politics of Industrial Change. Ithaca, NY: Cornell University Press.

9

Collective Responses to
the Urban Crisis:
Ideology and Mobilization

JEFFREY R. HENIG

☐ THAT THE INTERTWINED problems representing the urban crisis of the 1970s and 1980s have not sparked a large-scale collective response presents an anomaly. It presents an anomaly not only to many conservatives—who presume that the masses share only a tenuous commitment to the civil order—and to many radicals—who presume that objective class interests are destined to erupt into a forceful movement once the true nature of capitalism is revealed—but also to the liberal pluralists, who presume that the political disengagement of most Americans is a provisional state, quickly and easily shed once changing conditions threaten personal concerns.

Deteriorating infrastructure, freezes in public employment, cutbacks in services, and shifts of capital from city to suburb and Snowbelt to Sunbelt provide benefits for some at substantial costs to others. Yet a number of writers have noted that organization and resistance among the losers have been muted or ineffective (Browning et al., 1984; Fainstein and Fainstein, 1983; Friedland et al., 1984; Gittell, 1980; Katznelson, 1981). There are indications of a parallel decline of militant protest in Western Europe as well (Pickvance, 1985). This chapter

221

explores some of the reasons why the losers in the contemporary urban crisis have not become a more visible and vocal presence.

Mobilization will be considered as a multistage process, consisting of *perception* of threatening conditions, *evaluation* of the likely impacts and the appropriateness of a collective response, *calculation* of anticipated costs and benefits of alternative personal strategies, and *implementation* of organizational techniques (Henig, 1982a, 1982b). Obstacles to mobilization can emerge at any or all of these stages. Those harmed by the urban crisis may be unaware of the broader forces acting upon them. They may be aware of these forces yet regard them as harmless, benevolent, or outside the realm of public responsibility. They may recognize a stake in action yet consider such action too risky or too draining in terms of energy, money, and time, or they may judge the benefits too paltry, too improbable, or attainable through other means. Finally, they may decide that collective action is reasonable yet falter because of inadequate leadership, poor tactics, or lack of organizational skills.

The distinction between practical obstacles that hamper mobilization among individuals who are alert to their common interests and other obstacles that make it difficult for people to interpret accurately what their interests really are is significant. Although the latter are conceptually and empirically more elusive, they may provide the more valuable insights into the background of political quiescence against which the urban crisis today unfolds.

RESPONSES TO FISCAL RESTRUCTURING

Budgetary cutbacks have not gone unopposed. Ida Susser (1982) looked closely at the reaction of white, working-class residents of the Greenpoint-Williamsburg section of Brooklyn to general decline and the specific threat that a neighborhood firehouse would be closed, in 1975, as part of a money-saving plan. Several hundred residents took part in rallies and signed petitions. A smaller number occupied the "People's Firehouse" and held the engine hostage until local politicians acceded to their demands. Far from being apathetic, she concluded, "These residents have responded to their plight with energy and anger, fighting political holding actions for the survival of their neighborhood in the face of almost certain defeat" (Susser, 1982: vii).

This is not an isolated instance. In San Francisco and Minneapolis residents mobilized against plans to consolidate police precincts and close some neighborhood stations; in New York City lower-income and minority residents rallied to protest the closing of a municipal hospital; in the Poletown area of Detroit residents fought an urban renewal project that officials of the city and General Motors justified in the name of jobs and the local tax base; and in school districts all over the country parents have resisted proposals to save money by closing neighborhood schools.

In the face of such examples, some question whether the premise that the 1970s and 1980s have been marked by relative quiescence is legitimate after all. " 'Media-hype' to the contrary, activism did not end with the turn of the decade," Robert Fisher (1984: 125) indicates. Gail Cicotta, whose National People's Action was the most visible manifestation of the 1970s neighborhood movement at the national level, put the point more emphatically: "I keep hearing that everything's dead and there's no big cause since civil rights and the Vietnam War. But that's a myth. There's a neighborhood movement that started in the sixties. It's not as dramatic with everybody out in the street, but it's steadily gaining strength in every city and state" (Boyte, 1980: 33) Harry Boyte argues that we are in the midst of a "backyard revolution," marked by organizing efforts " 'more down to earth,' more practical, above all more enduring and rooted in the social fabric" than protests of the previous decade (Boyte, 1980: xi-xii).

Unfortunately, there is no currently available data source that would allow us to resolve empirically the question of whether grass-roots mobilization has declined or simply changed form. Those who sense a relative absence of collective response seem to stand on firmer footing, however, than those who insist that the response simply is harder to see. Commitment to the values of participation and community self-help does not require that one overplay the significance and solidity of those organizations that have emerged as visible counterpoints to the urban crisis. Organizations such as TWO in Chicago, SECO in Baltimore, and COPS in San Antonio are cited again and again for their remarkable achievements. It does these groups no injustice to acknowledge that they represent an exception rather than the rule.

Some of the organizations that constitute the so-called backyard revolution, moreover, are more ephemeral than their reputations might lead one to suspect. The Detroit Alliance for a Rational Economy (DARE) at one point seemed to be a model of an urban-based, multiracial organization that combined a positive plan for remaking the city with enough political savvy to help elect one of its leaders to the city council in 1977. Yet "DARE foundered, then disbanded on the divisive and demoralizing shoals of economic crisis, forced fiscal austerity," and Mayor Coleman Young's political mastery (Hill, 1983: 113). SECO—still cited frequently as an example of how residents, working together, can reverse the common cycles of neighborhood decline—split into two factions, neither of which has recaptured the dynamism of the early group (Fisher, 1984: 145-146). Adopt-a-Building, in New York City's Lower East Side, and the People's Development Corporation, in the South Bronx, were pioneers in efforts at sweat equity and urban homesteading. While they, too, continue to be touted as examples of a vital neighborhood-based movement, each suffered severe setbacks over the past ten years (Katz and Mayer, 1985: 32).

The Adams Morgan Organization (AMO), in Washington, D.C., provides another example. During the mid-1970s, AMO's activities helped to earn a reputation for the neighborhood as "one of the most developed communities in the country" in terms of political and economic self-sufficiency (Morris and Hess, 1975: 13). Ten years later, however, the group's meetings are poorly attended and its influence at city hall has all but evaporated (Henig, 1982c: 33-35).

Susser's account of the People's Firehouse effort in Brooklyn demonstrates clearly that low-income communities can mobilize collectively in response to the kinds of service cutbacks we associate with the contemporary urban crisis. But Susser herself recognizes that this might be a special case: Residents of that neighborhood were favored by a sympathetic media, local politicians who were responsive, and a valuable alliance with the local firefighters and their union. "Because such a massing of political influence is not common to most neighborhood issues, similar protests are likely to be defeated" (Susser, 1982: 181).

More typical may have been the experience on Norman Street itself, where Susser carried on most of her research and observation. There, a block association formed, partly in response to efforts by the Beame administration to encourage neighborhood-based self-help efforts as a way to compensate for service cutbacks. Attendance was poor and meetings unfocused. The association's major undertaking was the organization of a summer dance, and even this task proved overwhelming. A little over one year after it was initiated, the block association disintegrated. "In terms of tangible results, block association meetings had yielded little. In fact, they tended to contribute to a sense of hopelessness among the members as to the possibility of improving their environment" (Susser, 1982: 113).

Besides the lack of appropriate data, at least three other factors contribute to the absence of consensus about the scope and significance of political responses to the contemporary urban crisis. First, political organizations in low-income communities often work quite deliberately to present a facade that is more imposing than the substance behind it. Lacking other resources, these groups often must opt for the dramatic in the hopes of intimidating opponents, building self-confidence, or broadening the scope of conflict by drawing the attention and support of more powerful outside actors (Alinsky, 1971; Lipsky, 1970). It is somewhat ironic that sympathetic chroniclers of the neighborhood movement, all of whom are well aware of this bit of tactical legerdemain, are sometimes among the last to see through the saber rattling.

A second factor involves a question of timing. Most of the more optimistic portrayals of the post-1960s neighborhood movement based their observations on a period in which many organizations were being kept alive on the intravenous system of federal funds. Such organizations depended, in some instances, on direct and in-kind support through programs such as Vista, Legal Services, CETA, community services block grants, and local allocations of CDBG and revenue-sharing funds. In some cases these organizations were deliberately cultivated by local authorities as part of their efforts to stay in conformance with federal requirements for citizen participation in decision making. The dismantling of this support structure began in earnest in 1981, and its full implications have yet to be felt.

Finally, there is the question of what standard is most appropriate to judge current levels of political activity. Some trumpeters of voluntarism and neighborhood self-help offer no standard at all. Anecdotal accounts of busy and enthusiastic citizens are encouraging, but their significance is uncertain.

Arrayed on the other side are analysts who base their evaluation of the current situation on a demanding standard that has its roots in Marxian theory. This standard defines the possibility of a class-based, multiracial, multiethnic movement that links unions, neighborhood associations, antiwar groups, environmental activists, and civil rights organizations in a broad coalition (Piven and Cloward, 1982). Although useful as a means of keeping in perspective the limited nature of many collective enterprises, its abstract nature ultimately limits the utility of this standard. Measured against the idea of a class-based movement, the real world consistently comes up short. Important distinctions in the degree of effectiveness among existing organizations needlessly are blurred.

The standard used in this chpater is anchored in history rather than theory. Why, if the contemporary urban crisis is no less severe than that faced in the 1960s, do collective responses today seem more limited and restrained? In addressing this question, we must be cautious to avoid an overly romanticized vision of the late 1960s and early 1970s. Much of what went on was inflated by rhetoric and puffery, and the passage of time has left the memories of large rallies and dramatic marches sharper than those of disorganized meetings and protests in which onlookers, police, and the media outnumbered those actually taking part. At the same time, we can acknowledge an air of possibility that marked that era. "Suddenly, because much was uncertain, much seemed possible" (Katznelson, 1981: 3). This air generated momentum and elicited policy responses, and it is this air that largely seems absent today.

DOING IT WRONG: IMPEDIMENTS AT THE IMPLEMENTATION STAGE

That skill and leadership can alter the course of political events is recognized by scholars drawing from a broad range of theoretical orientations. Nelson Polsby (1980: 120), a pluralist, notes that "resources can be employed with greater or lesser skill," and suggests that this insight naturally should lead researchers "to pay attention to what practical politicians customarily see as the heart of their craft: the process of bargaining, negotiations, salesmanship and brokerage, and of leadership in mobilizing resources of all kinds." Rational choice theorists feel that leadership may be the key to "solving" the free-rider dilemma that plagues efforts to generate collective endeavors among self-interested individuals (Frohlich et al., 1971). Marilyn Gittell (1980: 90), writing from the perspective of the political left, states the case strongly: "The importance of leadership in directing and shaping the effectiveness of an organization cannot be overstated."

Belief that skill and leadership are critical if low- and moderate-income citizens are to force their concerns onto the public agenda has spawned training institutes such as the Industrial Areas Foundation, the Mid-American Institute, the Midwest Academy, the National Training and Information Center, and the Pacific Institute for Community

Organization. It has given birth to various "how-to" books and manuals, with titles such as *Rules for Radicals*, *How People Get Power*, *Starting a Group in Your City*, and *Roots to Power*.

The presumed importance of leadership and organizational skills gives rise to the possibility that it is shortages in these attributes that account for the relative lack of collective response among those injured or inconvenienced by the urban crisis. Susser's account of the ill-fated block association in Brooklyn lends a certain credibility to this hypothesis. Although members of the group deferred to a single leader, she

> had little sense of group dynamics. Meeting agendas were not followed, and the same topics were discussed repeatedly. Long silences were common. [The leader] made no attempt to converse with newcomers at meetings [Susser, 1982: 110].

Residents at the association meetings expressed concern about a burned-out building on the block, but the leader of the association was unable to channel that concern into collective action of any kind. Her "inability . . . even to locate an agency which would take responsibility for boarding up the burned-out house may have reinforced the inertia" that already infused the group (Susser, 1982: 111).

Because we are taking as our point of reference a higher level of activity in the 1960s, and not a state of class-based mobilization predicted in theory, the credibility of this explanation depends upon our accounting for a decline in available leadership and organizational skills. This imposes a bit of discipline on our speculation, especially because the experiences of the sixties and the various books and institutes mentioned above might easily be presumed to have broadened the pool from which capable leaders might emerge. At least three explanations for a decline in leadership and skills are worth discussing. These have to do with cooptation, cutbacks, and changes in the characteristics of the poor.

COOPTATION

Federal, state, and local governments responded to the issues of the 1960s by instituting reforms in the name of broader citizen participation. Regarded at the time as concessions forced by pressure from below, these reforms are now considered by some observers to be a double-edged sword. Community Action Agencies, neighborhood planning areas, community school districts, advisory neighborhood councils, community development corporations, and neighborhood-based service delivery mechanisms may absorb the energies of potential leaders, channeling their attention into narrow administrative and budgetary activities and making them dependent upon external sponsors who impose indirect, but highly effective, limitations on acceptable political activity (Piven and Cloward, 1979; Gittell, 1980; Katznelson, 1981). This belief that federal programs to empower the poor in actuality increased their dependency led Saul Alinsky to denounce them as "political pornography."

Leaders and potential leaders may be coopted into the private sector as well, though the political implications of this phenomenon are less frequently recognized. Civil rights reforms and policies of affirmative action have had little long-term success in elevating the relative economic status of the bulk of minority households. The median income of black households rose between 1967 and 1978 (up 11.4% in constant dollars, compared to about 7.5% for whites), but by 1983 it was even lower than it had been 16 years before. They have contributed, however, to an expansion of opportunities for a small but growing black middle class. In 1967 5.9% of black households earned $35,000 or more per year (in 1983 dollars), sixteen years later 11.1% had reached this level (though this too represents a decline from a peak, in 1979, of 12.7%; U.S. Bureau of the Census, 1984: 442). The responsibilities and demands associated with this upward economic mobility may remove from the pool of available leaders some of the best educated and most aggressive representatives.

Upward economic mobility, moreover, is associated with increased geographic mobility. The number of blacks living in U.S. suburbs increased by nearly 50% during the 1970s; approximately 1 of every 20 blacks who lived in a central city in 1970 had moved to that city's suburbs by 1975 (Goodman and Streitwieser, 1983: 301). Some analysts of the 1960s riots argued that a pool of educated and middle-class blacks who remained in inner city neighborhoods—either by choice or due to housing discrimination—played an important role in providing a political rationale and sense of legitimacy to the unrest (Banfield, 1974: 231). Although the walls of segregation and housing discrimination have not crumbled, they may have been breached sufficiently to draw the black middle class psychologically and physically further from those suffering most directly from urban ills.

FEDERAL CUTBACKS

Recent cutbacks in federal programs, as noted earlier, may have deprived low-income communities of the kind of direct and indirect resources that helped them, during the 1960s and early 1970s, to support a network of leaders and organizers. Rational choice theorists suggest that it is useful to consider these leaders and organizers as "political entrepreneurs." A political entrepreneur is "a rationally self-interested person who promises to supply some collective good—such as higher price supports for farmers, cleaner air, or lower taxes—establishes an organization to collect funds and other forms of support from members, works to produce the collective good, and retains as his personal 'profit' the difference between the cost of providing, or attempting to provide, the good and resources collected" (Wilson, 1973: 196).

Creating and maintaining a community organization or protest group are time- and energy-consuming tasks. Many phone calls must be made and answered, strategy sessions planned, evening meetings attended. Federal programs such as VISTA and CETA provided funds and positions that supported full-time organizers in many low-income communities, that, otherwise, did not have the wherewithal to entice leaders and organizers with the promise of material gain, or even material support. Susser's "Norman Street" again is illustrative. An immediate factor in the formation of the neighborhood block association was the employment of a block resident in a CETA-funded position in a community agency, where her "employer rated employees by the degree to which they organized their neighbors" (Susser, 1982: 109).

Rational choice theorists take pains to point out that the incentives to leaders may take a nonmaterial as well as a material form. "I do not wish to argue that group organizers are classic 'economic men' whose conscious motives are to secure the largest possible financial return," Robert Salisbury (1969: 26) indicates. It is clear, too, that the leaders of protests in the 1960s and early 1970s included many talented individuals, some of whom certainly could have obtained greater financial reward through alternative pursuits. The point, then, is not that the federal cutbacks have turned political leadership from a profitable to an unprofitable enterprise. More credible might be the hypothesis that a certain threshhold effect is involved. Unless material rewards for exercising leadership go beyond some point—enough, at least, to support a reasonable subsistence—leadership with the requisite skills will not be available and opportunities for collective mobilization will fizzle out in ill-timed media events, poorly run meetings, and misguided strategies.

CHANGING CONSTITUENCY

Finally, it is possible that the hardships of the current urban crisis fall on a constituency that, as a group, is less well endowed in the skills and experience that would facilitate political mobilization. The poor today include some groups with characteristics that may make them particularly difficult to organize. Female-headed households, for example, are difficult to organize because of the many pressures they face in the day-to-day struggle to earn some money, get the shopping done, and keep the children watched over. A relatively simple matter—such as attending an evening meeting—may loom as a major obstacle for a mother unable to count on a spouse to stay at home and care for the kids. Persons living in female-headed households currently make up half of the poor; in 1959 the comparable figure was only about 26%.

Hispanics are another group that has increased as a percentage of the poor. Some are illegally in the country, or harboring others who are so. Others are isolated from the political institutions around them by language barriers. Some come from nations in which even the mildest form of political activity carries substantial personal risks. All these factors present obstacles to those who would seek to organize them into a collective political force.

The 1970s, too, witnessed a major effort to deinstitutionalize many of the mentally and emotionally handicapped. The numbers involved are difficult to estimate. In 1960, there were about 722,000 beds in nonfederal psychiatric hospitals in the United States; in 1982 there were only 195,000 (U.S. Bureau of the Census, 1984: 106). Deinstitutionalization in some instances made it possible for the marginally handicapped to function in a much freer and more healthful environment. At the same time, however, it injected into the pool of the poor some whose mental and emotional state makes them incapable of dealing effectively with the broader political environment.

DECIDING AGAINST MOBILIZATION:
CALCULATING BENEFITS AND RISKS

A focus on the implementation stage of mobilization presumes that those with grievances are aware of their condition and have made a conscious decision to forge a political response. If genuinely felt grievances were being blocked from political expression at the implementation stage, we would expect some evidence that efforts to mobilize were taking place and aborting at an early stage in development. No record is kept of the meeting that no one comes to, the protest that goes unnoticed, the coalitions that go untried. I know of no reason, however, to believe that these occur more frequently now.

If there is little solid evidence that potential collective responses are foundering on the rocks of implementation, it is possible that those affected by the urban crisis simply have concluded that the likely benefits from such efforts will not outweigh the likely costs. As before, the question is formulated in relation to apparent changes over time. If the explanation lies at the calculation stage, we must explain why assessments of relative benefits should have become more bleak in the interim.

LESSONS LEARNED

There are at least two distinct schools of thought about what the sixties should have taught us regarding the efficacy of protest and grass-roots political activity. One holds that the combination of urban riots, calls for black power, and agitated demands to expand the political voice of the poor not only failed to succeed but left the intended beneficiaries worse off than they would have been had they opted for a more conventional, incremental strategy of accommodation.

Proponents of this view point to inner city neighborhoods that have never recovered from the physical and economic devastation caused by the riots. Even the nonviolent, formally sanctioned efforts to induce greater participation within low-income communities, according to this perspective, had a dark and self-defeating aspect. "Over and over again," wrote Daniel Patrick Moynihan (1970: 134-135), efforts such as those by the Ford Foundation and the federal antipoverty program "led first to the radicalization of the middle-class persons who began the effort; next to a certain amount of stirring among the poor, but accompanied by heightened racial antagonism *on the part of the poor* if they happened to be black; next to retaliation from the larger white community," and, once the actual weakness of the community forces was revealed, ending in "much bitterness all around."

Others read the record of history differently. Piven and Cloward are among those who suggest that the air of challenge and confrontation that marked the sixties was necessary in order to elicit progressive reforms. Rufus Browning et al. (1984), based on a study of ten cities' experiences from 1960-1980, conclude that protest was important as a complement to electoral mobilization, although not sufficient in and of itself to elicit the political incorporation of minority groups.

For our purpose, the immediate question rests less on the reality, however, than on the perception of that reality. If those who are disadvantaged by current policies believe that collective protests have proven to be counterproductive, nonaction may be a rational, calculated response.

CHANGING OPPORTUNITIES

Times change, and with time can come changes in the responsiveness of the institutions that confront us. Evidence that protest was effective in the 1960s might not be enough to convince a rational actor that such tactics would be equally effective today. Clark and Ferguson (1983: 140), for example, found that "black power" indicators played a statistically significant role in equations to predict local policies during the 1960s, but that their relative impact had faded by the late 1970s. Shifts in the structure of our political system, such as those associated with New Federalism initiatives and efforts to shift responsibilities from the public to the private spheres, may have diffused authority sufficiently to dissuade those with grievances from launching a collective response.

Paul Peterson (1981) has suggested that local governments are inherently incapable of aggressively pursuing redistributory policies, except in the short term. This is due largely to the permeability of local boundaries. Because citizens can move to a neighboring suburb without severing ties with family, friends, or place of employment, and because many businesses can relocate within a metropolitan area without leaving behind an experienced work force and established clientele, local governments risk sacrificing their tax base if they allow the ratio of taxes paid to services received to become overly burdensome. "The politics of redistribution at the local level is thus an arena where certain kinds of citizen needs and preferences seldom become demands" (Peterson, 1981: 182).

By moving decision making "closer to the people," New Federalism holds out the promise of reducing the costs of political mobilization. It undoubtedly is less expensive and less intimidating for those with grievances to present their complaints to the city council than it is to carry them to the state capital or Washington, D.C. But this will not convince many citizens to invest their energies in collective action if it is achieved at the cost of placing responsibility in the hands of local officials who are perceived as lacking the resources and power to exercise that responsibility with genuine authority. Piven and Cloward (1982: 130) make a similar observation: "If a good many popular economic grievances can be diverted into state and local politics, options for dealing with them will be greatly restricted."

Efforts to privatize public service delivery have proceeded coterminously with the New Federalism initiatives. At least 25% of local governments' solid waste collection and disposal, street repair, street light operation, traffic signal installation and maintenance, hospital management, legal services, and maintenance of municipal fleets are contracted out to private industry, according to a recent survey by the International City Management Association (Tolchin, 1985).

Like decentralization, privatization may diffuse responsibility and thereby increase the perceived costs of mobilizing for political goals. For all the intransigence and imperviousness to input they sometimes exhibit, public officials and public bureaucracies nonetheless are enmeshed in a formal and well-defined system for citizen access. The currency of this system consists of votes, pressure, and the reputation for power. Although the poor suffer disadvantages in competing in this system, they do not enter the arena unarmed. Privatization, however, may shift key decisions to an arena in which market power is the dominant currency, and the poor are well aware that this is an arena in which their victories come very hard indeed. "Use of the political process to control 'private' activity is vastly more difficult than employing it to affect government itself" (Fainstein and Fainstein, 1983: 241).

THE EXIT OPTION

Personal mobility can serve as a viable alternative to the exercise of political voice (Hirschman, 1970; Orbell and Uno, 1972; Fainstein and Fainstein, 1980). Faced with a deteriorating situation, some may choose flight over fight. Moving from the city to the suburbs, or from Snowbelt to Sunbelt, may provide a family with a more reliable escape from urban decline than would a possibly futile effort to seek a political resolution through collective means. Exit becomes a more likely response if the exercise of political voice has proven costly or ineffective in the past. Even if the effectiveness of voice remains relatively constant, though, voice might become a relatively less attractive alternative if opportunities to escape through personal mobility can be shown to have increased.

Has geographic mobility become more feasible in recent years, as a means to find relief for those affected by the urban crisis? The past twenty years have seen the erosion of certain long-standing obstacles to residential mobility by minorities and the poor. Fair housing statutes, as noted earlier, have dented, if not pierced, suburban walls of exclusion. Court rulings have made it more difficult for local jurisdictions to use residency requirements as a way to keep newcomers from voting or receiving welfare. Transportation costs, generally, are lower, and information about job and housing opportunities in other areas is more readily available.

Public policies intended to encourage citizens to "vote with their feet" may tip the balance further in the direction of exit over voice. The President's Commission for a National Agenda for the Eighties recommended a greater emphasis on "people-to-jobs strategies and programs, which assist people willing to migrate to the location of new opportunities" (Hicks, 1982: 56). Ohio, in this spirit, recently experimented with the use of job training funds to underwrite some of the job search and moving costs of unemployed residents who agreed to pursue out-of-state job leads. The gradual shift from public housing programs to programs—such as Section 8 and housing vouchers—which could allow recipients to apply their subsidies anywhere in the nation, could have similar effect.

UNDERSTANDING THE STAKES

Pluralism and rational choice analysis are two of the most influential theoretical perspectives dealing with political mobilization. Both presume that individuals are relatively aware of their interests and those aspects of their environment that bear most immediately on the prospect that their interests will be met. Both, accordingly, focus their analysis on the calculation and implementation stages. Failure to mobilize is attributed, ultimately, to personal choice or lack of skill.

The decision to assume that individuals are aware of their interests and environment is defended on several grounds. One argument is a pragmatic one: It works. Rational choice and, to a lesser extent, pluralist writers adopt many of the concepts and presumptions associated with traditional microeconomic theory. The assumption that individuals and firms have clear and relatively stable preference hierarchies and the assumption that they operate in an environment of perfect or near-perfect information have allowed economists to develop a tight, rigorous deductive model that seems to have predictive value when applied in certain economic realms. Other social scientists, envious of the apparent success and certain status that economists have garnered, have sought to extend the application of this model to behavior in nonmarket settings. Although most recognize that such models drastically oversimplify real-world dynamics, they argue that their successes are justification enough for their continued use.

To some, there is a deeper epistemological rationale as well. Behavioralists by training, these theorists are uncomfortable with the notion of interests except as they manifest themselves in actual behavior. To suggest that some group has a stake in mobilizing and yet does not do so calls for the analyst to flirt with notions of objective interests that are distinct from subjective interests or preferences. Nelson Polsby (1980: 196), for one, is doubtful that this can be done without simply having the researcher substitute his or her own values for those of the community.

Finally, there may be more political reasons for insisting that preferences that are not manifested in behavior not be considered preferences at all. John Stuart Mill made the dictum—every individual is the best judge of his or her own interest—into a central plank in liberal thought. To suggest otherwise, it is reasoned, to concede that a stranger might know my own interests better than I do myself, is considered not only presumptuous but threatening. It is an invitation to subjugation by others who might claim to be acting "for your own good."

Yet common sense and experience inform us that lack of information and distorted information are common in the political world. And those who think seriously about the nature of values, culture, and the development of self-concept recognize that these can be shaped and altered in response to a variety of external factors. Changes in the availability and content of information related to people's interests, or changes in the values and experiences that people apply to the information they do receive, might dampen the tendency toward collective political action by short-circuiting the impulse to act before either the calculation or implementation stages are reached.

CLARITY AND AVAILABILITY OF INFORMATION

To say that the world grows increasingly complex is to risk a truism that borders on the banal. Yet it is possible that the problems that constitute the urban crisis have changed in ways that make them fundamentally more difficult for the average citizen to grasp. Political inaction, if this is so, may reflect the fact that, confronted by disinvestment, service cutbacks, and changes in the tax structure, citizens are uncertain who the winners and losers will turn out to be.

From Moral Crisis to Fiscal Crisis

The definition of the urban crisis and the language with which it is discussed have changed. The urban crisis of the 1960s was a moral and political crisis. Its issues were framed in terms of "justice," "equality," "democracy," and "civil rights." Although these concepts have complicated intellectual referents, their emotional message is direct, simple, and intense. They appeal to ideas that are familiar and they carry a strong prescription for action.

Today's urban crisis, in contrast, is debated in more technical terms. Its dimensions are discussed in terms of bond ratings, investment tax credits, infrastructure, business climate, and efficiency. To many Americans, these terms are unfamiliar and forbidding. The message they carry is that these are complicated matters, that decisions should be deferred to those with expertise. The shift from a moral crisis to a fiscal crisis moves us toward a shrinking of the realm of governmental activities acknowledged to be political, in the direction the Progressives set half a century ago.

Indirect Benefits and Costs

The content of policy, as well as its terms of discourse, has changed in ways that may make determination of winners and losers more obscure. Local politics has always been a politics of distribution. When the goods being distributed consisted of construction and maintenance contracts, legal fees, and jobs, those who received the benefits were readily identifiable, and the value of the favor could be estimated by anyone with access to the formal budget. Increasingly, however, we see public benefits distributed through tax advantages and regulatory exemptions. These often apply to a broad class of actors whose specific identities are not immediately apparent. And the cost ultimately borne by the taxpayer may never appear in a governmental ledger sheet.

Several additional factors may have muddied the waters as far as determining losers in contemporary urban policy. During much of the 1970s and early 1980s, many cutbacks took the form of cuts in real, not absolute, growth. The purchasing power of AFDC benefits, for example, declined more than 30% nationally between 1970 and 1983 (Rubin, 1983). Proposals to cut programs or benefits become part of the formal agenda and are likely, therefore, to come to the attention of all but the most disinterested and alienated recipient. When inflation does the cutting, recipients may feel the impact only as a gradually worsening, undifferentiated ache, with no clearly defined time of origin and no immediately apparent cause.

Further cutbacks have come in the form of more restrictive eligibility requirements and stricter oversight. This, too, generates less interest, discussion, and media attention than would open challenges to the program's legitimacy.

Attacks on the Information Establishment

In the last several years, moreover, we have seen evidence of a more direct erosion of existing mechanisms for generating and disseminating information. Attempts to place limits on Freedom of Information guidelines, cutbacks at the Census Bureau and in the publication budgets of many federal agencies, constraints on the collection of race data used to monitor compliance with equal housing opportunity guidelines, loosening of reporting and planning requirements to state and local governments receiving federal grants, and efforts to constrain Legal Services activities radically make it potentially more difficult and certainly more costly to obtain reliable data about conditions of the poor.

DIMINISHING EXPECTATIONS AND A SHRINKING PUBLIC REALM

Once individuals perceive a condition in their environment, they must evaluate the condition in terms of their own knowledge and values in order to determine whether it does, in fact, affect their interests in a significant sense. The knowledge that citizens bring to bear on the situation—knowledge of social causality, of market dynamics, of historic parallels—shapes their expectations about the likely implications of known changes in their political and economic environment. Citizens, for example, may be aware that their local officials are offering tax incentives to promote economic development. Whether they regard this as an opportunity (more jobs) or threat (higher taxes for non-business taxpayers) will depend on other factors, including familiarity with similar efforts in other jurisdictions and personal experience. The values that citizens apply—the relative attachment that they place on such considerations as loyalty, neighborliness, stability, responsibility for others, individual freedom and growth—influence whether they are likely to interpret the expected outcome as desirable or undesirable, and, if undesirable, whether it is fitting for a public or private response.

This final section considers the possibility that broadly shared experiences of the 1960s and early 1970s have altered the ideological framework within which ongoing evaluations of individual interests and alternatives for action are made. The nation's defeat in Vietnam, the apparent failure of the War on Poverty, conservative backlash against civil rights enforcement, the inability of American industry to thrive in an increasingly competitive international market, layoffs of public employees and the near financial collapse of the nation's largest city— these experiences have fed a general sense of the fragility of our national well-being, contributed to lower expectations of progress and growth, undermined confidence that government can find the solutions to major problems, and even raised doubts that any solutions exist.

The Zero-Sum Perspective

Expectations play an important role in feeding the impulse to undertake collective political action. People rebel, it seems, not when things are at their lowest ebb but when the gap widens between their condition and the condition they expect for themselves (Davies, 1962; Gurr, 1970). Similar stimuli, in an era of growth, are interpreted differently than in an era of stagnation or decline. Declining services, physical deterioration, and job flight are less likely to stir indignation and action among those who have become resigned to a future of limited growth.

The 1960s were a time of economic growth and a widely shared perception of an expanding pie. The real income of all families, black and white, rose steadily between 1950 and 1970. After peaking in 1973, however, white family incomes dropped about 8.8% by 1983. After peaking in 1972, black family incomes fell about 11.3% by the same year (U.S. Bureau of the Census, 1984: 446).

Although Americans remain a fairly optimistic people, a sense that the ceiling on growth is in sight has become increasingly palpable. The Gallup Poll occasionally asks respondents to predict whether conditions will be better, worse, or about the same in the coming year. Only 7% answered "worse" in 1960. This figure rose steadily in the years the question was asked, reaching a high of 56% in 1980, and fluctuating sharply, but remaining high, subsequently. The data, moreover, mask some substantial differences among groups. About one-third of all

Americans, but more than one-half of blacks, predicted that 1983 would be worse than the preceding year (Gallup, 1983).

Related to lower expectations is a greater sense of fragility, a sense that whatever gains that are made may prove temporary. This sense probably has been heightened by sharp fluctuations in inflation and unemployment. Recent bank scares in Ohio and Maryland may have been a demonstration of this underlying insecurity.

Problems are less likely to generate collective responses when they are discounted by a strong perception that "things could be worse." News reports of major corporate closures, for example, may lead residents of slowly deteriorating cities to measure themselves against a Youngstown instead of a Houston. This not only generates a kind of second-order satisfaction, it can deflect serious consideration of actions that might alienate business and sources of capital. The argument that taxes, regulation, and political turmoil may spur capital flight is not a new one. In a context of lowered expectations and raised insecurities, however, the familiar argument carries a stronger punch. To the extent that this is the case, the depressed levels of collective reaction may reflect something deeper than a rational calculation that the benefits of action outweigh the costs. Broad categories of behavior may be ruled out as simply not worth considering.

Privatization of the American Psyche

If Americans are opting for personal instead of political routes to satisfaction—through their jobs, flight to the suburbs, devotion to their family—the explanation may lie less in an objective shift in the costs versus benefits of such alternatives than in a reformulation of the standards against which the array of opportunities are judged.

Most rational choice and pluralist analysts take for granted a standard based on a stable and fairly narrow sense of self-interest. The human being, according to this perspective, is "homo civicus": a creature naturally drawn to satisfactions available in the private realm. Political activity, as a "strategy to achieve his gratifications, will seem considerably less efficient than working at his job, earning more money, taking out insurance, joining a club, planning a vacation, moving to another neighborhood or city, or coping with an uncertain future in manifold other ways" (Dahl, 1961: 225).

As Hirschman (1982: 67) indicates, however, "the dogged pursuit of happiness along a private road is not, as we often think, 'what comes naturally,'" Rather,

It is presided over and impelled by an ideology which justifies it, not only in terms of its beneficial results for the individual pursuer, but as the surest and perhaps only way in which the individual can make a contribution to the public good. The ideological claims made for the private life thus sustain the individual's quest with two messages: one, the promise of satisfaction and happiness; and two, the assurance that there is no need for guilt feelings or regrets over the neglect of public life.

Hirschman suggests that there may be a cyclical pattern to the movement of societies from private to public to private concerns. The driving force of this dynamic is disappointment. The consumer who discovers that a newly purchased VCR brings neither happiness nor fulfillment may respond by seeking those goals in other market goods. The accumulation of disappointments, however, may lead ultimately to a sharp reorientation—a greater readiness to look for satisfaction in the public realm.

Public life holds its own frustrations, however. Activists become disillusioned as gains come slowly and at great expense in terms of energy and time. Favored reforms, when implemented, fail to live up to expectations. Social Security, AFDC, the War on Poverty, and civil rights legislation all exacted a toll on those who fought for their passage, and the personal security, equality, and justice they promised prove more elusive than their advocates dreamed.

The intense activism of the 1960s, according to Hirschman, is more than just a counterpoint to 1980s quiescence; it is, in a sense, the very source of the privatization of the American psyche that we see today. And the failure of personal consumption to generate satisfaction will, according to Hirschman, generate another round of public activity sometime in the future.

Loss of a Public Ideology

People need a reason if they are to act deliberately. In a culture that accents personal pleasures and individual routes to advancement, they especially need a reason if they are to act collectively. Just as the ideology of the market can provide a rationale for self-interested behavior, a public ideology can lead people to define their interests more broadly and to look more readily to political action as a means to achieve their ends.

The activism of the 1960s drew upon an ideology that recognized a central role for government (particularly the national government) as an effective tool for pursuing common ends. This ideology, in turn, drew upon an interpretation of American history that saw the New Deal as proof that the federal government could successfully manage the economy and establish programs to reduce hardship for the elderly, handicapped, and poor. Problems previously considered private matters or local concerns—caring for aging relatives, providing for the deserving poor—were given legitimacy as public issues and responsibilities. And the initial success of the government in addressing those problems contributed to a "can do" attitude that led many Americans to accept the premise that racism and poverty could be eradicated in their lifetime.

If government has the legitimacy, resources, and technical capacity to address such problems, failure to sustain progress could only be attributed to the lack of political will. With this as a background premise, the political instability generated by the urban riots and the antiwar movement fed a remarkable air of expectation. Katznelson (1981: 3) accurately captures the importance of this sense of the possible in overcoming the barriers that block collective action in more normal times:

> Suddenly, because much was uncertain, much seemed possible. . ... Since the mobilization of large numbers of people to act in risky and potentially costly ways on behalf of shared ends is so difficult to achieve, a common sense that dramatic alterations in deeply rooted racial and distributional practices were possible was the requisite for translating common threads of mass *ressentiment* into a willingness to engage in irregular political activity.

The ideology that bolstered this sense of the possible has suffered under an intellectual assault led by neoconservative theorists such as Edward Banfield, Nathan Glazer, James Q. Wilson, and Charles Murray. They argue that government—especially the national government—is a blunt instrument at best. They bolster their argument with examples of well-intentioned programs that seemingly backfired. Federal highway construction and mortgage guarantees fueled suburban flight. Urban renewal decimated urban ethnic enclaves and replaced low-income housing with parking lots. Social welfare policies nurtured a generation of the underclass habituated to dependence. These programs are part of a commonly shared history. As the neoconservative interpretation becomes the new "conventional wisdom," the parameters through which individuals assess their interests and weigh their alternatives are altered fundamentally.

CONCLUSIONS

Predictions of impending protests and mass political uprisings have become both familiar and quaint. The political right offers these predictions with an air of trepidation and grim resignation to a vision of human nature that makes the have-nots a perpetual threat to those that have. The left offers its predictions with an "I-told-you-so" spirit and an optimistic sense that class interests, once mobilized, have a historical mandate to reshape institutions broadly, not stopping or flagging until the system has been made more equal and more just.

These predictions are of a hearty nature. Like the tabloid headlines predicting a life-threatening collision between the Earth and a hurtling comet, they sprout each year with no sense of recognition that previous forecasts have gone awry.

This chapter has focused on the obstacles to mobilization, but it should not be taken as a prediction that we are entering a long and inevitable era of quiescence. The temptation to project the present into the future always is great, but the results often are deceptive. When Edward Banfield (1974: 335) wrote that "there is likely to be more rioting for many years to come," the context of ongoing disruptions gave his warning an unnerving air of reasonableness. To forecast an era of social peace based on sublimation, fatalism, or false consciousness among the deprived would be just as careless and, perhaps, just as likely to be wrong.

Because social science puts a value on the "predictiveness" of its theories, reticence to peer into the future might be regarded skeptically. Beyond the fact that those who have done so in the past often have ended up looking foolish, however, there is another reason to be wary. It has to do with the difference between organized, effective collective action and the dramatic, but somewhat haphazard, disruptions that took place in many ghetto areas between 1964 and 1968. Although both may draw on the same reservoir of indignation and discontent, the latter is more spontaneous, more episodic, more situational, and, accordingly, more difficult to foresee. Piven and Cloward (1979) argue that such disruptions ultimately are more effective than more routinized means of protest, but I believe that they misstate the case. The uprisings of the mid-60s drew their effectiveness from their coexistence with more organized efforts and their linkage with an ideological framework that they did not create.

We are witnessing a shrinking of the realm of the possible and a shrinking of the realm of the public, simultaneously. To suggest that this plays a role in limiting collective responses to today's urban crisis is to go further than those who, focusing on the calculation stage, reason that citizens simply have decided that collective political action does not pay. The latter perspective assumes that the likely grievants have reviewed all available evidence and courses of action; the former raises the possibility that ideology and experiences have cramped the way people think about themselves and their alternatives.

This analysis underscores the importance and influence of ideas. Pluralists and rational choice analysts have not come to grips with the effect of ideas on political behavior because they treat preferences as individual, idiosyncratic, and relatively fixed. Their neo-Marxist critics take ideology more seriously. They are sensitive to the ways in which ideology can skew the conceptions upon which individuals' calculations are based. Yet, they too trivialize the concept of ideology in the end.

By focusing on ideology as a tool of social control, neo-Marxist writers have tended to overestimate the ability of elites to manipulate ideas to their own ends. Ideas have power to move people only when they retain a footing in the soil of common experiences, commonly perceived. Neoconservatism, privatism, and the zero-sum perspective are potent precisely because they seem, to the average American, to make better sense of recent occurrences and to provide a more realistic guide to behavior than Great Society liberalism.

Those who wish to motivate others to action err if they proceed as if the battle for power can proceed in isolation from or prior to the battle of ideas. Institutes to train better organizers and efforts to shift the balance of power by building coalitions across different categories of the disadvantaged will have limited effect if unaccompanied by an effective theoretical challenge to neoconservatism, privatism, and the zero-sum mentality.

REFERENCES

ALINSKY, S. (1971) Rules for Radicals. New York: Vintage.
BANFIELD, E. (1974) The Unheavenly City Revisited. Boston: Little, Brown.

BOYTE, H. (1980) The Backyard Revolution: Understanding the New Citizen Movement. Philadelphia: Temple University Press.

BROWNING, R. P., D. R. MARSHALL, and D. H. TABB (1984) Protest Is Not Enough. Berkeley: University of California Press.

CLARK, T. N. and L. C. FERGUSON (1983) City Money. New York: Columbia University Press.

DAHL, R. (1961) Who Governs? Democracy and Power in an American City. New Haven, CT: Yale University.

DAVIES, J. C. (1962) "Toward a theory of revolution." American Sociological Review 22 (February): 5-19.

FAINSTEIN, N. I. and S. S. FAINSTEIN (1983) "Regime strategies, communal resistance, and economic forces," in S. S. Fainstein et al., Restructuring the City. New York: Longman.

————(1980) "Mobility, community and participation: the American way out," in W.A.V. Clark and E. G. Moore (eds.) Residential Mobility and Public Policy. Beverly Hills, CA: Sage.

FAINSTEIN, S. S., N. I. FAINSTEIN, and P. J. ARMISTEAD (1983) "San Francisco: urban transformation and the local state," in S. S. Fainstein et al., Restructuring the City. New York: Longman.

FISHER, R. (1984) Let The People Decide: Neighborhood Organizing in America. Boston: Twayne.

FRIEDLAND, R., F. PIVEN, and R. ALFORD (1984) "Political conflict, urban structure, and the fiscal crisis," in W. K. Tabb and L. Sawyers (eds.) Marxism and the Metropolis. New York: Oxford University Press.

FROLICH, N., J. OPPENHEIMER, and O. YOUNG (1971) Political Leadership and Collective Goods. Princeton, NJ: Princeton University Press.

GALLUP, G. (1983) The Gallup Report (no. 208). Princeton, NJ: Author.

GITTELL, M. (1980) Limits to Citizen Participation: The Decline of Community Organizations. Beverly Hills, CA: Sage.

GOODMAN, J. L., Jr., and M. L. STREITWIESER (1983) "Explaining racial differences: a study of city-to-suburb residential mobility." Urban Affairs Quarterly 18 (March): 301-325.

GURR, T. (1970) Why Men Rebel. Princeton, NJ: Princeton University Press.

HENIG, J. (1982a) Neighborhood Mobilization: Redevelopment and Response. New Brunswick, NJ: Rutgers University.

————(1982b) "Neighborhood response to centrification: conditions of mobilization." Urban Affairs Quarterly 17 (March): 343-358.

————(1982c) Gentrification in Adams Morgan: Political and Commercial Consequences of Neighborhood Change. Washington, DC: George Washington University Center for Washington Area Studies, Monograph No. 9.

HICKS, D. A. (1982) Urban America in the Eighties. New Brunswick, NJ: Transaction.

HILL, R. (1983) "Crisis in the motor city: the politics of economic development in Detroit," in S. Fainstein et al., Restructuring the City. New York: Longman.

HIRSCHMAN, A. O. (1982) Shifting Involvements. Cambridge, MA: Harvard University Press.

————(1970) Exit, Voice, and Loyalty: Responses to Decline in Firms, Organizations, and States. Cambridge, MA: Harvard University Press.

KATZ, S. and M. MAYER (1985) "Gimme shelter: self-help housing struggles within and against the state in New York City and West Berlin." International Journal of Urban and Regional Research (March): 15-45.

KATZNELSON, I. (1981) City Trenches. New York: Pantheon.

LIPSKY, M. (1970) Protest in City Politics. Chicago: Rand McNally.

MORRIS, D. and K. HESS (1975) Neighborhood Power. Boston: Beacon.

MOYNIHAN, D. P. (1970) Maximum Feasible Misunderstanding. New York: Free Press.

ORBELL, J. M. and T. UNO (1972) The theory of neighborhood problem solving: political action versus residential mobility." American Political Science Review 66 (June): 471-489.

PETERSON, P. E. (1981) City Limits. Chicago: University of Chicago Press.

PICKVANCE, C. (1985) "The rise and fall of urban movements and the role of comparative analysis." Environment and Planning D: Society and Space 3.

PIVEN, F. and R. CLOWARD (1982) The New Class War. New York: Pantheon.

———(1979) Poor People's Movements. New York: Vintage.

POLSBY, N. (1980) Community Power and Political Theory. New Haven, CT: Yale University Press.

RUBIN, R. J. (1983) Statement before the Subcommittee on Public Assistance and Unemployment Compensation, Committee on Ways and Means, November 3.

SALISBURY, R. (1969) "An exchange theory of interest groups." Midwest Journal of Political Science 13 (February): 1-32.

SUSSER, I. (1982) Norman Street: Poverty and Politics in an Urban Neighborhood. New York: Oxford University Press.

TOLCHIN, M. (1985) "More cities paying industry to provide public services." New York Times (May 28): 1.

U.S. Bureau of the Census (1984) Statistical Abstract of the United States: 1985. Washington, DC: Government Printing Office.

WILSON, J. Q. (1973) Political Organizations. New York: Basic Books.

10

The Crisis of Local Government
in Great Britain:
An Interpretation

C. G. PICKVANCE

☐ THE TERM "urban crisis" has both popular and social scientific uses. On the whole its popular usage has prevailed. The term has been applied to a motley collection of phenomena such as the U.S. urban riots in the 1960s, the fiscal crises of certain U.S. cities in the 1970s, and even the May 1968 revolt in France. These events were urban in location and disrupted social and economic life but had little else in common. In particular, the commonsense explanation that because they occurred in cities their causes were urban in the sense of lying within the city boundaries is untenable. It is generally accepted in social science that some social phenomena are "in the city" but not "of the city"—for example, foreign policymaking—and that even those that are in and of the city, such as traffic congestion or high land prices, are influenced by national and international processes.

Yet the paradox is that every effort to identify those processes that epitomize the urban only uncovers processes that occur in nonurban areas too (Saunders, 1981a: 249-258). For example, traffic congestion or high land values are in and of cities but are also found outside cities; the process of concentration of activity that gives rise to them is only contingently urban in a geographical sense (but see Scott, 1980). The

AUTHOR'S NOTE: *I am grateful to Ed Page for helpful comments.*

three most influential analytical social science (as opposed to common-sense) definitions of the urban in recent years have been urban as collective consumption, urban as local political process, and urban as spatial proximity (Castells, 1977; Pickvance, 1985). In each case the urban refers to a social process that spills over the urban-rural divide. Collective consumption, or the involvement of the state in consumption provision, is a major social process but occurs in both urban and rural areas. The same is true of local political processes, and spatial proximity gives rise to certain interests such as territorial defense in both urban and rural areas. Urban does not, however, have a transhistorical theoretical meaning. The processes that constitute the urban differ between societies (Castells, 1983); collective consumption has only been a significant process in advanced capitalist countries in the last century and is now under challenge.

This chapter will focus on one crisis in Britain that is urban in a social scientific sense: the crisis of local government. This overlaps to some extent a second urban crisis, the crisis of collective consumption, because most education and social service expenditures and some housing expenditures are a local government responsiblity. (Collective consumption also refers to health and social security.)

The term "urban crisis" is not in fact commonly used in Britain. This is due partly to a cultural reluctance to admit the existence of crises; by contrast in France *la crise* is a constant point of reference in everyday conversation. And partly it is because the economic plight of Britain's cities is seen as part of a national economic crisis, and because there is greater attention to the regional unevenness of its incidence than to its urban unevenness. On the one hand, every conurbation is losing population and employment—there are no growing conurbations. Growth in population and jobs is occurring in small and medium-sized towns and fringe areas. There was an inverse relationship between settlement size and population growth rate between 1971 and 1981 with Greater London losing 10.1% of its population and urban-rural fringe and "accessible rural" areas gaining 7%. An even more marked inverse relationship is found for manufacturing employment between 1959 and 1975; a less marked inverse relationship is found for services employment, which constitutes 64% of all employment (Fothergill and Gudgin, 1982). On the other hand, the regional unevenness of the economic crisis is very marked and this is more salient in the U.K. political system than is its differential incidence by settlement size. The regions with the highest unemployment rates and levels of outmigration in 1981 are the same as those in 1931: Northern Ireland, Scotland, Wales, and the North of England (Law, 1980).

The term "urban fiscal crisis" also has little resonance in Britain. Newton's (1981) article carries the title "The local financial crisis in Britain: a non-crisis which is neither local nor financial." This epithet is somewhat exaggerated but as we proceed we shall see why such terms seem out of place in the British context.

This chapter is divided into two parts. First I outline the phases of the crisis of local government in Britain. Second, I discuss its causes and draw out implications for theories of state intervention and social mobilization.

THE CRISIS OF LOCAL GOVERNMENT SINCE 1976

The period since 1976 in Britain has been remarkable in that local government has been almost continuously in the headlines. This is a new development. Previously local government had been newsworthy at the time of institutional reforms (the reorganization of London local government in 1965, and of local government elsewhere in 1974) or because of conflicts over services such as comprehensive education, slum clearance, and highrise housing. In the present section I first present a brief overview of British local government, and then consider in turn government attempts to control its spending, and limit its power to levy a tax, and to abolish the Greater London Council and the six conurbationwide authorities. The effects of these measures and the extent of their opposition are also discussed.

LOCAL GOVERNMENT IN BRITAIN: ORGANIZATION AND FINANCE

Local government in Britain has a wide range of responsibilities. In addition to police, roads, fire service, refuse collection, and town planning, it is responsible for education, council housing (30% of all housing), and personal social services. Education accounted for 47% of local government current spending on final consumption in 1983, followed by personal social services (12%), police (11%), and roads and public lighting (6%). In the capital budget the main items are housing (45%), roads and public lighting (12%), and education (6%). In total, local government accounts for 23.8% of all government spending, and employs 13.8% of all employees, 35% of them being part-time. Local elections are contested by national political parties with strong local branch structures but there is no tradition of partisan appointments of local government officials by incoming parties. Local government is highly professionalized and resistant to public pressure: Openness to citizen pressure is seen as a threat to bureaucratic rationality rather than a virtue as in the United States (Newton, 1976). Its responsibility for welfare state services means that there is a concern with territorial equality of service provision and tax burden, and an element of central control and central funding, though this is often exaggerated by participants and observers alike. Organizationally there is a two-tier structure. In England and Wales higher-tier ("county") councils cover whole conurbations and nonmetropolitan counties (they range from 280,000 to 7 million in size); lower-tier ("district" or in London "borough") councils cover smaller units within metropolitan or nonmetropolitan counties (ranging from 10,000 to 1 million). (See Newton, 1980.)

Local councils draw their *current income* from three sources: government grants; rents, fees, and charges for certain services; and rates. In 1982 the total of £36627 million was made up of government grant £16091m (of which block grant £12849; 43.9%); fees, charges, and rents £8561m (including £3147m surplus from the "housing revenue account" from which loan interest and depreciation has to be paid; 23.4%) and rates £11975m (32.7%; Central statistical office [CSO], 1984: Table 8.2). *Government grants* are mostly made in the form of a block grant, but specific grants are made for transport, police, and some housing and education purposes. They are distributed between councils according to a complex formula that takes into account an area's resources, level of needs, and the relative cost of meeting them, but does not fully compensate for such inequalities. *Rates* are a local property tax levied on the "rateable value" of domestic and business property—this is based on its rental value. It is the sole tax source for local councils; there is no local income tax.

Income for *capital purposes* is derived from government grants, surpluses on current account, and the sale of assets such as council houses. In 1982 the total of £5863m was made up of government grants £382m (6.5%); surpluses on current account £3404m (58.1%); and capital receipts £2077m (of which council house sales accounted for £2036m; 35.4%). (See CSO, 1984: Table 8.3.) In addition councils borrow to finance capital spending. In 1982 councils in fact reduced their outstanding debt as their capital spending of £5042m was less than their capital income. Throughout the 1970s their debt increased by some £2 billion per year, however.

After this brief overview of local government organization and finance, we now turn to the first aspect of the crisis of local government.

ATTEMPTS TO CONTROL LOCAL GOVERNMENT SPENDING

We first outline government initiatives and their success and then discuss the incidence of spending cuts and political responses to them.

Government Initiatives

The first attempts to control local government spending go back to 1976, halfway through the term of office of the 1974-1979 Labour government. In that year the minister responsible for local government announced, "The party's over." He proposed an end to growth in local government expenditure: The real growth of 6.2% per annum between 1970-1971 and 1974-1975 would be replaced by a decline in real terms of 3.1% per annum between 1974-1975 and 1979-1980. This would be achieved by a 0.8% increase in current expenditure and a 6.6% per annum fall in capital expenditure (Cmnd. 6393, 1976: 139).

Total local government spending between 1976 and 1979 was cut by less than intended, but nevertheless fell by 2.4% per year in real terms (see Table 10.1). The brunt of the cuts was borne by local government capital spending, which fell 9.4% per year in real terms between 1976 and 1979. Because it had also fallen sharply in 1974-1976 due to the unexpectedly high rates of inflation (16% to 24%), the 1974-1979 period saw cuts in capital spending that exceeded any under the Conservative government. These cuts mainly involved house building and translated into a 37% cut in new council houses built—from 127,320 completed in 1977 to 79,896 completed in 1980. The attraction of cutting spending on house-building was that the labor force affected consisted largely of nonunionized employees of private building firms. For a government relying on trade union support, this was an important consideration; any attack on current spending would have affected a sector of unionized employees. In addition, it was administratively easier to make a decison not to build something, and there was little chance of protest from future residents.

In 1979 the Conservative government of Margaret Thatcher was elected. Its rhetoric emphasized the creation of an "enterprise culture" by "rolling back" the public sector and freeing private enterprise of controls. The implication for local government was clear. As part of the public sector it faced continuing cuts in spending. In addition, councils

TABLE 10.1   Trends in Central and Local Government Spending and Income 1974-1983, in Real[a] Terms

	Simple Annual Rates of Change[b]			
	1974-1976 Labour	1976-1979 Labour	1979-1983 Conservative	1974-1983 Whole Period
Central government spending	2.9	1.9	1.6	2.1
Local government spending	−2.1	−2.4	−1.0	−1.6
Capital spending[c]	−12.2	−11.5	−9.0	−7.6
	(−12.2)	(−9.4)	(−4.6)	(−6.3)
Current spending	1.9	0.2	0.5	0.7
Central grants to local authorities for current purposes	14.7	−4.3	0.6	1.7
Income from rates	−2.3	1.8	4.3	2.0

SOURCE: CSO (1984: Tables 7.1, 8.2, 8.3).
a. The deflator used is the general government deflator.
b. Rates of change are calculated by reference to different base years in each column, hence the absolute value of a 1% change is not the same across columns.
c. Capital spending is measured in the first line net of receipts from council house sales. The figures in parentheses have been calculated after adding in these receipts, and are preferred in the text.

were encouraged to contract out more of their activities to private firms, and were forced to sell council houses to their tenants.[1]

The evolution of council spending between 1974 and 1983 is shown in Table 10.1. After the real cuts of 2.4% per annum under Labour between 1976 and 1979, the Conservative period of office 1979-1983 has seen continuing real cuts of 1.0% per annum. As in the Labour period this has been achieved entirely via cuts in capital spending; current spending has continued to rise in real terms (by 0.5% p.a.).[2] These cuts in council spending have been the object of bitter conflict. This has centered around a series of measures introduced by the Conservative government to bring council spending "under control."

From the government's point of view the problem was how to reduce total council spending and spending by individual councils with a fair degree of predictability. On the face of it, partial or complete removal of central government grant, which represents 43.9% of council current income, would achieve cuts of any level a government wanted because most councils could not raise their income from other sources (rates, charges) sufficiently to compensate. However, this "big stick" approach was not adopted because its effects are very unpredictable and uneven between councils. The percentage of government grant varies between councils, so that those rich in property wealth or with "low needs" receive less. Such councils would find it easier to make good the shortfall of income, unlike councils with little property wealth or "high needs." The nonuse of the big stick approach is one index of the power of local government to resist spending cuts. As a result, the methods used to control spending concentrated directly on spending rather than on income. Indeed, the political unacceptability as well as technical defects of using cuts in central grant to control current spending[3] is indicated by the fact that such grants actually *increased* in real terms (by 0.6% per annum) over the period 1979-1983 (Table 10.1). The conflicts over successive attempts to control spending directly are now described.

The Conservative government has always hoped that councils that spend too much by its standards would be voted out of office by their electors. In the 1979-1981 period there were several initiatives to increase local responsiveness to council activities. Councils were obliged to produce an annual report to inform electors of their policies and spending, and the idea was proposed (but abandoned in the face of hostile reaction) that councils wishing to levy a supplementary rate (i.e., an extra levy in the middle of the year) should carry out a local referendum. However, in the end this reliance on electors was abandoned. Many councils that spent more than the government wanted did so either because of public support (Labour councils have a tradition of higher spending and higher rates) or because local elections were decided on the basis of national party popularity, thus insulating councillors from adverse local reaction (Dunleavy, 1980). In either case the hoped for rejection by voters failed to materialize.

As a result, an interventive approach was introduced in 1980, with the passing of the Local Government Planning and Land Act. This had two aims: (1) to control current spending directly by imposing graduated penalties on councils whose spending exceeded targets set by central government—these penalties took the form of reduced central grants—and (2) to control capital spending directly by obliging councils to obtain authorization for planned spending. By setting targets for individual councils the government hoped to control their current spending without controlling their income sources. Two types of targets were devised: a volume target based on a rate of increase over a previous year's spending and an absolute target based on the government's judgment of what each council should spend to meet needs in their areas.

These proposals caused an uproar because they threatened councils' most jealously guarded freedom. Councils have always argued that they know the needs of their area better than government, and should have the right to spend accordingly, raising extra income from rates. The new absolute target meant that government was usurping the right to decide the area's needs. Councils argued that this was simply a way of allocating a global spending target between areas and had no connection with local needs. Labour councils felt they were being victimized by the government, but the opposition crossed party boundaries. It was conducted by the three local authority associations that represent metropolitan authorities (all Labour), nonmetropolitan higher-tier, and nonmetropolitan lower-tier authorities (both Conservative-dominated). Their main claim was the "constitutional" one that councils had a mandate for their spending policies and could not be interfered with by central government. This opposition did not prevent the system from being introduced, but did affect its form. Because conservative councils were particularly vulnerable to volume targets as they traditionally spend less than Labour councils and had less "fat" to cut away, the government decided that in the first two years the volume target would not be applied to protect them. By introducing absolute targets too, Labour councils with their traditionally higher spending levels could be penalized with little fear of affecting Conservative councils. In this way the party's political as well as macroeconomic basis of the policy was made clear.

The penalty system has led to a state of permanent confrontation between government and councils. Yet the great irony is that it led to relatively small overall cuts in council spending; between 1979 and 1983 total local government spending fell by only 1.0% per annum in real terms, and current spending even increased (by 0.5% per annum; see Table 10.1).[4] There were two reasons for this. First, as mentioned earlier, for political and technical reasons central grant to councils for current spending has not been used as the primary means of controlling spending and has in fact continued to increase in real terms. Central grant in fact increases (but tapers off) as councils spend more. Second, the penalty system has been operated in such a restrained way that it has failed to bite. Some penalties were not applied at all to avoid alienating Conservative councils. Some of the targets set were "soft"; one calculation even showed that councils (mostly Labour) that spent most received the highest target increases (Smith, 1983). And certain Labour authorities, notably the Greater London Council and the Inner London Education Authority, exceeded their spending target by so much that they incurred the maximum penalty (the complete loss of central grant) and made good their lost grant by setting higher rates. Both reasons reflect the political strength of local government vis-à-vis central government, particularly when Conservative control of numerous councils is combined with Conservative national power.

Responses to Government Spending Controls

Before discussing political responses to the penalty system and spending cuts, two points must be made about them that indicate the relative power of local government. First, as was argued above, their very form was the result of extensive lobbying by councils and local authority associations. Second, a most striking feature of the penalty system and cuts is that they did not involve any challenge to council responsibilities. A dramatic change could have been achieved by removing responsibilities from local government but this has not been done. For example, the transfer of education, which accounts for 35.2% of all local government spending (1983), to central government has been discussed on and off but never carried out. Instead the legislation within which councils carry out their responsibilities has remained largely unchanged. The main exception has been the 1980 "right-to-buy" act that compelled councils to sell council houses to tenants. Previously councils had had the right to sell council houses but most Labour councils and a minority of Conservative councils had not done so. The reason why changes in council's powers were not necessary is that most legislation is permissive, giving councils power to carry out certain activities, rather than compelling them to do so. It was thus possible to encourage councils to spend less without breaching their statutory obligations. Nevertheless, the removal of council responsibilities would have encountered great opposition, and the power of local government is indicated by the fact that is has not been tried.

Turning now to the political responses after the penalty system and spending cuts were introduced, the first is the use of legal cases to claim the government is acting unlawfully. A number of private individuals have undertaken lawsuits against councils on the grounds that they were failing in their statutory responsibilities; and some councils have tried to prove that central government was acting illegally in forcing spending cuts on them. Great hopes were raised but in only one instance did these cases succeed, and in that case (a complaint about grant penalties), the victory was technical and did not lead to more money. This is because legislation is mostly permissive and the wording has proved too loose to allow successful legal challenges. Legislation that had been perceived as enshrining "welfare state" rights did not in fact protect any particular level of service provision.

The second and most striking response to the cuts introduced by the penalty system was Liverpool's rebellion in 1984. In 1983, control of the Liverpool council passed to a left Labour group ("Militant") with a strong public sector trade union base (the council is the city's largest employer). The group claimed that adherence to the government's target would lead to a tripling of rates or a loss of 5000 jobs. It thus decided to refuse to pass a legal budget in 1984. This defiance was not supported by the national Labour leadership, which has no sympathy for the Militant group and had been trying to expel it from the party. The government failed to persuade the council to back down and it continued to operate for 3½ months. Meanwhile negotiations with the government were opened and a compromise reached. During this period the councillors risked fines and imprisonment but no legal action was taken against them. The government continued to make its weekly grant payment, thereby condoning the council's position. The final settlement was a victory for the council because the government offered financial aid and permission for various accounting maneuvers that were probably worth £50m (but see Midwinter, 1985). On July 12, 1984, the council passed a legal budget involving a 17% rate increase and the rebellion was over.

Liverpool's action was unique in England. Its defense of council service levels and employment was possible because of the council's determination and unity, and the close integration of Labour party and public trade sector unions. In Scotland, however, there were also cases of defiance of the government. In 1980-1981, the Dundee council opposed the compulsory sale of council houses and ran a campaign based on close liason between labor and skilled manual trade unionists; public sector unions were also involved. Also in 1980-1981 the Lothian council resisted government spending cuts for a time. Here the social base of the movement was very different: the Labour majority on the council was led by young middle-class councillors committed to involving the community groups in their campaign (Elliott and McCrone, 1984). Gyford (1984) has shown that many such councillors are one-time community activists. Neither campaign was ultimately successful. The Liverpool and Dundee cases indicate an older style of mobilization based on Labour party links with industrial unions, whereas Lothian indicates a new community-oriented style. The striking point, however, is the paucity of these campaigns of defiance—respect for the law is strongly embedded in British political life and it is rare to find sufficient unity among Labour councillors or support from trade union or community organizations to engage in illegal action.

A third type of response to the spending cuts was the exploitation of legal loopholes by councils. This became known as "creative accounting." It allowed councils to avoid spending controls by the use of reserve funds and other devices. For example the budget for Hackney, a Labour-controlled inner-London borough, announced for 1984-1985 was £82m but its actual planned spending was £106 million. Such tactics threatened the government by depriving it of accurate information on which to base its plans for council spending. A related response to the penalty system was that councils levied higher than necessary rates in order to build up their reserves because if they were penalized their government grant would be cut. This natural response to uncertainty was estimated by the Audit Commission (a regulatory authority) as having led to an extra £1.2 billion being levied in rates over the three years 1981-1982 to 1983-1984, which compares with total rates income of £35 billion—a paradoxical result for a government seeking to hold down council spending.

To sum up, opposition to the spending cuts primarily took the form of protest over the penalty system by local authorities and their associations. Lawsuits have been notably unsuccessful and illegal defiance rare and short-lived. The role of industrial conflict and community protest is referred to below.

Effects of Spending Cuts on Employment and Services

Despite the relatively small cuts in council spending of 1% per annum between 1979 and 1983, the effects on jobs and services have been considerable. These will be discussed in turn.

Whereas between 1976 and 1979, jobs were largely protected, this has not been the case since 1979. Although, as we have seen, current spending rose in real terms by 0.5% per year, total council employment fell by 3.4% between 1979 and 1984 (see Table 10.2). On the one hand, some types of employment have increased: police, social services, recreation, and housing administration (where the task of calculating

**TABLE 10.2   Change in the Number of Local Government Employees
(full-time equivalents) March 1979 to June 1984**

	1979	1984	Total Change
Construction	156.1	130.7	−16.3%
Refuse collection and disposal	59.9	51.0	−14.9%
Education − manual and clerical	473.5	421.0	−11.1%
− professional	638.8	606.2	−5.1%
Recreation and parks	87.0	94.2	+8.3%
Police	123.0	134.1	+9.0%
Social services	233.6	263.9	+13.0%
Housing	53.8	62.4	+16.0%
Other	522.0	503.4	−3.6%
Total	2347.7	2267.0	−3.4%

SOURCE: Travers (1983), Department of Employment, *Employment Gazette* December 1980 and December 1984.

housing benefits has been transferred to councils). The job losses, on the other hand, have been concentrated on manual jobs in construction, refuse, and education. Council construction workers are employed partly on new building but mainly on maintenance of council housing. Their numbers have declined as the sale of council houses has led to a decline in the stock—by 10% since 1979. All education employment has been affected by the fall in number of school-age children and closure of schools but teachers and lecturers have been less affected than clerical and manual workers. Manual workers such as school cleaners and school meals staff have, with refuse collectors and street cleaners, been the main target of contracting out to private enterprise.

These cuts in employment conceal a rise in the number of part-time employees (though this varies greatly between councils; see Travers, 1983; Webster, 1985) and changes in the conditions of employment of manual workers, as well as the disappearance of full-time jobs. These have led to numerous industrial conflicts. In addition, in the small minority of councils that have contracted out services, existing refuse collectors and school cleaners have often made an "in-house" bid, offering to do their present work under worse conditions. Professional jobs are more often lost through natural wastage, but part-time jobs with short-term contracts have often been terminated. Industrial conflict has thus frequently accompanied job losses but strikes have rarely been successful in protecting jobs.

The effect of spending cuts on services has taken three forms: reductions in the quantity and quality of provision, and higher charges. In council housing house completions have fallen 57% between 1979 and 1984, the state of repair of existing dwellings has declined, and rents have been increased (helping encourage council house sales). In education the range of subjects taught is declining, books and equipment are in short supply (average council spending on books is £10 per pupil), class sizes are not being allowed to fall as numbers of school-age children decline, and school buildings are in poor repair. As a result, parents are raising funds for essentials and even acting as volunteer helpers in schools. Contracting out of school cleaning has often meant lower standards as private firms employ fewer people . In social services, there is a change in the character of the service. Residential homes for children and the elderly have been closed in favor of fostering and community care, placing a bigger burden on relatives and the voluntary labor of women. The unpaid labor of carers for elderly people saves the government over £4 billion per year according to one estimate (Webster, 1985). Webster also reports that the population over age 65 increased by 10.9% from 1975-1976 to 1982-1983, whereas those in residential care fell by 8.5%, the number of home helps fell by 6.8%, and the number of meals served per 1000 fell by 5.6%. Charges have been introduced for planning applications.

In view of this deterioration of council services one might have expected an extensive upsurge of public protest. Industrial action in defense of the jobs of service providers has of course been to preserve services too, but on the whole service *consumers* have been inactive. In a number of towns "anticuts" campaigns were formed to defend services but these were mainly led by the trade unions involved and drew in little new support.

To sum up, government attempts to cut council spending via the penalty system, to introduce contracting out of a few services, and to privatize public housing have had limited success. But the extent of the changes has been less than political rhetoric (of left or right) would suggest.

RATE-CAPPING

The power to set rates has been a major way in which councils have been able to increase their current income and maintain their spending in the face of cuts or low increases in government grant. (Table 10.1 shows that income from rates increased sharply in real terms after 1979.)

This power is effective partly because there is public support in many areas for local government spending and partly because where there is not councils may be safe from electoral sanction. It is not surprising, therefore, that in 1983 the government introduced a bill to interfere with councils' power to set rates. A similar measure had been operating in Scotland since 1981. Before discussing this second aspect of the local government crisis, a word is necessary about the economic and political significance of rates.

In both the 1979 and 1983 election manifestos, the Conservatives pledged themselves to find an alternative to the rating system. Rates are unpopular with individuals because they are based on property and disregard the number of earners in a household and its gross income, except at the lowest income levels where a rebate scheme operates. Also, because the tax base lacks buoyancy, the rate in the £ has to be increased each year to secure a higher yield because property revaluations are rare. More significant is the sustained campaign by business interests against rates. Two lines are taken. The absolute level of rates is objected to as reducing profits and threatening employment, and rates are criticized as "taxation without representation" because business ratepayers have no votes at local elections (except as residents). Evidence on the former point is anecdotal but a government-commissioned research project failed to detect any ecological correlation between rate levels and employment change. Moreover, much council spending supports business interests rather than being a drain on business profits, for example, the provision of loss-making car parks, conference centers, ports, entertainment and recreation facilities. On the second point, it is perfectly true that business has no council representation. But this confuses formal power and effective power. Business has considerable effective power through behind-the-scenes contacts and in particular by the incorporation of business priorities into civic initiatives to promote local economic development such as those mentioned. It is of course not surprising that businesses should prefer to pay lower taxes, but what is new is the attention given by the Conservative government to this special pleading. As in others of its manifestations (such as enterprise zones; Shutt, 1984) the "enterprise culture" turns out to require not laissez-faire but massive state transfers to the "wealth-creators"—perhaps better termed "wealth guzzlers." On the other hand, Labour councils such as the Greater London Council have made great play of the fact that rate-borne expenditure is a highly progressive redistributive mechanism—

because business ratepayers in London pay one-third of all rates and the poorest receive rate rebates.

Hence by taking power to fix rates levels the government is responding both to its own supporters and to its opponents. The Rates Act was passed in 1984 following extensive opposition by the three local government associations. As in the case of the penalty system, their opposition was couched in terms of the defense of the "constitutional" autonomy of councils. The Act contains a general power to set a limit (or "cap") on rate increases for all councils and a selective power to cap the rates of councils on a list of high-spending councils. It also obliges all councils to consult business representatives before setting a rate. The only concession granted to opponents of the measure was that the general power would not be applied to councils that had spent within their targets for the previous three years.

In July 1984 the first list of councils whose rates were to be capped in 1985-1986 was issued. All but two of the eighteen councils were Labour-controlled and included the GLC and ILEA, which had defied the penalty system so blatantly. The sixteen Labour councils agreed on a policy of defiance. This was given limited support by the national Labour party leadership—unlike their neglect of Liverpool's rebellion in 1984. The potential stakes are very high because failure to declare a legal rate opens councillors to fines, bankruptcy, and imprisonment. The Labour leadership is ambivalent about being seen to support illegality.

In any event, all sixteen councils had by July 1985 passed a legal rate. This was because the permitted level of rate increases was fairly generous (again a reflection of the power of local government) and because in most councils the Labour group was divided from the outset over a policy of defiance. The size of the permitted increases exacerbated the divisions because defiance could be branded as leftist posturing rather than an essential step to protect jobs and services. In addition to the rate-capped councils, Liverpool is committed to a repeat of its successful 1984 rebellion and has passed an (illegal) deficit budget.

In sum, rate-capping is technically a very effective weapon for central government in controlling council spending, but its use depends on the balance of political opinion for and against it. So far this has prevented it being very effective economically. Its main effects have been to exacerbate political conflict.

THE ABOLITION OF THE GREATER LONDON COUNCIL
AND METROPOLITAN COUNTY COUNCILS

To understand the abolition proposals, a word on recent history is necessary. As we have seen, the GLC (and ILEA) led the opposition to the penalty system by demonstrating that rates could be used to replace lost central government grant (GLC rates rose by 64% between 1981-1982 and 1982-1983). This was symptomatic of the way the GLC has been the focus of opposition to the Conservative government. The six metropolitan county councils have all been Labour-controlled since 1981 but have been much less vocal opponents of the government.

The GLC's fame and notoriety centered on the cheap fares scheme it introduced on London bus and underground services in 1981, managed by London Transport. The policy was intended to increase ridership and divert people from private to public transport. The essence of the policy was to cut fares (by one-third) and make good the gap between fares income and running costs by raising rates. Because one-third of all rates income in Greater London is paid by nondomestic ratepayers (commerce and industry), the effect was to make business pay more toward public transport. The redistributive effect of the cheap fares scheme was explicitly acknowledged by the GLC's Labour leader, Ken Livingstone (1984: 265), who argues that the GLC is "the best redistributor of wealth we [Labour] have ever been able to take control of."

In order to raise its rates income, the GLC levied a supplementary rate. This had two effects. It enabled the GLC to spend at a level much in excess of its target. It thus suffered the ultimate penalty of complete loss of its central government grant. But its ability to use rates to replace lost grant demonstrated the ineffectiveness of the penalty system in preventing overspending by certain councils. Moreover, the popularity of the scheme was shown by the shift in public opinion from 3:1 against, before the scheme was launched, to 2:1 in favor after six months (Livingstone, 1984: 272). The second effect was that suburban Bromley council challenged the legality of the GLC's use of rates in this way and was ultimately successful. The GLC was subsequently obliged to raise fares again in 1982, but in 1984 an Act was passed abolishing London Transport and replacing it by an appointed board responsible to central government. Nevertheless, throughout the 1981-1984 period the GLC served as a focus of opposition to the Conservative government, and was arguably more effective than the Labour parliamentary opposition.

"Can you afford to keep my daughter *and* Ken Livingstone?" *Standard*,
October 29, 1981 (*Michael Heath*)

SOURCE: London *Standard*. Reprinted with permission.

The proposal to abolish the GLC and MCCs gave the local
government crisis a third aspect. The proposal was part of the 1983
Conservative manifesto and its inclusion was partly due to the failure to
reform the rating system, a 1979 manifesto pledge. The overt rationale
for abolition was set out in a White Paper *Streamlining the Cities*
(Cmnd. 9063) published in October 1983. It is functional, economic, and
political. The GLC and MCCs have few functions, little day-to-day
responsibility for certain of them (public transport, police), and are
dependent on the cooperation of lower-tier authorities for others. They
thus tend to search for a wider, strategic role that inevitably leads to
conflict with lower-tier councils and central government. Their

spending has also increased faster than that of other authorities, hence abolition would lead to "considerable savings." Many observers would acknowledge friction and duplication but would point to the need for a strategic authority in spheres such as public transport, planning, and traffic. In addition, it is argued that the GLC and MCCs are too remote and abolition will return local government in the big cities to the people. It is not clear how this will happen, however, as the proposal is to transfer the councils' functions to joint boards (made up of nominees of the lower-tier councils), and to central government, as well as to lower-tier councils directly.

However, quite a different rationale can also be detected. It is purely and simply party political. According to Norman Tebbit, a senior cabinet minister, "The GLC is typical of this new divisive form of socialism . . . so we shall abolish the GLC" (March 1984, quoted in Forrester et al., 1985: 5). Or as a Conservative backbencher put it: "If we are honest with ourselves, the purpose of this bill is to change the political complexion of the G.L.C.—and that is the greatest compliment we can pay to [Ken] Livingstone" (F. Sylvester, reported May 11, 1984). In other words it is the political capital made by the GLC and MCCs that is the key to abolition plans. In support of this is the fact that no commission of inquiry has been undertaken into local government in the seven conurbations, nor has any estimate been made of the savings that would be achieved. A report commissioned by the six MCCs, however, estimates that their abolition would lead to £50m extra costs.

Once again, opposition to this initiative has not been restricted to the Labour party. The former Conservative Prime Minister, Edward Heath, described the abolition plan as laying "the Conservative Party open to the charge of the greatest gerrymandering of the last 150 years of British history" (April 11, 1984, quoted in Forrester et al., 1985: 67). Numerous organizations such as environmental groups, church and voluntary bodies, and even the roads lobby (the British Roads Federation) protested against it. In 1984 a bill to pave the way for abolition went through Parliament. A major provision of this bill was defeated in the House of Lords (to provide that the GLC and MCCs would be run by boards of nominees from lower-tier councils from May 1985 to March 1986) but its other provision (to cancel the May 1985 elections) was approved. In the 1984-1985 session, the abolition bill itself passed through Parliament and became law. The House of Lords inflicted some defeats on minor features but these were reversed in the House of

Commons. The only concession to critics is acceptance of an advisory Londonwide planning body.

Opposition to the abolition of the GLC and MCCs has been much less widespread than that to the penalty system or to rate-capping. While the proposals are seen as antidemocratic, the GLC is widely criticized for acting as an antigovernment platform—though "74% say no" to abolition according to a poll of Londoners. Many lower-tier councils have been hostile to the GLC and MCCs ever since their creation. Cities such as Birmingham, Manchester, and Liverpool resented their loss of status in 1974 when they became lower-tier authorities in metropolitan counties. They are keen to see the removal of the higher-tier authorities, particularly as they will regain control of certain functions either directly or through nominees on boards. Whereas Conservative councils did battle alongside Labour councils on the other two issues, on the abolition issue party politics and divided interests led to a split in the local government ranks and allowed the plan to be passed.

AN INTERPRETATION OF THE LOCAL GOVERNMENT CRISIS IN BRITAIN

So far we have outlined the crisis of local government in Britain. In this section we shall seek to explain its occurrence and form and relate our explanation to the main theories in the field. In contrast to the prevailing interpretation that takes government rhetoric at face value and assumes spending cuts to be colossal and central control of local authorities nearly complete, we shall stress the role of local government interests in resisting government intentions. We shall deal in turn with the economic crisis, the social forces impinging on local government, and the absence of urban movements.

THE LINK BETWEEN ECONOMIC CRISIS AND LOCAL GOVERNMENT CRISIS

The economic crisis is an essential background to the crisis of local government in Britain but there is no straightforward link. The closeness of the link in a particular country will depend on the economic importance of local government, the extent to which political institutions cushion local government from local economic decline, and prevailing ideologies regarding public spending and welfare state spending. These will be discussed in turn.

We saw earlier that U.K. local government accounts for nearly one-quarter of all government spending due particularly to its responsibility for education. This suggests that the effect of national economic crisis on local government as a whole will be more immediate in the United Kingdom than in those countries where local government is mainly responsible for "housekeeping" functions such as police, refuse, fire, and planning.

A second way in which economic conditions affect British local government as a whole is through the way individual councils are buffered against local economic decline. This happens through the existence of central grants and their use to partly compensate councils in areas with least property wealth. The effect of this is two-fold. Councils are protected from the vicissitudes of their local economies in a way they would not be if they received no central grants and raised all their resources locally, and the pressure of responding to local economic decline is diverted at least partially to central government. The implication of this is that it is in systems where local government has a strong institutional position that it is protected from urban fiscal crisis.[5] This runs counter to the usual argument that "fiscal crisis is the price of local freedom" (Szelenyi, 1984: 17) and that British cities cannot experience urban fiscal crisis because they "do not have anything like the same degree of autonomy [as U.S. cities]" (Elliott and McCrone, 1984: 194. See also Newton, 1980: 114).

This raises an interesting comparative issue between the United States and United Kingdom. If the institutional strength of local government is the key explanation of its ability to deflect financial pressures elsewhere, then this must be greater in the United Kingdom than the United States. Conversely if it is local autonomy that explains the likelihood of urban fiscal crisis, this should be greater in the United States than the United Kingdom. Evidence of the institutional power of U.K. local government is presented below. Here we shall consider whether the empirical evidence on local autonomy reveals a greater level in the United States than the United Kingdom, as the standard explanation requires.

First, the concept of local autonomy needs clarification. It has at least three dimensions: a local government's freedom to set the level of its income (via taxes, charges), the proportion of its income raised locally, and its freedom to spend its income as it chooses. The independence of these dimensions is supported by the fact that British councils resisted attacks on the first and third types of local autonomy, but did not want less central grant and more local funding (which has been the trend since 1977). Similarly the phrase "he who pays the piper calls the tune" suggests that the source of funding is the only determinant of autonomy, but this is fallacious because in the U.K. central grants to local councils are accompanied by few controls on how they are spent—this is even true of specific grants. I would therefore agree with Wolman (1982: 178) that local autonomy in the first and third senses does not necessarily decline when central funding increases.

Second, the empirical evidence on local autonomy does not support the alleged U.S.-U.K. contrast. Consider the three dimensions: local governments in the United States are subject to "much stricter" control over their power to raise income (Wolman, 1982: 177) than those in the U.K. prior to rate-capping; there is little difference in the proportion of income raised locally (39% for U.S. local governments in 1978-1979, and 44% for U.K. local government in 1982); and specific grants are far more important than block grants in the United States, unlike the U.K. (McKay, 1980; Wolman, 1982). Thus it is plausible to argue that on all three dimensions U.K. councils have more autonomy than U.S. local governments. If the standard argument was correct, this would make them more prone to fiscal crisis than U.S. local governments, which is not the case. Thus I would suggest that it is the weakness of U.S. local governments in the relation to state and federal government (Newton, 1976) and not their alleged autonomy that explains their tendency toward urban fiscal crisis. As will be argued later, it is the power of local government in the U.K., not its lack of autonomy, that has enabled it to deflect financial pressures onto central government and ratepayers. This power derives from the influential position of professionals, with their slogan "local autonomy," and the large number of Conservative councils at a time when the government is Conservative.

The third way in which the economic crisis affects local government is through ideologies regarding public spending and the welfare state. The attack on local spending in the U.K. is predicated on the assumption that it is crucial to macroeconomic policy. This is in complete contrast with the United States according to Wolman (1982: 178), where "concern about the noncongruence of local authority expenditure levels and total public sector spending targets does not exist." The different scale of local government in each country is obviously relevant, but so are economic ideologies.

Ideologies are not determined by economic circumstances but have a life of their own. They serve to bridge the gap between economic realities and the interests of different groups. The key ideological change needing explanation in the U.K. is the decline in the Keynesian use of public spending to maintain demand and hence full employment. Keynesianism was accepted because it seemed to work and because full employment was a policy goal desired by employees and conceded by the state and employers because of the strength of the labor movement. In the early 1970s it became clear that the slump in demand was worldwide and could only be counteracted through an internationally coordinated recovery. Because this was politically impossible, the economic preconditions of full employment policy disappeared, and Keynesianism was abandoned. Instead, given the weakening of the labor movement, the state and employers could pursue a defensive policy to restore corporate profitability and increase competitiveness (e.g., through lower wages and more flexible work practices). The implications for public expenditure were that it should be cut in total and redistributed away from "welfare state" items to "productive" uses. The key theory in this new ideology was Bacon and Eltis's (1976) deindustrialization thesis that argued that the "nonmarketed" sector of the economy was a drain on the "marketed" sector, and a cause of inflation. This led to a volte-face over the desirability of public expenditure because most state activity outside the nationalized industries lay in the nonmarketed sector.

The effect of the economic crisis on local government after 1976 was thus mediated by this new economic ideology and as shown in Table 10.1 led to a decline in local government spending while central government spending continued to rise.

The suddenness of this shift of view regarding public spending was a shock for theories of right and left, both of which had seen the growth of public spending and the welfare state as ineluctable. The explanations for this growth pointed to the realm of values (the pursuit of full employment, the rise of collectivism), the imperatives of technology and labor processes, pressure groups (such as political parties and enlightened officials), and class conflict (where the welfare state was part of the "post-war settlement" with the working class). (See Gough, 1979, Pickvance, 1982.) However, only those theories that gave a role to class conflict or political conditions could cope with the changed realities. Functionalist theories, whether they stressed technological requirements or the requirements of capital accumulation for public expenditure, failed miserably. On the face of it the crisis of public expenditure supports O'Connor's (1973) theory that the contradictory requirements of supporting accumulation and ensuring legitimation lead to a "fiscal crisis of the state." In fact this contradiction is largely imaginary. In most political conditions state aid to accumulation through corporate subsidies, tax reliefs, and tax incentives to the wealthy are entirely public and are defended as in the national interest; such measures do not need to be concealed or accompanied by "legitimation" expenditure. They would only lead to social conflict in political situations where a class perspective was widely held—these are very rare. Once again the role of mediating institutions and ideologies is clear (Pickvance, 1980).

SOCIAL FORCES AFFECTING
LOCAL GOVERNMENT RESISTANCE
OF FINANCIAL PRESSURES

So far I have indicated some general reasons why in Britain the economic crisis should have an impact on local government. We now turn to the social forces that have affected the form of the crisis of local government. These can be seen by examining the business rates issue, the use of councils as political platforms, and the defense of council autonomy.

Business rates have been an object of complaint for a long time like any other tax. Their transformation into an issue depended partly on the coming to power of a government sympathetic to business and partly on economic conditions. Corporations can claim tax reliefs against national taxes, but not against rates; as the real level of rates increases (see Table 10.1) and as profits are squeezed, rates thus become more salient as an unavoidable and increasing cost. The increased use of councils as antigovernment platforms is partly due to the revival of interest in "local socialism" by Labour following the overwhelming general election defeats of 1979 and 1983 (Boddy and Fudge, 1984). As a general tendency, parties excluded from national power give priority to local power as a first stepping stone, for example, the Liberal party's association with "community politics" and Labour's municipal social-ism period (Buck, 1981).

Finally, the centrality of the issue of council autonomy in the local government crisis is due to the institutionalized power of councils and particularly their permanent staff of professionals. This is a key point. Councils have defended the institution of local government but not the welfare state services it provides (Cochrane, 1985). The separation between these issues is clearly seen in the following quote referring to an incident in the 1983 Labour general election campaign:

> Kinnock [Labour leader] . . . was furious at the failure to exploit the Tories' shocking neglect of primary and secondary schools. . . . He had the idea of placing a statutory obligation on local authorities to ensure that all children were educated to a "national minimum standard" in the basic subjects. . . . He wanted, by law, to stipulate the maximum size of class permitted and to guarantee nursery provision for all children whose parents wanted it.
>
> *The idea was killed in its infancy by the powerful local government lobby within the* [Labour] *party who were worried at the threat to local autonomy* [Hugill, 1985; emphasis added].

Local autonomy is treated as a self-evident good by councils, but rarely justified. The notion that it is required by professionals who can be relied on to meet local needs is attractive, but in the light of the British experience of spending cuts, nondefense of service levels, and disproportionate job loss among manual local government employees, is false. Indeed Wolman (1982) argues that many of the alleged benefits of local autonomy are achieved in the United States despite its absence.

Theories of local government present it as the sphere of "competitive politics" (as opposed to "corporate politics" involving corporations and unions at national level; Saunders, 1981b) and as the place where monopoly capital makes alliances with nonhegemonic classes (Castells, 1981). In light of our argument these images do not seem helpful, at least in the British case. The competitive politics argument underestimates the institutional power of professionals. This power is backed by the relative insulation of many councils from local electoral pressures. Because local government elections are contested by national parties, local policies are rarely at issue, and election results reflect the popularity of the parties nationally (Dunleavy, 1980). There is a chance this may change; as the number of councils where no party has a clear majority increases the autonomy of professionals is curtailed, but so far this is not a major trend. Castells's argument about class alliances is rooted in the uneven spatial development of French capitalism and does not have general force. I would argue that local government is less open to medium and petty bourgeois interests than to a distinct set of civic interests, promoted by professionals whose essence is the advancement of economic activity in the area. The driving force is economic competition between local governments and the effect on existing local business is a minor consideration, as when councils dominated by small business persons seek to attract large supermarkets (Smith, 1985).

URBAN MOVEMENTS

Finally we turn to the role of consumers of local government services. One of the most striking theories of the last decade was Castells's argument that the expansion of collective consumption led to a new sphere of politicization and the emergence of a new type of social protest. In the extreme case, urban movements would link up with political parties and trade unions to challenge established power relations (Castells, 1977, modified in Castells, 1983). In reality, with a handful of exceptions, urban movements have failed to have such effects (Ceccarelli, 1982; Pickvance, 1985). In the U.K. those dependent on local government services have notably failed to defend them against cuts. Why should this be?

Despite the new political rhetoric about self-reliance and the nonresponsiblity of government for individual welfare, there has been little change in public support for the welfare state. But while popular attachment to the welfare state is widespread, it coexists with a concern about quality, tax levels, and value for money (Taylor-Gooby, 1985). The lack of consumer protest about service cuts is partly due to the form in which services are provided. In particular there is a paternalistic and centralized tradition of provision where the consumer has no rights and is not encouraged to participate in decision making about the service. This reflects the general professionalization and secrecy of British government. For certain services a stigma is also attached—recipients have failed to provide for themselves, and should be grateful for whatever they are offered. One exception to the above arguments is the sale of council houses, for which there is widespread support—tenants may purchase them at discounts of up to 60%.

Equally important is the belief that service deterioration is inevitable given local government spending cuts, that councils have no autonomy. There is an element of truth in this belief but to a larger extent it results from a deliberate attempt by councils to manage potential protest by passing the blame upward. Local government in Britain has tremendous discretion in spending—legislation is mostly permissive and central grants are accompanied by few controls. By claiming that poor services are due to a lack of autonomy, rather than a lack of resources, councils channel the debate onto their preferred terrain—the extent of autonomy.

Additional reasons for the lack of urban movements over service cuts are the social groups involved (e.g., the handicapped and infirm;

Webster, 1985), their individualization (e.g., schools offer an institutional base for opposition, but social services in their increasingly individualized form do not), the form of the cuts (which have often been small, gradual, and involved natural wastage or decisions not to build new facilities), and the possibility of exit to private provision.

CONCLUSION

To conclude, it has been argued that the financial pressures on local government in a country are neither a direct reflection of the economic crisis nor due to an inherent fiscal crisis of state. Economic conditions are mediated by the economic importance of local government, by political buffering institutions (which depend more on the federal or unitary character of the political system than on local government autonomy), and by ideologies about public spending.

The form the local government crisis takes depends on how these financial pressures impinge on central government, local government, and local income sources (ratepayers and those paying for services); and how local government distributes the pressures on it among capital spending, job losses, and service levels. The outcome is historically specific and depends on the distribution of economic, political, and ideological power between the groups concerned, with each attempting to deflect pressure onto the others.

In the British case we have shown that despite its expressed wishes central government has failed to cut local government spending significantly, and has maintained the level of the grant to local government for current spending; meanwhile ratepayers have paid an increasing amount in real terms (Table 10.1). These trends are measures of the power of local government in deflecting financial pressures away from itself and onto central government and ratepayers. Hence there has been no urban fiscal crisis. This confirms what we saw earlier—that the penalty system and rate-capping were potentially powerful weapons against local government but were not used to their full extent due to the resistance of local government. This resistance has two bases: the institutionalized power of local government professionals and the political fact that the majority of councils are Conservative, thus limiting the ability of a Conservative government to impose its wishes on local government.

Within local government we have seen that the main effects of spending cuts have been on capital spending, and on manual rather than professional jobs. Again a political interpretation is possible: Private sector building workers are nonunionized and unlikely to resist; manual workers are unionized and have protested but contracting out and privatization (council house sales) have affected them disproportionately. Finally service levels have been cut, or have failed to keep pace with demand, in the absence of movements of service consumers. A plausible interpretation of the form taken by the crisis of local government in Britain is that it reflects the strength of professional local government interests, facilitated by the extent of Conservative control of local councils, vis-à-vis all other groups. Moreover it is not surprising that the dominant theme adopted in the defense of local government is that of local autonomy, rather than that of service protection, because it is the ideology of local government professionals.

This conclusion is advanced for Britain, but it is hoped that the framework used, stressing economic crisis, the economic and political character of local government, ideologies, and the balance of power between different social groups and institutions will suggest lines for the comparative analysis of local government crises elsewhere.

NOTES

1. The term "privatization" is used where ownership of an asset passes from the public sector; "contracting out" refers to the employment of private firms to undertake responsibilities.

2. It should be noted that these figures refer to changes in real terms; they are not the same as planned changes. For example, the lower than expected rate of inflation in 1982 and 1983 means that real increases in current spending were higher than planned. Also, it is not the case that a zero change means that needs are being met at a constant level because the number of people eligible for certain services is increasing (e.g., the old).

3. As far as capital spending by councils is concerned, government grants are of negligible importance as a source of income. Until 1979 capital spending was in fact controlled through controls on borrowing; but these became less effective after 1980 as the role of loans in financing borrowing declined, and the use of surpluses on current account increased. Even in the 1970s controls on borrowing were not very effective because they specified the amount borrowed but not its timing (Ball, 1980). Hence there has been a shift to direct controls on capital spending.

4. Government controls on capital spending were very successful from 1981-1983. Indeed a new "problem" emerged for central government—that of aggregate underspending by councils. This was due to the difficulty of predicting the timing of capital projects, and to councils' reluctance to undertake projects that would entail higher current spending. In 1983-1985, however, underspending was replaced by overspending as a problem. This was because sales of council housing boomed and councils—which may

spend part of the proceeds—are allowed to carry forward a certain amount of authorized spending from year to year.

5. This is connected with the difference between unitary and federal political systems. Redistributive policies such as grants for areas experiencing economic decline are much easier to operate in a unitary political system than a federal system where territorial units have greater political weight and resist deviations from an equal per capita distribution of federal spending. Another characteristic of unitary systems is also relevant to the possibility of municipal bankruptcy in Britain. Although it has recently been shown that a local council could technically go bankrupt because borrowing by councils is secured against revenues and a council might fail to set a legal rate to cover spending (Grant, 1984), it is empirically unlikely. A government lending agency, the Public Works Loans Board, has the power to bail out bankrupt councils and although this is not an obligation, it is difficult to imagine it not being exercised. This reserve power is characteristic of a unitary political system.

REFERENCES

BACON, R. and W. ELTIS (1976) Britain's Economic Problem: Too Few Producers? London: Macmillan.

BALL, I. D. (1980) "Urban investment controls in Britain," in D. Ashford (ed.) National Resources and Urban Policy. London: Croom Helm.

BODDY, M. AND C. FUDGE (1984) Local Socialism? London: Macmillan.

BUCK, N. H. (1981) "The analysis of state intervention in nineteenth-century cities," in M. Dear and A. J. Scott (eds.) Urbanization and Urban Planning in Capitalist Society. New York: Methuen.

CMND. 6393 (1976) Public Expenditure to 1979-80. London: Her Majesty's Stationery Office.

CASTELLS, M. (1983) The City and the Grassroots. London: Edward Arnold.

————(1981) "Local government, urban crisis, and political change." Political Power and Social Theory 2: 1-19.

————(1977) The Urban Question. London: Edward Arnold.

CECCARELLI, P. (1982) "Politics, parties and urban movements: Western Europe," in N. I. Fainstein and S. S. Fainstein (eds.) Urban Policy Under Capitalism. Beverly Hills, CA: Sage.

Central Statistical Office (1984) United Kingdom National Accounts (1984 edition). London: Her Majesty's Stationery Office.

COCHRANE, A. (1985) "The attack on local government: what it is and what it isn't." Critical Social Policy 12: 44-62.

DUNLEAVY, P. (1980) Urban Political Analysis. London: Macmillan.

ELLIOTT, B. and C. McCRONE (1984) "Austerity and the politics of resistance," in I. Szelenyi (ed.) Cities in Recession. London: Sage.

FORRESTER, A., S. LANSLEY, and R. PAULEY (1985) Beyond Our Ken. London: Fourth Estate.

FOTHERGILL, S. and G. GUDGIN (1982) Unequal Growth. London: Heinemann.

GOUGH, I. (1979) The Political Economy of the Welfare State. London: Macmillan.

GRANT, M. (1984) "Rate capping, the law and insolvency." Public Finance and Accountancy (March): 19-24.

GYFORD, J. (1984) "From community action to local socialism." Local Government Studies 10: 4, 5-10.

HUGILL, B. (1985) "New champion of parents' rights." New Statesman (April 12).

LAW, C. M. (1980) British Regional Development Since World War I. London: Methuen.

LIVINGSTONE, K. (1984) Interview with M. Boddy and C. Fudge in M. Boddy and C. Fudge, Local Socialism? London: Macmillan.

McKAY, D. H. (1980) "The rise of the topocratic state: US intergovernmental relations in the 1970s," in D. Ashford (ed.) Financing Urban Government in the Welfare State. London: Croom Helm.

MIDWINTER, A. (1985) Setting the rate—Liverpool style. Local Government Studies 11, 3: 25-33.

NEWTON, K. (1981) "The local financial crisis in Britain: a non-crisis which is neither local nor financial," in L. J. Sharpe (ed.) The Local Fiscal Crisis in Western Europe: myths and realities. London: Sage.

———(1980) "Central government grants, territorial justice and local democracy in post-war Britain," in D. Ashford (ed.) Financing Urban Government in the Welfare State. London: Croom Helm.

———(1976) "Feeble governments and private power: urban politics and policies in the United States," in L. H. Masotti and R. L. Lineberry (eds.) The New Urban Politics. Cambridge, MA: Ballinger.

O'CONNOR, J. (1973) The Fiscal Crisis of the State. New York: St. Martin's Press.

PICKVANCE, C. G. (1985) "The rise and fall of urban movements and the role of comparative analysis." Environment and Planning D: Society and Space 3: 31-53.

———(1982) The State and Collective Consumption. Milton Keynes: Open University Press.

———(1980) "Theories of the state and theories of urban crisis." Current Perspectives in Social Theory 1: 31-54.

SAUNDERS, P. (1981a) Social Theory and the Urban Question. London: Hutchinson.

———(1981b) "Community power, urban managerialism and the 'local state,' " in M. Harloe (ed.) New Perspectives in Urban Change and Conflict. London: Heinemann.

SCOTT, A. J. (1980) The Urban Land Nexus and the State. London: Pion.

SHUTT, J. (1984) "Tory enterprise zones and the labour movement." Capital and Class 23: 19-44.

SMITH, P. (1983) "How targets went wrong." Public Finance and Accountancy (December): 28-31.

SMITH, S. L. (1985) "A political economy of urbanization and state structure: urban and industrial change in two selected areas." Ph.D. thesis, University of Kent, Canterbury.

SZELENYI, I. (1984) "Introduction," in I. Szelenyi (ed.) Cities in Recession. London: Sage.

TAYLOR-GOOBY, P. (1985) Public Opinion, Ideology and Social Welfare. London: Routledge & Kegan Paul.

TRAVERS, T. (1983) "Local government de-manning." Public Money (June): 64-67.

WEBSTER, B. (1985) "A women's issue: the impact of local authority cuts." Local Government Studies 11, 2: 19-46.

WOLMAN, H. (1982) "Local autonomy and intergovernmental finance in Britain and the United States," in R. Rose and E. Page (eds.), Fiscal Stress in Cities. Cambridge: Cambridge University Press.

11

Retrospect and Prospect in Urban Crisis Theory

M. GOTTDIENER

☐ MOST CRISIS ANALYSIS comes directly after crisis. It catches the wave and makes instant experts of us all. It sets off a mad rush to be first in the publishing wars; first in the race to match concrete events with commentary. Years after crisis, academics wedded to it create a form of nostalgia. They cling to explanations gone stale. In the case of the recent urban crisis, for example, nostalgia buffs see a still nascent economic apocalypse when even formerly depressed cities hum with new life. They extoll so-called urban social movements when, in reality, our cities are monuments to the catastrophic failure of militant political strategies and left-liberal mythology.

It is somewhat refreshing, therefore, to stand back and survey the record of crisis events and crisis literature after some time has passed. We have seen that the social events of the 1960s and the fiscal stress of the 1970s were linked to each other by the process of urban restructuring taking place in cities over the past thirty or more years. It is this socioeconomic change that has produced changes in local politics—rather than the latter being connected to the former by some direct mechanism of political economy. Social transformations in recent years involve a massive exchange of population—white flight to the suburbs and a minority implosion from the South and the Third World.

Economic transformations experienced by cities are as equally graphic and involve the shift from manufacturing to service industries and replacement of the infrastructure of the factory town by downtown office buildings and the facades of high-rise consumption—hotels and luxury apartments.

With regard to crisis management, central city restructuring concerns a host of particular changes that defy categorization by old labels. Society-centered approaches find their limits in failing to follow state-initiated change. In contrast, state-centered analyses miss the intrinsic overlap between public and private initiatives responsible for massive urban restructuring that makes up the very essence of resource control by the local state. Finally, dichotomies such as society-centeredness versus state-centeredness fade away as we attune ourselves to the failure of positivist thinking, because economic forces have meshed with political processes and cultural mediations to effect change and restructuring in ways too complex to model by simple cause and effect.

This book has focused on the aftermath of the urban crisis and adjustments to it. It is profitable to compare what has been said above with what others have asserted regarding city change and, more specifically, about the origins and management of fiscal strain. To begin with, certain economic forces have been at work remaking city economies despite a prevailing discourse that casts the central city in metaphors of decline. Like Mark Twain's obituary, announcements about the death of the frostbelt were somewhat premature. In particular, conventional readings of census data that were devoid of analytical insights, such as Sternlieb and Hughes (1975) or Kasarda (1980), seem to have missed what other more penetrating urbanists observed, namely, the compositional linkages between frostbelt and sunbelt that married the success of growth poles in the new regions to headquarter and banking centers in the older areas (see, for example, Mollenkopf, 1983). Boom and bust patterns were not regional, as conventional analysts led us to believe, but compositional or activity-specific, and explained better by uneven development in every area.

Alex Ganz's chapter highlights the remarkable success of most central cities in bouncing back from a cycle of decline. This new phase of health is not due to some magical mode of high technology or an alchemist's discovery promising new ways of making money. Rather, cities have survived because of what they have always represented and done best—the capturing of externalities or, as Lamarche (1977) once remarked, the exploitation of "the useful effects of agglomeration." At a deeper level we know now that certain fractions of capital, such as multinational banking interests, possessed a special stake in revitalizing downtown (Gottdiener, 1985), and that state spending on capital improvements subsidized this renaissance at the expense of city residents (Friedland, 1981).

In fact, what is new and different about the current perspective on the urban crisis is the way it challenges the common assumptions propagated in the past regarding city decline. Both Friedland (1981) and Hoffman (1983) illustrate this point well. Using O'Connor's (1973) categories regarding capital streams, for example, Friedland shows clearly that fiscal spending has a dimension ignored by critics of social welfare policies, namely, investment in social capital or infrastructural and real estate development projects. Such state-sponsored efforts, beginning with the urban renewal projects of the 1950s and 1960s, have transformed the very face of cities stimulating privately sponsored development as well, especially luxury housing and highrise office space. In short, although attention was paid in the past to excessive local government spending on social welfare programs so that conservatives could argue the need for cutbacks in order to fight fiscal strain, ample evidence now indicates that the lion's share of such burdens and indebtedness was caused by massive state spending in the service of capital.

Subsidization of capitalist development may not be the function of local government that most Americans desire, but it certainly is the underlying basis for the relation between the local state and the economy. One need not be a Marxist nor follow O'Connor's capitalist stream approach to acknowledge the fundamental imbalance in our society between developmental and redistributive programs of local government in favor of the former. Little wonder that cities seem to work better at promoting growth than social justice. Furthermore, the present phase of restructuring differs somewhat from that prior to the 1980s. Whereas in the era of publicized urban renewal, the state/economy marriage was highly visible, current modes of subsidization are relatively invisible and include the brokerage by the city of low-interest bond money to the business sector and the provision of generous tax abatements as a bribe by places for capital location choices. Recent evidence suggests that this subsidization of new development has little influence on the choices made by capital as all localities vie for the right to host growth (Judd and Smith, 1983). Were such hefty incentives operating the other way, however, toward balanced development and social justice, a different type of city might exist.

Fiscal strain research also challenges Marxian analysis in addition to conservative ideology. In the past, Marxists asserted that tying local state fortunes to capitalist development would prove fatal to the polity. The costs of growth to the public could never be recovered by its benefits because of the very nature of private expropriation of all wealth. They argued that state subsidization of capital would prove to be a burden manifested in fiscal crisis no matter how successful state-supported development schemes would be (see, for example, O'Connor, 1973; Hill, 1978; Friedland, 1981). Yet, the chapters in this book do not bear this prediction out. On the whole, fiscal strain has been managed well because cities have discovered new ways of running themselves in the shadow of default as Matzer, Sbragia, and the Rubins all suggest. The mounting crisis of funding envisioned by Marxists as resulting from the confluence of increasing state spending according to three separate capital streams simply has not occurred. In fact, we now have some evidence from analysis following these streams that the structural argument for crisis hinging on collective consumption is itself false. City regimes have been very effective in cutting back on socially sustained user benefits and in controlling the mass of impoverished and deprived central city residents from organized acts of violence.

Management of strain as studied by the authors in this book highlights at least three new phenomena that warrant further research. First, although redevelopment has been successful, it has assumed an uneven social form. Our metropolitan centers are really two cities: the one that goes to work is reserved for the affluent and the tourists; the other, which languishes in unproductive social forms, is reserved for the working poor, minorities, and the urban underclass. This contrast is quite graphic, as anyone touring our central cities can attest, and represents an extreme crisis of inequality produced by the uneven nature of city growth.

In the past, analysts concerned about social inequality dealt with the political significance of uneven development. On the one hand, a line of argument was developed by Piven and Cloward (1971, 1979) that explained ghetto insurgency as the consequence of the isolation of marginalized groups in the democratic process. As the social crisis of the 1960s faded into the fiscal distress of the 1970s, new observations took up this thread and wove it into the discourse that asserted the political nature of fiscal austerity. It was suggested that hard-fought gains achieved by the militancy of the 1960s on the part of organized labor and minorities were now "targeted" for extinction by a capitalist orchestration of crisis and recovery (see, for example, Marcuse, 1981; Piven and Cloward, 1979; Tabb and Sawers, 1978). In short, the dynamic process linking activism, welfare statism, and the political participation of new urban constituencies, on the one hand, with sociospatial changes and the concerted control of economic restructuring by the capitalist class, on the other, was to be explained by a theory alleging a voluntaristic, capitalist conspiracy orchestrating city events and city politics.

Several chapters herein have called this approach into question. Although agreeing with social control analysts that the contemporary urban crisis is largely a manufactured event, Eric Monkkonen questions the direct relationship between marginalization and activism, thereby also calling into question the explanation of state welfarism as a means of social control. To be sure, cities in stress have used the occasion to badger municipal unions and, in some cases, attack their standard of living. Yet this is not a consistent feature of crisis. Stein et al. note that in many cities hiring rather than firing remains a means of promoting political support for local leaders, and the Rubins show us how crisis itself may set off a wave of municipal expansion, especially for more police. With regard to social inequality, however, Marxists were correct to call this crisis to our attention. But this too is not a voluntaristic product of politicized capitalist interests. Uneven sociospatial development is a process intrinsic to capitalist growth (Browett, 1984; Gottdiener, 1985). Ganz, Judd, and Henig each show that inequality is a byproduct of political choices that sought to follow and reinforce the logic of capital under the sign of growth rather than promote the general welfare of all urban residents. Furthermore, it is most discouraging that we are no better prepared today to deal with the social engineering this human crisis requires than we were in the 1960s except to note that state welfare programs administered by large bureaucracies have had little effect (Murray, 1984; Auletta, 1982).

A second area of new work concerns the way the preceding chapters have illuminated the relation between the economy and the state as compared with efforts in the past. Marxian political economy seems to have erred in tying economic crisis theory directly to political effects. The fiscal crisis of the 1970s, in particular, is overwhelmingly a property of political institutions, as Pickvance suggests. This does not mean, however, that we can hypothesize some abstract political realm of action, call it the state, that is independent of a second realm, call it the economy. Rather, economic forces and political process meet in the realm of local politics and work themselves out according to a contingent logic that is beyond the reach of austere deterministic models to comprehend. For this reason it is possible to conclude that there is no general theory of fiscal crisis for the local level; only an inquiry into the underlying forces that are responsible for the variation between cities in the management of strain. Although capital has the ability to hem in possible choices and alternative outcomes in this process, especially through ideological mechanisms, institutional factors deriving from a society's structure of political organization figure strongly in the behavior of city regimes under stress. In addition, fiscal strain research uncovers the important role that ideologies of city living play in the conception of crisis. The discourse about the purpose of cities and their conceived limits figures prominently in local political confrontations between the users of space and the promoters of its exchange value.

The political and ideological basis of the urban crisis is illustrated by studies that uncover how capital has been able to manipulate success-fully representative political forms for private purposes. In Cleveland, Todd Swanstrom shows that cities weakened by the decline of the traditional frostbelt economy, despite being wealthy in other ways, can fall prey to predatory capitalist interests motivated by power as well as greed. In the case of Cleveland, default was not used to anyone's special benefit nor was it caused by the general economic crisis that Marxists have supposed. It was a political outcome played in a game of *chicken* between brinkmanship banks demanding resources from the city and a populist mayor who became a willing partner in the confrontational scenario written by greedy finance capital. That Cleveland and cities like it were abandoned by national levels of politics and presidential domestic policy to their fate at the hands of the city's banks should not be forgotten, especially in light of the remarks above.

The record of Cleveland shows, above all, that conservatives, such as Novak (1982), are dead wrong. Local government should not merely promote a "positive business climate" in the belief that the marriage between the public and the private sectors is a happy one in the name of social and economic progress. Like the Black Widow spider, business has a way of turning predator, and, in times of economic recession, devouring not only other businesses in mergers but the assets of the public interest as well.

Alberta Sbragia's work here and elsewhere substantiates an approach that goes beyond both mainstream and Marxist political economy by pursuing the same themes isolated above. The study of city budgets should be tied to the study of city sources of revenue. Only for the case where city revenues are dependent on taxation would changes in the general conditions of capital accumulation warrant linking economic crisis to fiscal effects. In most cases, cities are linked directly to their fortunes in the municipal bond market—to the finance fraction of capital. Sbragia indicates that neither the process determining borrowing nor the structure of lending is as simple as might be supposed from the urban crisis literature. This observation is reinforced by Pickvance's comparative study. In Great Britain, local governments obtain considerable funding from the central government, thereby freeing them from dependency on private sector sources. This works to insulate local areas from the interests of capital and for the benefit of the community as a whole.

In recent years the influence of capital in the United States and the demand for local state subsidies of development because of the declining fortunes of local economies have been so strong as to force local regimes to use their link to finance capital as a means of providing business with cheap money (Sbragia, 1983: 70). The socialization of capital by the local state is even more extensive and pervasive than studies on the direct partnerships between public and private sectors have led us to believe. Irene and Harry Rubin document the fact that such active socialization of capital has been a result rather than a consequence of fiscal crisis, tending to invert some of the original ideas on this subject. In their chapter they suggest that, although there may be a political economy explaining the causes of fiscal crisis, there must also be a political economy studying the response to the threat of crisis, real or not. This political economy is tied just as strongly to an understanding of the ways that local states transfer value across space by subsidizing capital because of some ideologically induced fear that the specter of crisis holds for local places.

The latter inquiry is qualitatively different from original fiscal crisis theory. Rather than viewing crisis as caused by the logic of monopoly capital expansion and its contradictions, crisis has become its own independent variable and, in turn, can be viewed as producing its own effects on both the economy and local politics. This phenomenon, which is both political and ideological rather than economic in origin, constitutes a rich research area that deserves further work.

Third, and last, the management of fiscal strain by local bureaucrats has assumed importance as a field of study in its own right. This does not mean, however, that we need to follow Nordlinger (1981) or Block (1980) and abandon a society-centered approach for a state-centered one. To be sure, King and Gurr (1983: 5) are correct in their assertion:

> State managers and those whose positions and livelihood depend upon the state have intrinsic interests in the perpetuation of the state independent of the interests of all other social groups.

Yet, this interest seems to be manifested as a compulsion to bring sophisticated, rational techniques of decision making to the management of local government that is attuned to, and even driven by, society-centeredness.

John Matzer, Jr.'s, chapter documents the increasing level of technical rationality and professional expertise assumed by state managers in the wake of fiscal crisis. As indicated above, this has combined with general economic recovery through restructuring to belie, in spectacular fashion, the dire predictions of 1970s analysts forecasting fiscal doom. However, the shift to instrumental fiscal management has not been without its own political problems. Politicians require flexibility. The domain of politics is not an area that can be surrendered to mundane calculations of dollars and cents. City budgets represent expenditures in response to political expediency and not rational planning.

As Shefter (1977), Yates (1977), and O'Connor (1973) have all suggested, politicians modulate the demands of citizens through the instrument of a budget so as to work toward a public peace. To be sure, we can no longer agree with conventional political analysts, such as Shefter, or Marxists, such as O'Connor, that changes in these demands and the need to satisfy new constituencies or achieve social control through local spending bring about crisis. Yet the use of the budget in meeting the special interest demands of local politics, despite the progressive increase in the level of management expertise, remains a singular paradox of fiscal adjustment. In this observation we are compelled to agree with those who suggest that there is no "general interest of capital" that rules state intervention in advanced capitalist society, because of its complex class structure. Active in the administration of local areas is this clash between the increasing need for technical expertise to manage stress and local politicians relying on the often contradictory demands of constituencies for reelection. Thus local urban politics, expressive of racial and gender interests and fractions of capital as well as those of the working class, remains a salient force to be reckoned with while state managers modulate their intervention in society in pursuit of their own needs.

It is precisely for this reason that the chapters by Stein et al. and Judd break new ground. In the former, by focusing directly on municipal expenditure levels in contrast to the factor of total spending, the authors introduce the fruitful notion that future studies of city budgets should assume a compositional approach. The role of factors internal to city politics, and not just the limits set by the external operating environment within which all cities find themselves, remains an important aspect of budgetary determination. In the second chapter, Judd suggests that a spark of hope has been ignited by the election victory in Chicago of Harold Washington. The needs of neighborhoods and the forgotten urban poor may be addressed by a new generation of minority-led city governments. What is still needed is direction from the higher realms of the state, especially a renewal of socially conscious politics at the national level itself.

In effect, political conflict and the competition between various urban groups remains with us. City politicians manage this conflict at the heart of local politics as well as the budgets themselves; in fact, the former is accomplished through the latter. The study of strain concerns this meeting ground among the demands of business for state subsidization of capital accumulation, progressively increasing levels of technical rationality called forth as a means of combating the spending crisis that this produces, and the political expediency of running cities in a representative democracy with a strong need for social justice to combat uneven development. At present this three-way clash among state managers, business interests, and the people has been resolved in favor of the former two groups. Future events may, however, realign priorities in a new civic equation.

A picture emerges from the chapters presented here, one in which we find the city being asked to stand alone and face capital without benefit of guidelines or directed policies from other levels of government. As both Swanstrom and Pickvance note, in the countries of Europe alternative sources of municipal financial resources that are insulated from the direct influence of economic agents exist for the benefit of local governments. No such separate structure is present in the United States. Cities must fend for themselves. It should not be surprising, then, to find local areas highly dependent on promoting economic growth despite its obvious perils, while remaining critically weak in pursuing social justice and proper planning. Consequently, this observation points to the fundamental role that our existing political institutions play in so much of what happens within cities. Were structural changes in place since the 1960s to combat the domination of cities by capitalist restructuring, urban life would be much different than it is today.

Some may argue that the federal government has been instrumental in sheltering cities from the direct dependency on private capital through urban-related programs and block grants. I do not intend to suggest that spending by the feds on redistributive and socially relevant projects has ceased. Clearly it has not. Yet the past decade testifies to a devastating failure of political leadership with regard to the articulation of a much-needed urban policy—some overarching theme and vision that could have provided a direction for the aimless drift of crisis and restructuring. Because capital possesses a narrow focus of concerns centered on profit realization, and because local government must perform a juggling act placating a variety of special interests including those of state managers, neighborhood associations, and fractions of capital, the influence of business and the needs it exhibited in a period of economic restructuring have been given priority over the social needs produced by that same period. Even in cases where neighborhood participation in decision making has increased, it has been confined to very narrow practical concerns concordant with the needs of fiscal austerity in the boosting of economic growth (see Moskowitz and Simpson, 1983; Cunningham, 1983). Unlike the British case, local issues have not been contested by national politics or party organizations with overarching political ideologies. They are played out in a vacuum of political vision and leadership. Consequently, over the past several decades of restructuring, capital has won in a very big way whereas uneven development adjacent to the pristine towers of downtown has taken a toll in inequality and pathology that future generations will find hard to face.

Adding up the observations of the distinguished contributors above, a theme suggests itself that characterizes crisis adjustment and change. The very nature of local politics has been altered and, in my opinion, for the worse, following three decades of urban crisis and change. A freestanding process that allowed the public to challenge effectively the power of capital has been sacrificed over the years. The quality of local political life has itself declined. Government is currently constrained by accounting balance sheets, the nightmare of capital flight, and the specter of corporate bankers banging on the city's door for the past payment of bills. In place of a direct connection between the city and its residents, who supported the type of government they wanted through their own taxes and votes—a state of affairs that Monkkonen says characterized early regimes in this country—we now possess a local urban government far removed and insulated from its people. Technical managers administer cities running scared from default. Powerful nonelective super-agencies raise tax exempt bond money to pursue development without benefit of public participation. Fiscal austerity itself beats back the plaints of the have-nots and supplants other more negotiable goals of city administration. The reduction of the urban vision to instrumental capital growth, it seems, gains hegemony everywhere.

The political structure of our cities is rotten at its core because the mechanisms that once aggregated collective demands created by needs generated in everyday urban life have long since atrophied. Yet, as Henig has shown, political activism within cities has not disappeared. Like Katznelson (1981), Henig turns his attention to the ideological and structural traps that await local insurgency. Quite simply, it was a mistake for activists to have assumed that organizing at the grass-roots level was sufficient for social change. Local politics is a labyrinthine maze of trenches and false tunnels that dissipates the collective energy of grass-roots protest. Local political activism has been debilitated because the levels of politics at both the state and nation have failed to produce the type of intermediate party structures that could sustain grass-roots demands for change with overarching extralocal auspices and a vision of social justice.

The transformative politics of the future should learn these lessons of the past well. Gone are the halcyon days of the 1960s when localized neighborhood skirmishes with capital or the state were picked up and promoted by national organizations advocating social change, as was the case with CORE's championing of the New York City rent strike (Lipsky, 1970). As Pickvance (1985) suggests, mythologists of urban social movements have failed to take into account the critical role that the contextual environment of political organization has played in the early success of neighborhood mobilization. Analysts familiar with the history of organizing powerless interests in the United States have long recognized the critical role that context plays in the relative success of insurgency (see, e.g., Jenkins and Perrow, 1977).

In the era of activism prior to the 1980s, so much emphasis was placed on organizing at the grass roots to match the militancy of top-down liberal politics that contemporary analysts seem unaware that today there is no top to work down from. The so-called contextual factors, such as strong national party support and leadership from the president in promoting social welfare, have all evaporated in the blinding glare of austerity ideology, while pentagon capitalism sets our social priorities and plunges the country into the very crisis of debt that austerity ideology convinces us it will avoid. To address the present social realities of our cities, much more is needed than a singleminded focus on grass-roots populism. The mesopolitical structure of society itself requires revitalization.

It is simply too easy to explain this state of affairs as a crisis orchestrated by capital for its own convenience. A political failure of monumental dimensions has accompanied sociospatial restructuring in favor of capital. In a sense, left-liberalism reached its own limits during the 1970s in mobilizing people around its social concerns and we have just begun the inquiry into what those limits were. Activist-observers close to the neighborhood mobilization phenomenon are the first to admit that such organizing at the level of everyday life has yet to mature to the stage of "social movement" (Boyte, 1980). Yet the need to label insurgency as a social movement is a "theoretical problem" of Marxian academics that is largely irrelevant to an understanding of what it means to build a viable urban praxis (see Gottdiener, 1984). In today's cities the ordinary needs of residents articulated in neighborhood forums that are not progrowth-related seem to be labeled as insurgent demands, as if they are somehow out of place. This is so because the present political structure possesses no room for the interests of the users of urban space. One does not require a social movement to address common concerns of everyday life; only a democratic political structure of self-management representing government by all the people.

The great disjuncture between the quotidian occurrence of neighborhood activism organized around the needs generated by everyday life (see Kotler, 1979; Susser, 1982; Bookchin, 1984) and the hegemony of exchange value in the social space of the city is so great as to have paralyzed the existing political apparatus in its long-standing quest for social change. This is so because of the failure of the mesolevel of politics—of parties and leadership, of mayors and governors, of organizers and social welfare reformers, and, finally, of a left-liberal tradition so enamored with economic growth itself that threats to "progress" become the very legitimation for the interests of capital in the politics of state.

REFERENCES

ALCALY, R. and D. MERMELSTEIN [eds.] (1977) The Fiscal Crisis of American Cities. New York: Vintage.

AULETTA, K. (1982) The Underclass. New York: Random House.

BERRY, B. and J. KASARDA (1977) Contemporary Urban Ecology. New York: Macmillan.

BLOCK, F. (1980) "Beyond relative autonomy: state managers as historical subjects." Sociologist Register: 227-242.

BOOKCHIN, M. (1984) The Ecology of Freedom. Palo Alto, CA: Cheshire.

BOYTE, H. (1980) The Backyard Revolution. Philadelphia: Temple University Press.

BROWETT, J. (1984) "On the necessity and inevitability of uneven spatial development under capitalism." International Journal of Urban and Regional Research 8, 2: 155-176.

BURCHELL, R. and D. LISTOKIN [eds.] (1981) Cities Under Stress. New Brunswick, NJ: Rutgers University Press.

CECCARELLI, P. (1982) "Politics, parties and urban movements: Western Europe," in S. Fainstein and N. Fainstein (eds.) Urban Policy Under Capitalism. Beverly Hills, CA: Sage.

CLARK, T. and L. FERGUSON (1983) City Money. New York: Columbia University Press.

CUNNINGHAM, J. (1983) "Power, participation and local government: the communal struggle for parity." Journal of Urban Affairs 5, 3: 257-266.

EYERMAN, R. (1984) "Social movements and social theory." Sociology (February): 73-82.

FAINSTEIN, S. and N. FAINSTEIN [eds.] (1982) Urban Policy Under Capitalism. Beverly Hills, CA: Sage.

FRIEDLAND, R. et al. (1981) "Central city fiscal strains: the public costs of private growth." International Journal of Urban and Regional Research 5, 3: 356-375.

————(1978) "Political conflict, urban structure and the fiscal crisis," in W. Tabb and L. Sawers (eds.) Marxism and the Metropolis. New York: Oxford University Press.

GOTTDIENER, M. (1985) The Social Production of Urban Space. Austin: University of Texas Press.

————(1984) "Debate on the theory of space: towards an urban praxis," pp. 199-218 in M. Smith (ed.) Cities in Transformation. Beverly Hills, CA: Sage.

GOTTMAN, J. (1972) "Urban centrality and the interweaving of quaternary activities," in G. Bell and J. Tyrwhit (eds.) Human Identity in the Urban Environment. Baltimore, MD: Penguin.

HABERMAS, J. (1975) Legitimation Crisis. Boston: Beacon.

HAWLEY, A. (1981) Urban Society: An Ecological Approach. New York: John Wiley.

HILL, R. (1978) "Fiscal crisis, austerity politics, and alternative urban policies," pp. 213-240 in W. Tabb and L. Sawers (eds.) Marxism and the Metropolis. New York: Oxford University Press.

HOFFMAN, J. (1983) "Urban squeeze plays: New York City crises of the 1930's and 1970's." Review of Radical Political Economy 15, 2: 29-57.

JENKINS, J. and C. PERROW (1977) "Insurgency of the powerless farm worker movements (1946-1972)." American Sociological Review 42: 249-268.

JUDD, D. and M. SMITH (1983) "Economic restructuring and the politics of growth, welfare and territorial preservation." Presented at Association of Schools of Planning, San Francisco, CA, October 21-23.

KASARDA, J. (1980) "The implications of contemporary redistribution trends for national policy." Social Science Quarterly 61: 373-400.

KATZNELSON, I. (1981) City Trenches: Urban Politics and the Patterning of Class in the U.S. New York: Pantheon.

KING, D. and T. GURR (1983) "State fiscal crisis and urban decline." Presented at APSA meetings, Chicago, September 1-6.

KOTLER, M. (1979) "A public policy for neighborhood and community organizations." Social Policy (September/October): 37-43.

LAMARCHE, F. (1977) "Property development and the economic foundations of the urban question," in C. Pickvance, Urban Sociology: Critical Essays. New York: St. Martin's Press.

LEFEBVRE, H. (1969) The Explosion. New York: Vintage.

LIPSKY, M. (1970) Protest in City Politics. Chicago: Rand McNally.

MARCUSE, P. (1981) "The targeted crisis: on the ideology of the urban fiscal crisis and its uses." International Journal of Urban and Regional Research 5, 3: 330-354.

MINGIONE, E. (1981) Social Control and the City. New York: St. Martin's Press.

MOSKOWITZ, E. and D. SIMPSON (1983) "Neighborhood empowerment and urban management in the 1980's." Journal of Urban Affairs 5, 3: 183-192.

MURRAY, C. (1984) Losing Ground. New York: Basic Books.

NORDLINGER, E. (1981) On the Autonomy of the Democratic State. Cambridge, MA: Harvard University Press.

NOVAK, M. (1982) "Mediating institutions: the communitarian individual in America." Public Interest 68: 3-20.

O'CONNOR, J. (1981) "The fiscal crisis of the state revisited." Kapitalistate 9: 41-61.

———(1973) The Fiscal Crisis of the State. New York: St. Martin's Press.

PICKVANCE, C. (1985) "The rise and fall of urban movements and the role of comparative analysis." Environment and Planning D: Society and Space 3: 31-53.

———(1980) "Theories of the state and theories of urban crisis." Current Perspectives in Social Theory 1: 31-54.

PIVEN, F. and R. CLOWARD (1982) The New Class War. New York: Pantheon.

———(1979) Poor People's Movements. New York: Vintage.

———(1971) Regulating the Poor. New York: Pantheon.

SBRAGIA, A. (1983) The Municipal Money Chase. Boulder, CO: Westview.

SHEFTER, M. (1977) "New York's fiscal crisis: the politics of inflation and retrenchment." Public Interest 48 (Summer): 98-127.

SMITH, M. [ed.] (1984) Cities in Transformation. Beverly Hills, CA: Sage.

STERNLIEB, G. and R. HUGHES [eds.] (1975) Post-Industrial America. New Brunswick, NJ: Rutgers University Press.

SUSSER, I. (1982) Norman Street. New York: Oxford University Press.

TABB, W. and L. SAWERS [eds.] (1978) Marxism and the Metropolis. New York: Oxford University Press.

THERET, B. (1983) "Collective means of consumption, capital accumulation and the urban question." International Journal of Urban and Regional Research 6, 3: 345-371.

TOURAINE, A. (1981) The Voice and the Eye. New York: Cambridge University Press.

YATES, P. (1977) The Ungovernable City. Cambridge, MA: MIT Press.

About the Contributors

ALEXANDER GANZ is Research Director at the Boston Redevelopment Authority, where he marshals analytic reports useful for planning and development of the city. Earlier, he was Lecturer in Urban Economics at the MIT Department of Urban Studies and Planning. Prior to that he was Chief Economist of an MIT-Harvard Joint Center for Urban Studies Advisory Group helping a regional development authority build a new industrial city on the Orinoco River in Venezuela. He has a B.A. degree from Rutgers University, and has been a guest lecturer at Harvard University, Boston University, and universities in Venezuela, Colombia, Argentina, and Chile.

M. GOTTDIENER is Associate Professor in the Department of Sociology at the University of California, Riverside. His principal interests are contemporary social theory, semiotics, and urban analysis. He is the author of *The Social Production of Urban Space* and coauthor of *The City and the Sign: Introduction to Urban Semiotics.*

JEFFREY R. HENIG is Associate Professor of Political Science and Associate Dean of the School of Public and International Affairs at George Washington University. His research and writing have focused on neighborhood organizations, anticrime efforts, and urban gentrification. He is the author of *Neighborhood Mobilization: Redevelopment and Response* (1982) and *Public Policy and Federalism: Issues in State and Local Politics* (1985).

DENNIS R. JUDD is Associate Professor of Political Science and Fellow in the Center for Metropolitan Studies at the University of Missouri, St. Louis. He has published numerous articles on urban revitalization, national urban policy, and state politics. His books include *The Politics of Urban Planning*, *The Politics of American Cities* (second edition), and *Restructuring the City* (coauthor). He is currently writing books on public policy and American politics. He is coeditor of the *Urban Affairs Quarterly*.

JOHN MATZER, Jr., is the City Administrator of San Bernardino, California. He has also managed Beverly Hills, CA, Skokie, IL, and Trenton, NJ. He is the author of three books including *Creative Capital Financing Strategies for Local Government*. He is a Distinguished Professor of Administration at California State University, Long Beach.

ERIC H. MONKKONEN is a Professor of History at UCLA. He has written several books and articles on criminal justice history and social history, most recently editing *Walking to Work: Tramps in America, 1790-1935* (1984) University of Nebraska Press. He is now writing a book on U.S. urban history, *America Becomes Urban*.

MAX NEIMAN is Associate Professor of Political Science at the University of California, Riverside. His research interests include urban policy, theory, and urban planning politics.

C. G. PICKVANCE is Reader in Urban Studies in the Urban and Regional Studies Unit at the University of Kent at Canterbury. He has held visiting positions at universities in Toronto, Montreal, Istanbul, Amsterdam, and Canberra. He has written numerous papers on housing, local government, urban protest, spatial policy, and urban theory. He is author of *The State and Collective Consumption* (Open University Press, 1982) and is Review Editor of the *International Journal of Urban and Regional Research*.

HERBERT J. RUBIN is an Associate Professor of Sociology at Northern Illinois University. He has written a text on applied social research entitled *Applied Social Research*. Along with Irene Rubin, he has just completed a book *Community Organizing and Development* that reflects his current interests in community and economic development.

IRENE S. RUBIN is Associate Professor in the Public Administration Division at Northern Illinois University. She has done studies of fiscal stress at the state, local, and federal levels. Recent books include *Running in the Red* and *The Politics of Retrenchment* (coauthored), both about city government. Her most recent book, *Shrinking the Federal Government*, is about the effects of the Reagan Administration on five federal agencies.

ALBERTA M. SBRAGIA is an Associate Professor of Political Science and the Director of the West European Studies Program at the University of Pittsburgh. In 1983-1984, she spent a year at the Harvard Business School as a visiting Associate Professor. She has edited *The Municipal Money Chase: The Politics of Local Government Finance* (Westview, 1983) and authored articles on various aspects of finance and public policy in Italy, France, Great Britain, and the United States. She is currently working on a book comparing "the political economy of public investment" in the United States and Great Britain.

ELIZABETH G. SINCLAIR is a 1985 graduate of Rice University and is currently a research associate with Peter Hart and Associates, Washington, DC.

ROBERT M. STEIN is an Associate Professor of Political Science and Acting Chair of the Department of Political Science, Rice University. His main areas of research include state, local, and urban government and intergovernmental relations. His work has appeared in the *American Political Science Review, American Journal of Political Science, Journal of Politics, Western Political Quarterly, Social Science Quarterly,* and *Public Choice.*

TODD SWANSTROM is Assistant Professor of Political Science at the State University of New York at Albany. In 1984 he served as Staff Director of the Albany Strategic Planning Project, which resulted in a long-term plan for New York's capital city. He earned his M.A. from Washington University, St. Louis, in 1971 and his Ph.D. from Princeton University in 1981, both in political science. His interests, both in academic and practical spheres, revolve around identifying the potential for progressive public policies at the local level.

M-719

W

(Form L-9)